Voucher Wars

Voucher Wars

Waging the Legal Battle over School Choice

•

Clint Bolick

CATO
INSTITUTE
Washington, D.C.

Library of Congress Cataloging-in-Publication Data

Bolick, Clint.
  Voucher wars : waging the legal battle over school choice / Clint
Bolick.
      p. cm.
    Includes index.
    ISBN 1-930865-37-6 (cloth : alk. paper) -- ISBN 1-930865-38-4 (pbk. alk.
    paper)
      1. Educational vouchers--Law and legislation--United States. 2. School
choice--Law legislation--United States. I. Title.

KF4137.B65 2003
344.73'076--dc21   2002041605

Cover design by Elise Rivera.

Printed in the United States of America.

CATO INSTITUTE
1000 Massachusetts Ave., N.W.
Washington, D.C. 20001

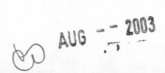

For Shawnna

Contents

Acknowledgments

Voucher Wars recounts an enormously challenging yet intensely rewarding collective struggle over the past 12 years. In these pages, I have tried to name a fraction of the committed, principled, energetic individuals who helped achieve the wonderful triumph for parental choice in the U.S. Supreme Court. For all in the school choice movement, my heartfelt thanks and admiration.

Voucher Wars is the latest in a long and wonderful collaboration with the Cato Institute. I am especially grateful to David Salisbury, David Boaz, David Lampo, and Amy Mitchell for their help in creating and promoting *Voucher Wars*.

Special thanks to Susan and George Mitchell, the dynamic duo who have done so much to foster school choice in Milwaukee and around the nation, for refreshing facts that had faded from my memory.

I also thank my colleagues at the Institute for Justice for their friendship, inspiration, support, and devotion to the cause of freedom; as well as our clients, supporters, directors, and allies who have made this work possible. In particular, I thank Chip Mellor for reviewing the manuscript, Gretchen Embrey for dredging up old legal documents, Maureen Blum for filling in some missing facts, Stacy Craanen for logistical support, and John Kramer and Lisa Andaloro for promoting the book. It is a terrific team that constantly defies the odds, and I am honored to be a part of it.

Introduction

Voucher Wars is the story of a freedom movement. It comprises men and women who are diverse in ethnicity and ideology and united by a common passion and determination to extend educational opportunities to children who desperately need them. It is a freedom movement because it involves challenging one of the biggest and most pernicious government monopolies in the free world. It is the movement to secure greater parental autonomy and educational opportunities for the millions of American families that lack the most basic power over the education of their children.

My colleagues and I have had the tremendous honor of serving as the movement's lawyers for the past dozen of its formative years. It is from that vantage point that I tell this story. I present it not merely or even primarily to make an historical record, but to share the lessons—some joyful, others painful—that we've learned along the way, so that future freedom advocates can learn from our mistakes and from our accomplishments.

This particular story spans the course of a dozen years, from the adoption of the nation's first urban school choice program in Wisconsin in the spring of 1990 to the decision of the U.S. Supreme Court in *Zelman v. Simmons-Harris*[1] upholding the Cleveland school choice program in June 2002. In reality the story neither begins nor ends with those 12 years. The roots of parental choice trace to the origins of the American experiment, and as a form of education policy it has barely begun to realize its potential. Indeed, even the legal battles are far from over. But when the history of the school choice movement is finally chronicled one day, I believe these dozen years will be recounted as pivotal—viewed, I hope, as the period in which the essential groundwork was laid for a new era of freedom in our nation's educational system.

---

[1] *Zelman v. Simmons-Harris*, 122 S.Ct. 2460 (2002).

Litigation was a constant feature of that crucible period. It began shortly after I first contacted Wisconsin State Rep. Polly Williams following the enactment of the Milwaukee Parental Choice Program in spring 1990. It took a while for me to reach her—she couldn't imagine what some white lawyer from Washington, D.C. could possibly want from her. When I finally spoke to her, I congratulated her and asked whether she was ready for the lawsuit. To that query she uttered the painfully immortal words, "What lawsuit?"

Since that conversation, my colleagues and I have litigated 16 school choice cases from California to Puerto Rico. The cases have encompassed about 40 court arguments and 80 briefs totaling approximately 2,400 pages. If you lined up corner-to-corner every page and exhibit we filed during that time, it would stretch more than a mile. And that from lawyers who pride ourselves on getting to the point.

During those 12 years as my colleagues and I toiled in the legal trenches, different courts produced about 50 rulings in our cases. We lost many more times than we won. Aboard that legal roller coaster, we experienced every possible emotion, from soaring exhilaration to searing anguish. That is because every case, every argument, could determine the educational fate of thousands of children, which amplified intensely the effect of every win and loss. For that reason, school choice has become a deeply personal cause, our own personal and institutional interests deeply enmeshed with those of the people we represent. In every case, our adversaries were trying to pry our clients' little fingers from the only decent educational opportunities they had ever experienced, and we were fighting even more desperately to prevent it. Our job was to get kids into good schools and keep them there. Despite the many setbacks along the way, I am proud to say that in 12 years of litigation, not one child in the 50 states was forced to leave a private school as a consequence of an adverse court decision. It has been an experience I would not trade with any other lawyer, and it has been so rich that I have burned with urgency to share it with others. I'm grateful for the opportunity to do so.

When the contemporary school choice movement started over the past few decades, its leading protagonists probably could have met comfortably in a telephone booth. In an amazingly short period, it has grown into one of the most sophisticated, passionate, and ecumenical movements in American history. I've never encountered a group of people—activists, philanthropists, public officials, clergy, lawyers, parents—so motivated by good faith, willing to put aside ideological differences in pursuit of a common cause, even at enormous personal sacrifice. That is probably why the movement has come so far, so fast; and it is essential that we replicate that type of effort wherever we seek to expand freedom.

Against the backdrop of the broader school choice movement, this book offers only a smidgen of a glimpse. I have described the movement's development primarily as it relates to the litigation side of the battle, and that of course is only a small part of a much bigger story. In that regard, I compare my colleagues and myself to relief pitchers in baseball: we have an important role to play only if someone else has set up the game to be saved. In that regard, this book offers a glimpse into the anatomy of a public-interest law strategy, and illustrates how litigation can be an effective tool for public policy change.

But about the school choice movement there is much more to be told, a saga of heroes ranging from parents to politicians to activists to philanthropists to policy wonks and theorists, that extends far beyond the scope of this book.[2] Still, from the vantage point of the litigation, I hope the reader will be able to grasp the essence and historical significance of the movement in which we have been fortunate to play a part.

Whatever the legal issues in a particular school choice lawsuit, our core argument throughout has been that parents, not government, should have the primary responsibility and power to determine where and how their children should be educated. That we ever should have had to fight so long and so hard to establish such a basic principle is a testament to the strength, determination, resilience, and ferocity of the reactionary forces dedicated to the status quo. The teacher unions, which form the cornerstone of the education establishment, are the most powerful special-interest group in America. At the national level, they essentially own the Democratic Party; at

---

[2]In this regard, I strongly recommend two outstanding books, Daniel McGroarty, *Break These Chains: The Battle for School Choice* (Rocklin, Calif.: Prima Publishing, 1996), and Mikel Holt, *Not Yet "Free at Last": The Unfinished Business of the Civil Rights Movement* (Oakland: Institute for Contemporary Studies, 2000), which chronicle the early days of the Milwaukee program.

the state level, they wield enormous influence over elected officials in both parties; at the local level, they frequently control school boards (which is why the nostalgic cry among some conservatives for "local control" is a self-defeating goal). The education establishment has dedicated itself and all of the resources at its disposal to defeat meaningful school choice anywhere and everywhere it presents itself—as if its own pathetic existence depends on it. With luck, it does.

The stakes are enormous. For the education establishment, the cause is about preserving its virtually monopolistic vise grip over American education. For the parents—and for society—the stakes are much, much higher. Nearly a half-century after *Brown v. Board of Education*, nearly half of all black and Hispanic children do not graduate from high school; and many of those who do, lack the most basic skills to pursue even entry-level jobs. As a result, many poor children in inner-city schools have as much likelihood of winding up on welfare or in jail as of going on to college or productive livelihoods. That is because our K–12 system of education, especially in large urban centers, is a government monopoly much more beholden to special-interest demands than to consumers. Within that system, economically disadvantaged families suffer worst: poor children, who need quality education to escape conditions of poverty, are usually relegated to the worst schools; and their parents, who lack the resources to move or enroll their children in private schools, have little ability to better their children's fate. Until we alter the distribution of power, we will consign additional generations of children to educational cesspools. In climbing out from this morass, it seems to me we should not worry about whether a particular reform proposal is too radical; we should worry about whether it is radical enough.

At its essence, the school choice movement is a civil rights crusade—an effort to vindicate the sacred and unfulfilled promise of equal educational opportunities. It's not just about ideas, but about the real lives of real people. Over the years, I've met hundreds of low-income parents in cities across America. Many of them are single parents; few have high school diplomas let alone college degrees. But they know that in order for their children to succeed, they must somehow secure for them a high-quality education. Unfortunately, the system has written them off—both the parents and their children.

Too often, the government schools and their liberal patrons are disdainful of low-income parents, contending that they are part of the problem, not part of the solution. The schools assume that the children are incapable of learning, and subject them to what President George W. Bush has characterized as the "soft bigotry of low expectations." When little is expected of children, of course, it becomes a self-fulfilling prophecy.

But in most inner-city private schools, conditions are markedly different. Not because they have greater resources than their public school counterparts (they typically have far fewer)—or because they are selective (they usually accept all applicants)—but because the operative philosophy is markedly different. The parents are not discouraged from involvement, they are *required* to play a role in the school and in their children's education. The children are expected to behave, and expected to achieve—and they do. I've walked the hallways of dozens of inner-city private schools, and the biggest difference is in the children's faces: regardless of the obstacles they face in their lives outside of school, they are kids who are going somewhere. That look of self-confidence, of determination, of earned pride: that is all the fuel, all the reward, that my colleagues and I could possibly desire. And with the victory in the U.S. Supreme Court, those children are safe now.

The road from a Saturday hearing in a steamy Madison courtroom in August 1990 to the decision of the U.S. Supreme Court on June 27, 2002, was a long and arduous one. Sometimes the effort seemed hopeless: the adverse court decisions were mounting, the resources arrayed against us were overwhelming. But we had an inspiration far more potent than anything the other side could hope to muster: the families who were counting on us to win. On that sunny February day when the case was argued in the U.S. Supreme Court—the day when hundreds of parents and children gathered from all across the nation in solidarity for school choice, the day when the stalwart Cleveland Councilwoman Fannie Lewis emerged from the Court and raised her arms high and proclaimed "We won!"—it was clear beyond question that every ounce of sweat was worth it, and more.

Along the way, the movement aided the litigation as much as the litigation helped the movement. The *Zelman* decision came down our way, decisively, and yet with nary a vote to spare on the Court. It was so close that if a single person involved in the effort had failed to make a single one of the myriad sacrifices endured over the course of those 12 years, it might have come down differently. But the sacrifices were made for the good of the cause, and a modern revolution was won.

And yet, there is so much left to do. The decision opens doors—but the titans of the education establishment are still determined to block them. Legal obstacles remain, requiring continued concerted action to face them down. And school choice activists have to make good on the opportunities newly available by creating new school choice programs. The *Zelman* decision only removes barriers; by itself it cannot change the educational status quo. But if the school choice movement continues to exhibit the passion, the unity, the goodwill, the ingenuity, and the perspicacity it has exhibited so far, I am certain it will help our nation finally deliver on its promise of opportunity.

Voucher Wars is the story of this movement, of its successes and failures, of its impact on our society, and of those who are fighting for and against it, that I will try to relate in the following pages. Not to spoil the suspense, but it's a story with a happy ending. I hope the lessons my colleagues, our allies, and I have learned over the past 12 years will make some contribution, however modest, to the broader fight for freedom.

Now, this is not the end. It is not even the beginning of the end. But it is, perhaps, the end of the beginning.

—Winston Churchill after the British defeated the Germans at El Alamein (1942)

1. Laying the Groundwork

It is almost surrealistic that my colleagues and I have had to spend the past dozen years litigating to establish the basic legal premise that parents may exercise school choice. In a nation supposedly committed to free enterprise, consumer choice, and equal educational opportunities, school choice should be routine. That it is not demonstrates the clout and determination of those dedicated to preserving the government's monopoly over public education.

To listen to the education establishment, one would think that school choice is a scary, radical, alien concept. And indeed, the defenders of the status quo have managed to convince voters in initiative after initiative that school choice is a threat to public education.

And yet, school choice is not new. To the contrary, private schools, often using public funds, have played a key role in American education. Even today, America's post-secondary system of education—the world's envy—is characterized by widespread school choice. Students can use the G.I. Bill, Pell Grants, and other forms of government aid to attend either public or private schools, including religious institutions. Parents can use childcare vouchers in private and religious settings. Indeed, under federal law, tens of thousands of disabled children receive schooling in private schools at public expense. It is only mainstream K–12 schools in which the government commands a monopoly over public funds.

Thomas Paine, the most prescient of the founding fathers, is credited with first suggesting a voucher system in the United States. He was interested in promoting the goal of an educated, enlightened citizenry; and in his time the idea of the government operating schools was actually an alien concept. So instead he proposed providing financial support to people who could use those funds to purchase education in private schools.

Most early American "public" education took place in private schools; and even when states started creating government schools,

1

teachers often were ministers.[1] The concept of "separation of church and state," which never quite made it into the Constitution, certainly did not apply to education.

In 1869, Vermont adopted a school choice program for communities that did not build their own public schools, and Maine did so in 1873. Both states to this day pay tuition for children in such towns to attend public schools in neighboring communities or in private schools. In Vermont, 6,500 children in 90 towns attend private schools at government expense; in Maine, 5,600 children in 55 towns do so. Interestingly, those programs, in existence for more than a century and a quarter, have not destroyed public schools, and indeed both states boast a well-educated population.

But the goal of universal common schools, fueled by the ideas of Horace Mann, helped make government schools the norm in the late 19th century. Private schools thereafter typically served two groups: the elite and those who dissented from the Protestant theology that dominated public schools. The latter, of course, were primarily Catholic immigrants who created their own schools. That phenomenon bitterly annoyed Protestant public school advocates, most notably Sen. James G. Blaine (R-Maine), who struck back in the latter decades of the 19th century. Blaine tried in 1876 to enact a federal constitutional amendment that would prohibit any government aid to religious private schools—not to advance separation of church and state, but to protect the Protestant hegemony over public schools and taxpayer funding. Blaine came close, but failed to secure passage of an amendment to the federal Constitution. Undaunted, Blaine's allies lobbied state legislatures and succeeded in attaching the "Blaine amendments" to approximately 37 state constitutions, prohibiting the expenditure of public funds in "aid" or "support" of sectarian (i.e., Catholic) schools.[2]

Anti-Catholic bigotry grew even more virulent in the early years of the 20th century, cresting in the form of an Oregon law whose passage, secured by the Ku Klux Klan, required all children to attend

---

[1] For an excellent discussion of the evolution of American public education, see Joseph P. Viteritti, *Choosing Equality: School Choice, the Constitution, and Civil Society* (Washington: Brookings Institution, 1999), pp. 145–68.

[2] An excellent historical account of the Blaine movement is Joseph P. Viteritti, "Blaine's Wake: School Choice, the First Amendment, and State Constitutional Law," *Harvard Journal of Law & Public Policy*, Vol. 21 (1998): p. 657.

government schools. In the landmark 1925 decision in *Pierce v. Society of Sisters*, the U.S. Supreme Court struck down the law, declaring

> The fundamental theory of liberty upon which all governments in this Union repose excludes any general power of the State to standardize its children by forcing them to accept instruction from public teachers only. The child is not the mere creature of the State; those who nurture him and direct his destiny have the right, coupled with the high duty, to recognize and prepare him for additional obligations.[3]

This principle of parental sovereignty, proclaimed in answer to pernicious efforts to destroy private educational options, remains a cornerstone of American constitutional jurisprudence—though it remains constantly under attack.[4]

Still, the anti-Catholic movement succeeded in squelching any serious effort to allow parents to use public funds in religious schools until the 1960s. That was the heyday of the Warren era of the U.S. Supreme Court, whose jurisprudence took a very expansive view of the Establishment Clause. On issues of public assistance to students in religious schools, such as textbooks, instructional materials, and transportation, the Court's decisions zigged and zagged. But permeating those decisions was hostility toward any policy that might have the consequence of aiding religion.

The modern case for school vouchers was first made by the Nobel laureate economist Milton Friedman, who introduced the concept of "vouchers" into the American lexicon.[5] Acknowledging that Americans would not support the government's getting out of the education business altogether, Friedman advocated the next-best thing: instead of providing education as a monopoly supplier, the government would finance it, in both public and private schools. Every child would be given a voucher allowing the student to redeem it at a school of the parent's choice, and the schools would

[3] 268 U.S. 510, 535 (1925).

[4] The most recent major precedent in this area is *Troxel v. Granville*, 530 U.S. 57 (2000), the so-called "grandparents' rights" case, in which the U.S. Supreme Court reiterated the principle that parents should have primary control over their children. Of special interest are the dueling opinions of Justices Clarence Thomas, who concurred in the judgment, and Antonin Scalia, who dissented.

[5] Milton Friedman, "The Role of Government in Education," in Robert A. Solo, ed., *Economics and the Public Interest* (Westport, CT: Greenwood, 1955).

compete for the vouchers. Friedman's proposal contained two insights that formed the intellectual foundations of the contemporary school choice movement: that parents, rather than government, should choose where children attend school; and that the rules of economics are not suspended at the schoolhouse doors.

Friedman's ideas gained currency mainly in conservative intellectual and policy circles, but in the broader realm of public policy they remained a decidedly minority perspective. The handful of school choice activists, such as Martin and Mae Duggan, who created the St. Louis-based Citizens for Educational Freedom, were passionate and persistent but few in number.

The support base for school choice began to expand and diversify in the 1970s when two liberal Berkeley law professors, Jack Coons and Steven Sugarman, began to consider school choice as a means of delivering educational equity. If forced busing plans had failed, Coons and Sugarman argued, why not give vouchers to poor and minority parents so they could choose the best education for their children? Although Coons and Sugarman adapted Friedman's proposals to their own ends, the differences were substantial: Friedman advocated universal vouchers while Coons and Sugarman wanted to target them to disadvantaged populations; Friedman preferred a lightly regulated system while Coons and Sugarman believed substantial government oversight would be necessary. Still, the divergent proposals suggested a prospect for alliance among freedom-seeking conservatives and libertarians on the one hand and equity-seeking liberals on the other that would make the school choice programs of the 1990s a reality.

In the 1970s, the widespread closure of Catholic schools created a crisis for the public schools that would have to absorb them. In response, New York and Pennsylvania—two states with large Catholic school populations—enacted "parochiaid" laws designed to financially prop up religious schools. The assistance took the form of direct subsidies to the schools and financial assistance to private school parents.

In 1973, the U.S. Supreme Court struck down parochiaid in *Committee for Public Education v. Nyquist*.[6] Because the aid was restricted to private schools—most of which were religious—and those who

---

[6] 413 U.S. 756 (1973).

patronized them, the Court concluded that the "primary effect" of the aid programs was to advance religion. But in a footnote, the Court reserved an important question: "whether the significantly religious character of the statute's beneficiaries might differentiate the present cases from a case involving some form of public assistance (e.g., scholarships) made available generally without regard to the sectarian-nonsectarian, or public-nonpublic nature of the institution benefited."[7] *Nyquist* put an end, for the time being, to notions of school choice while at the same time suggesting a possible course—what later would be dubbed "neutrality"—upon which school choice proponents could craft new innovations.

The idea might have died with that Supreme Court decision had the government schools turned out a consistently decent product, but they did not. Particularly alarming was the decline in urban public schools. In 1954, the U.S. Supreme Court had proclaimed in *Brown v. Board of Education* that education, "where the state has undertaken to provide it, is a right which must be made available to all on equal terms."[8] Massive resistance led to stern remedies, especially forced busing, which were well-intentioned but had the devastating impact of ruining inner-city schools and, ironically, exacerbating conditions of segregation. Whites (and middle-class blacks) fled to the suburbs, depriving urban public schools of their support base and leaving poor, mostly minority student populations in rapidly worsening schools.

The problems of urban public schooling were symptomatic of a broader decline in public education. The 1983 study *A Nation at Risk* chronicled a systemic crisis in American education. Meanwhile, starting in the early 1980s, social scientists, including the eminent sociologist James Coleman, began producing findings that private and religious schools were succeeding where government schools were failing in educating minority schoolchildren from low-income families—findings that have continued unabated ever since.[9]

[7] Ibid., p. 782 n.38.

[8] 347 U.S. 483, 493.

[9] James S. Coleman, Thomas Hoffer, and Sally Kilgore, *High School Achievement* (New York: Basic Books, 1983). An excellent recent study to the same effect is Derek Neal, "The Effects of Catholic Secondary Schools on Educational Achievement," *Journal of Labor Economics*, Vol. 15 (1997): p. 98.

Finally setting the stage for a school choice movement in the 1990s was a pathbreaking Brookings Institution study by John Chubb and Terry Moe, *Politics, Markets & America's Schools*.[10] Chubb and Moe set out to discover why suburban public schools and inner-city private schools generally produced good academic outcomes, while inner-city public schools were disasters. They found that whereas the first two types of schools were characterized by strong leaders with a clear mission and a high degree of responsiveness to parents, inner-city schools were not. Instead, urban public school districts were run by bloated bureaucracies whose principal constituencies were not parents, but politicians and unions. A crucial distinguishing factor was the element of choice: suburban parents could send their children to private schools or move to different communities if they were dissatisfied with their public schools; likewise, private schools were entirely dependent on satisfied parents. But inner-city public school parents were captives: they had no choice except to send their children to whatever public school they were offered. And in school districts with tens if not hundreds of thousands of students, they were powerless to do anything about it. Introducing choice in inner-city public schools—crucially, giving parents the power to exit the system altogether—would force the system to respond to its customers rather than to politicians and special-interest groups, Chubb and Moe concluded. Their findings created a scholarly foundation for school choice not merely as an escape valve for children in failing government schools, but as an essential prerequisite for systemic public school reform.

At the same time, a remarkable Pennsylvania lawyer, William Bentley Ball, was somehow managing to navigate a hostile judicial environment and to produce legal precedents favorable to religious liberty and parental autonomy. Among other landmark cases, Ball litigated *Wisconsin v. Yoder*,[11] in which the U.S. Supreme Court held that Amish children could not be held to comply with compulsory high school requirements that were contrary to their religious beliefs. Ball kept the flickering promise of *Pierce* alive and laid the jurisprudential groundwork for the legal defense of school choice in the 1990s and beyond.

---

[10] Washington: Brookings Institution, 1990.
[11] 406 U.S. 205 (1972).

What was lacking was political leadership; what was abundant was a wide divergence over how to proceed. Division was apparent even among libertarians, a natural support base for expanded educational freedom. Many if not most libertarians believe in a strict separation of school and state—as Ayn Rand put it, for the same reasons that we support separation of church and state—because it is inherently dangerous to allow the government to create and instill an educational dogma. But some believe it as an ideal, with a pragmatic desire to move incrementally in that direction through school choice, while others support it as a nonnegotiable absolute. The problem with the latter perspective is that if there is one idea that surely derives support from a vast majority of Americans, it is that it is a proper and important role for government to provide (or at least enable) education; and the absolutist perspective leaves intact (indeed, it aids and abets) a status quo in which nearly 90 percent of American schoolchildren are enrolled in government schools. In any event, even among the majority of libertarians who support school choice, some support a broad range of efforts (including vouchers) to expand competition and parental autonomy, while others support only tax credits and deductions, which do not entangle the government with private schools. All libertarians, of course, favor limiting the government's power to regulate private schools.

As the 1980s ended, the pressure for educational alternatives was palpable and growing, but leadership and direction were all but nonexistent. If those two ingredients were found, the stage would be set for the birth of a potent school choice movement.

As the school choice movement was coming of age, so was I. A New Jersey boy, I was born into a working-class family that had little interest in big issues of public policy. But my family placed a premium on education. My father was a welder who had only an eighth grade education, and he died when I was eleven. But from my earliest school days his eyes would glow with pride whenever I came home with good grades, and he gave me five dollars any time I received straight As. (I've continued that tradition with my own sons, albeit with painfully inflation-adjusted rates.)

From the beginning, though, three characteristics manifested themselves that would propel me into a career as a defender of school choice. First, growing up as a puny kid, I developed a keen appreciation for the underdog. Second, I loved teaching. Some of my earliest recollections as a kid involve lining up my stuffed animals and teaching them whatever I'd learned that day (an enterprise that seemed more suited to my talents than the time I gave my favorite teddy bear a haircut). And finally, I developed a love for politics.

So when I headed to college at bucolic Drew University in northwestern New Jersey, I pursued a double major in political science and history as well as a K–12 teacher certification. Drew offered no teaching program, so I enrolled in a reciprocal program at the College of St. Elizabeth in nearby Convent Station, New Jersey. In addition to the fringe benefit of being the only male student in an otherwise all-girls college, "St. E's" proved an epiphany for me. Having been raised as an armchair Presbyterian, I had never set foot in a Catholic institution of any sort. My experience there makes me wonder how on earth Catholic schools got saddled with the label "parochial," because they exemplify the values of true liberal education. Not only did I receive first-rate teacher training, but I was exposed for the first time to a full range of ideas about education policy. At Drew, I received a red "X" when I quoted Milton Friedman on an economics exam; but St. Elizabeth's thoughtfully presented not only Milton Friedman's voucher proposal but even more radical ideas such as the unschooling philosophy of John Holt.

Much as I enjoyed Drew and St. E's, three events catapulted me toward a different career path. The first was a summer internship in Washington, D.C., hosted by the Fund for American Studies. I arranged an internship with a then-unknown rising-star freshman senator, Orrin Hatch. Though I admired Hatch and enjoyed the experience, it opened my eyes to the reality of our nation's capital: a town filled with power-seeking people who spend most of their time compromising their principles. I quickly realized that I was not dispositionally suited to politics.

A second formative experience was my clinical and student-teaching experience. Observing an inner-city public school for the first time, I was shocked at the disorder, low expectations, and poor teacher quality. Meanwhile, during my student-teaching experience at posh suburban Milburn High School, I spent more time correcting grammar than teaching history. My attempt to engage students in a contemporary world history class by replacing the boring textbook with the novels *We the Living* by Ayn Rand and *This Perfect Day* by Ira Levin was firmly rejected by my supervising teacher. Though I had received a decent-enough education in my own suburban public high school, it was evident to me that the quality of even the best public schools was suspect, and the worst was appalling.

Fortunately, at around the same time, I was taking a two-semester course in constitutional law with Drew's professor emeritus, Robert Smith. I had never previously considered a career in law. I had never known a lawyer and the profession appeared boring and mercenary. But constitutional law was magical. Cases like *Brown v. Board of Education*, which literally changed the world, captivated my imagination. Cases were decided on principle, win or lose, often in black and white rather than shades of gray. I decided that it was law, not politics, where an idealist could achieve positive change, without compromise. And that I could make a bigger difference for education in the courtroom than in the classroom.

Luckily for me, my last-minute decision to attend law school was made in blissful ignorance of how few attorneys ever get to litigate constitutional cases at all, let alone do so for a living. So I packed my car for the sunny climate at the University of California at Davis and a bright imagined future as a constitutional lawyer.

Talk about a dismal three years! (Was it only three?) Davis was the most ideologically hostile and intolerant place I had ever encountered. Any philosophy was welcomed by my fellow students, so long as it occupied the range between Lenin and Mao. Adding insult to injury, constitutional law makes up only a fraction of the legal curriculum, which is dominated by such subjects as contracts, torts, and wills and estates. My grades were miserable. But I made good use of my time, running for the state legislature as a Libertarian and learning how to think on my feet, and filing lawsuits against the president of the university and the City of Davis for various unconstitutional acts. In a final act of rebellion, I spent graduation day in the wine country rather than listening to our all-too-fitting commencement speaker, Ralph Nader.

I can't be too tough on Davis, though, because somehow along the way I developed some decent lawyering skills. I wanted to work for Bill Ball, but he had too much work to take on a young associate. Happily, I was hired into my other dream job at Mountain States Legal Foundation, a conservative public-interest law firm in Denver.

9

Its acting president was Chip Mellor, a fellow libertarian idealist who saw a spark in me and nurtured it.

My first solo project was an amicus curiae (friend of the court) brief in 1983 in *Mueller v. Allen*.[12] The case involved a Minnesota statute that provided tax deductions for educational expenses, including private school tuition. The case was difficult because the overwhelming majority of benefits—allegedly 96 percent—were claimed by private and religious school families, because few public school families incurred educational expenses. But it was the first case to raise the question left open by the footnote in *Nyquist*: whether an aid program that was neutral on its face could survive scrutiny under the Establishment Clause.

Though the program's impact was modest, I perceived the case as important for school choice. Any truly significant school choice program—such as vouchers or tax credits[13]—would have to overcome the hurdle of the Establishment Clause; and if this modest program couldn't survive, it was hard to imagine a program that could.

On its face, the Establishment Clause would not seem to present an insuperable barrier. The First Amendment begins with the admonition, "Congress shall make no law respecting an establishment of religion," and then continues, "or abridging the free exercise thereof." That combination sounds like a command of governmental neutrality toward religion; it would not seem to permit (much less require) official hostility to or discrimination against religion. But over the years, liberals on the Supreme Court morphed the First Amendment from a prohibition against establishment of religion into something akin to a complete separation of church and state. It led to some odd jurisprudence: tax exemptions for religion were permissible, but tax benefits for religious school parents were not; secular textbooks and transportation were fine but other secular aid was not; government school teachers could provide remedial instruction to religious school students but only outside of religious school premises (leading to the use of trailers outside many private

---

[12] 463 U.S. 483 (1983).

[13] A tax deduction merely reduces the amount of taxable income, while a tax credit reduces the amount of taxes. A "refundable" tax credit goes even further, providing a refund even for people who do not pay taxes.

schools). *Mueller* provided a chance to begin creating harmony out of constitutional cacophony.

In our amicus brief, I wanted to try a fresh approach.[14] I rounded up some right-of-center education reform groups to represent, but added to them the New Coalition for Social and Economic Change, an organization founded by Clarence Pendleton, President Reagan's controversial chairman of the U.S. Commission on Civil Rights and the former head of the San Diego Urban League.[15] Articulating the Coalition's "empowerment" philosophy, I argued that the real "primary effect" of school choice was to expand educational opportunities, particularly for people outside of the economic mainstream. It was the first articulation of an argument—and the first deployment of the tactic of forging nontraditional alliances—that my colleagues and I would repeat frequently in subsequent years.

The Supreme Court, in a five-to-four decision by Justice William Rehnquist (joined by Justice Lewis Powell, who had authored the *Nyquist* decision a decade earlier), upheld the tax deductions and provided the analytical framework by which future school choice programs might be judged. The program differed from *Nyquist*, the majority found, because the aid was transmitted to religious institutions only on the basis of parental decisions, and the range of educational options included both public and private choices. As Justice Rehnquist explained, "The historic purposes of the [Establishment] Clause simply do not encompass the sort of attenuated financial benefit, ultimately controlled by the private choices of individual parents, that eventually flows to parochial schools from the neutrally available tax benefit at issue in this case."[16] That seemed to provide a very congenial standard for school choice programs.

The Supreme Court would not revisit the issue for a few years. In the meantime I left Denver to answer the siren call of the nation's

[14] An amicus brief can be a wonderful thing. It allows a nonparty to make any argument, even a nonlegal one. Some groups waste the opportunity by merely repeating the parties' arguments. At the Institute for Justice, we employ the "Mr. Ed Rule" for amicus briefs, taken from the black-and-white television-era show about the talking horse: we speak only when we have something to say (or someone distinctive to say it).

[15] Pendleton was so controversial that pundits at the time referred to Clarence Thomas, the low-key chairman of the U.S. Equal Employment Opportunity Commission, as the "other Clarence."

[16] *Mueller*, p. 400.

capital, first at the EEOC, then with the U.S. Department of Justice's Civil Rights Division, where I honed my litigation skills. During my brief period of government service (which I compared with a stint in the Marine Corps: not always pleasant, but good for building character), I wrote my first book, *Changing Course: Civil Rights at the Crossroads*.[17] There I developed an alternative civil rights agenda based on the original principles of America's civil rights vision that emphasized individual empowerment over race-based entitlements.[18] One central facet of the agenda was school choice, empowering economically disadvantaged families to opt out of failing government schools.[19] The argument was grounded in two core constitutional principles: parental liberty, emanating from the *Pierce* line of cases, and equal educational opportunities, drawing upon *Brown*.

Stephen King needn't worry about the competition: the publisher produced only about six hundred copies of *Changing Course*; but the book helped distill my thinking and strategy. It also brought me to the attention of Landmark Legal Foundation, a Kansas City-based conservative public interest law firm that wanted to open a Washington, D.C. office and create a new niche. The group's then-president, Jerry Hill, made me an offer I couldn't refuse: the chance to turn my book into a litigation program. I accepted eagerly and in 1988, with seed funding from the Lynde and Harry Bradley Foundation, I opened the Landmark Center for Civil Rights in the basement of a townhouse across the street from the Supreme Court.

My plans were big but my "operation" oh-so-modest. It lacked even a secretary and filing cabinets when the office opened, and a flood destroyed most of my papers during the first week of operation. When I discovered the disaster, I had to take off my shoes and socks, roll up the pant legs of my suit, and wade out into the muck in the courtyard to clear out the drain. I asked myself, "Clint, what have you gotten yourself into?"

---

[17] Transaction Books, 1988.

[18] I subsequently refined those ideas in *Unfinished Business: A Civil Rights Strategy for America's Third Century* (Pacific Research Institute, 1990); *The Affirmative Action Fraud: Can We Restore the American Civil Rights Vision?* (Cato Institute, 1998); and *Transformation: The Promise and Politics of Empowerment* (Institute for Contemporary Studies, 2000).

[19] Other facets of the agenda included freedom of enterprise and private property rights, which also are mainstays of our work at the Institute for Justice.

12

But I absolutely loved it: a shingle of my own, practicing constitutional law full-time in the shadow of the Supreme Court at the ripe young age of 30.

My first case was not a school choice case, but an "economic liberty" case. Of all the freedoms that Americans cherish, the least-protected is the right to earn an honest living. If the government tries to take a person's welfare check away, a Legal Services Corporation lawyer can tie the government in knots with all manner of due process arguments; but if the government regulates a person's business out of existence, there's precious little a court will do to stop it. That seems backward in a nation doctrinally committed to opportunity—especially given that the Fourteenth Amendment to the U.S. Constitution was intended in part to protect economic liberty. But the federal courts had not struck down an economic regulation as a violation of civil rights in 50 years.

Wanting to vindicate constitutional protections for economic liberty, I cast about for a case, and found it in the person of Ego Brown, a shoeshine entrepreneur who set up street-corner stands in downtown Washington and gave training and jobs to enterprising homeless people. Dusting off an old Jim Crow-era law forbidding street-corner shoeshine stands, the District of Columbia closed down Ego's business. One could sell almost anything on the streets of the nation's capital, from hot dogs to flowers to photo opportunities with cardboard Ronald Reagans, but not a shoeshine. As the Center for Civil Rights was getting off the ground, I filed a lawsuit challenging the law.

When I sought a preliminary injunction while the case was proceeding, the federal district court turned it down. I was devastated: the lawsuit was Ego's only hope, and I had failed. I thought about hanging it up as a public interest lawyer. But when I read the decision, it turned out the court had turned down the injunction on procedural grounds. On the substance, the court found that we had a substantial likelihood of prevailing on the merits. And sure enough, we did—on the first day of spring in 1989, the court struck down the law as unconstitutional.[20] Not only that, but ABC's *World News Tonight* got hold of the story and made Ego Brown its "Person of

---

[20] *Brown v. Barry*, 710 F. Supp. 352 (D.D.C. 1989).

the Week." I'll never forget Peter Jennings's closing words about Ego: "He's made us all a little bit freer."

The Ego Brown case made me realize that, in a very small way, we were onto something. Indeed, as I had learned in my constitutional law class in college, litigation could in fact change the world. The experience demonstrated that humanizing a case, and arguing in the court of public opinion, could make a huge difference. I began to comprehend the concept of empowerment as a positive and coherent alternative to a liberal orthodoxy that looked to the state, rather than to individuals themselves, as a source of salvation. And I discovered that in a court of law, David really could slay Goliath.

It also made me realize that if I was going to pursue those types of cases, I had better develop some stamina. By definition, empowerment cases are uphill battles, with powerful special interests fighting hard to preserve their advantaged legal status. That also meant we might have to endure some pretty painful losses along the way. It turned out that in both regards—the power of the opposition and the endurance of painful losses—I hadn't seen anything yet.

And that's pretty much where things stood for me in 1990 when the school choice movement scored its first epical victory in Milwaukee, and I stepped forward to offer my services: an idealistic young lawyer with largely unproven ideas, lousy law school grades, little courtroom experience, a basement office now reeking of mildew, and almost no resources at my disposal. But my rates were good.

2. Polly

In 1990, the desperate conditions in the Milwaukee Public Schools called for desperate solutions. A student in MPS had less than a fifty-fifty chance of graduating; for children from families on government assistance, only 15 percent graduated. Those who did graduated with an average grade point of less than 2.0—just above a D. School-children in Milwaukee, especially those from poor families, had little prospect of acquiring the essential skills they needed to go on to college or to productive livelihoods.

It was, of course, a pattern reflected in virtually every large city in the United States.

The Milwaukee school system, controlled by teacher unions, was militantly opposed to systemic reform, and had successfully resisted all such efforts. But they had never encountered Polly Williams, a maverick Democratic state legislator who represented some of the poorest neighborhoods in Milwaukee, and was determined to try something different. Williams was a rebel. A former welfare mother, Williams had chaired Jesse Jackson's presidential campaign in Wisconsin and served as a member of Alderman Michael McGee's militant separatist brigade. She knew there were good schools in her community, most of them formerly Catholic schools that had been shut down and reopened as nonsectarian private schools geared toward the city's black and Hispanic populations. Though the schools' tuition was low, too few of Williams's constituents could afford them. So Williams mixed a dose of Milton Friedman and a dose of Malcolm X and came up with the nation's first urban school choice plan.

At the same time, the Bradley Foundation and its president, Michael Joyce, also were exploring school choice options as a means of arresting MPS's alarming decline and the flight of middle-class families to the suburbs. They had a willing ally in the trailblazing Republican governor, Tommy Thompson. For most conservatives, urban policy was at best an afterthought and at worst an albatross, but Thompson viewed with gusto the opportunities created by the failures of the welfare state.

The three-way marriage of Bradley, Thompson, and Williams was hardly a match made in heaven, but it was politically potent. Together they worked out a pilot school choice program for Milwaukee that would allow about one percent of the district's students— approximately one thousand in all—to use a fraction of state funds (roughly $2,500) as full payment of tuition in participating nonsectarian private schools in Milwaukee.

It was in scope a very modest program. Choices were restricted to private schools within the Milwaukee city limits. The program was limited to nonsectarian schools, in part because of Williams's distrust of Catholic schools. It was proposed only for a two-year pilot period. And rather than stand-alone legislation, it was made part of the budget bill, significantly easing prospects for passage. The program gained crucial support from the city's innovative Democratic mayor, John Norquist, and Howard Fuller, a former civil rights activist who would later serve as the reform-minded superintendent of the Milwaukee Public Schools.

In spring 1990, with Williams as the principal catalyst, the Wisconsin Legislature enacted the pilot school choice program as part of the state budget, and Thompson signed it into law. But the governor's handiwork wasn't finished. A remarkable feature of Wisconsin law is that the governor can use his line-item veto power not just to excise spending items in the budget but also to cross out words. So Thompson lined out the language limiting the program to a pilot period, in one fell swoop creating what he fervently hoped would be a permanent school choice program.

Despite the historic feat of enacting the nation's first urban school choice program, the media reacted with complete disinterest. I happened upon a brief mention of it in the *Washington Times* and my pulse quickened. Finally!

The only name mentioned in the article was Polly Williams, and I instantly started trying to reach her. She couldn't understand why some Washington lawyer wanted to talk with her, and she resolutely ignored my calls. It was maddening: this was what I hoped my entire career would be about, and I couldn't even get the program's architect to return my call.

In a moment of inspiration I turned to a dear friend and mentor, Bob Woodson, founder and president of the National Center for

Neighborhood Enterprise, the widely acknowledged godfather of the movement to empower low-income people with market-oriented reforms. Bob had assisted with the Ego Brown case. He has enormous credibility among low-income communities in cities across the United States, and he was able to persuade Polly to take my call.

When I finally spoke with her, I congratulated her on her path-breaking legislative success and asked if she was ready for the lawsuit. "What lawsuit?" she retorted.

I took her response as both good news and bad news. Good news in that she obviously did not have another lawyer. Bad news in that she had no idea what she and her program were in for.

My colleagues and I often joke that in public policy, no good deed goes unchallenged in court. In fact, one way to measure a policy reform's saliency is whether or not it's challenged; if some aggrieved special interest group doesn't sue, it's a pretty safe bet that the reform hasn't accomplished much. That means that any successful reform strategy is necessarily at least a two-step process, legislative and judicial. Subsequently, in working with allies on school choice legislation, our role has been to build a successful legal defense into the legislation itself, to help bulletproof it against the inevitable legal challenge.

We understand all that very clearly now; but at the time I only dimly perceived it. Still, I exhorted Polly that she needed to anticipate a legal challenge. The nation might not yet realize the magnitude of her accomplishment, I explained, but one group—the teachers unions—surely did, and we could safely bet that they would use every tool at their disposal to undo it. You can't rely on the state to defend your program effectively or passionately, I told her; you need to play an active role in the litigation. After our conversation, she agreed with the strategy in concept and also consented to meet with me in Milwaukee to make a pitch to represent her.

So I flew out to Milwaukee, the first of scores of trips. It wasn't exactly hardship duty—I quickly discovered that Milwaukee's hometown airline, Midwest Express, is the finest in the nation, with spacious leather seats and freshly baked chocolate chip cookies. I came to call the trip from Washington to Milwaukee the "cookie run."

So my stomach was full but still nervous as hell. What if I was wrong about the litigation? Wouldn't they want a big firm or at

17

least a hometown lawyer to defend it? Even if I got the chance, was I up to the task? Compounding my own inexperience, our resources at Landmark were meager and precarious, to put it mildly. Though we now had a second lawyer and had moved to a larger office near Union Station, we had trouble making payroll or paying our suppliers. Could we realistically go up against one of the nation's most powerful special interest groups?

My internal concerns turned out to be nothing compared with the grilling I received when I met with Polly at an office in her neighborhood. In person, Polly turned out to be a feisty, indignant, and eloquent silver-haired grandmother with a burning passion for her "neighborhood" and a willingness to venture outside usual political alliances to achieve her objectives. But she was deeply skeptical of white conservatives and their motivations. I drew some comfort, though, from her evaluation of the political situation. "Liberals say they care for us, and they give us all sorts of programs, but the one thing they won't give us is power over our own destiny. Conservatives don't give a damn about us, but the one thing they're willing to give us is the keys," she quipped. "I'm beginning to like conservatives better."

But Polly wasn't the real taskmaster; she left that duty to her aide and alter ego, Larry Harwell. Larry is an intimidating guy. Though a professional legislative tactician, he should have been a lawyer: he interrogated me for two straight hours and didn't give an inch. What were my motives? No, what were my motives, *really*. Why did I think there would be a lawsuit? What would the issues be? What was my strategy? How much would it cost? Nothing? How could that be?[1] Where did we get our money? Who would be in charge? Would I be willing to work with a local black lawyer?

To those questions I responded that I wasn't sure what the attack would be, but that it would come soon, in an effort to prevent the program from opening in September. Once kids started in new schools, I explained, it would be tough for the unions to convince a court to force them out. I told them I believed it essential that the parents be separately represented in the lawsuit. Polly and Larry

---

[1] Among the joys of public interest law are that you get to choose your cases and your clients, you don't have to charge anything, and, in our case, you get to sue bureaucrats.

would be in charge of overall strategy, but I would be in charge of the litigation. I was happy to work with any lawyer they wished as local counsel,[2] but in terms of legal decisions I would call the shots.

Somehow I survived the ordeal. Though I didn't receive an immediate verdict, Larry assured me that if they decided in my favor, it would be a serious, no-looking-back commitment. He told me I was "all right." And in return, despite myself, I was already beginning to feel not only admiration but affection for the guy.

Then the three of us took a drive around the neighborhood. It was generally well-kept but obviously poor, with a plethora of boarded-up buildings. At one traffic light I saw a large man who appeared to be mentally retarded striking an elderly woman with her purse. I said, "Larry, shouldn't we go help that lady?" He looked back at me and delivered the first of many doleful stares. "When I go into y'alls' neighborhood, I see strange things, too. Like people *watering their lawns*. But I don't stop and tell them what they should be doing." And with that we drove off. I was chastened and educated, and not for the last time.

Our principal destination was to look at the neighborhood schools. The government schools were obvious hellholes. Some of them looked as if they were abandoned, but Polly assured me they were operational and in fact bursting at the seams with children. If I had been concerned about the plight of inner-city schoolchildren before, this experience sobered me all the more. Indeed, if every American could visit inner-city public schools and witness firsthand the conditions there, I'm confident we'd have much less resistance to systemic reform proposals.

Finally we drove past a public school that appeared to be in stellar condition, right in the middle of an impoverished neighborhood. "Tell me about that school," I asked.

"That's a magnet school," Polly replied. "It's good, but our kids don't go there. It's for white kids from the suburbs." Inner-city kids could also attend schools in the suburbs through a program called Chapter 220, she explained, but her constituents didn't want to do

[2] Any time lawyers appear in court outside a jurisdiction in which they're licensed, they have to associate with a local lawyer who will vouch for them and appear on the pleadings (a procedure called *pro hac vice*, or admission to the bar for a particular case). We also like to find local counsel who can give us credibility and provide sound intelligence about local courts.

19

that. They wanted the same thing as middle-income parents: good schools in their own neighborhoods. And that's why Polly had sponsored the school choice program, because the good schools in her neighborhood were mostly private and (despite low tuition) economically inaccessible to most of the residents.

I returned to Washington invigorated and more determined than ever to represent the parents. Unbeknownst to me, Polly and Larry attempted to find a black lawyer to take the case. Their efforts proved unavailing and instructive: no black establishment attorney would touch the case. Finally Larry called and offered me the job, provided I would try to find a black lawyer to serve as local counsel. I eagerly agreed.

We didn't have to wait long to learn the other side's strategy. To my dismay, it consisted not of one front but two. First, as anticipated, the teachers unions filed a state court lawsuit challenging the constitutionality of the program. In addition, they unleashed the state's Superintendent of Public Instruction, Bert Grover. Despite having two Sesame Street names, Grover was no friend of children, and declared himself an unrepentant opponent of school choice. In an attempt to sentence the program to death by bureaucratic strangulation, Grover imposed a blizzard of regulations upon private schools. The program required only that participating private schools accept students on a random selection basis and accept the voucher as full payment of tuition. Under Grover's rules, all public school rules would also apply to participating private schools, as well as obligations under the federal Individuals with Disabilities Education Act.

Meanwhile, the lawsuit was filed in Madison, the (very liberal) state capital, and named as its lead plaintiff Felmers Chaney, the head of the Milwaukee chapter of the National Association for the Advancement of Colored People. The lawsuit alleged that the program violated three provisions of the state constitution: the "private or local bill" clause, the guarantee of a "uniform" public education, and the public purpose doctrine. I had no idea how to size up the claims, but they appeared potent.

Why the double-barreled assault on such a tiny program? The union and its allies recognized the historic importance of the program, and its potential for replication. The Milwaukee Parental Choice Program changed the educational status quo in two fundamental ways. First, power over basic educational decisions was being transferred, for the first time in the nation's history, from bureaucrats to parents. Second, government schools would have to compete, also for the first time, for economically disadvantaged children and the financial resources now at their command. If this precedent were allowed to stand, it could destroy the education establishment's monopolistic stranglehold over urban public education. The union and its allies perceived they were fighting for their very survival, and were leaving absolutely nothing to chance.

The overall legal strategy was brilliant. The plaintiffs had neutralized their obvious equitable disadvantage by aligning with a civil rights group. Private schools would not sign up for the program under the rules, so Grover could (and did) claim that the schools were not interested in assisting poor children. The challenge that their double-barreled strategy presented was overwhelming. To get the program up and running, the parents, who were not organized, would have to successfully defend the program's constitutionality *and* challenge the regulations, with the state as its ally in the first instance and its adversary in the second. And we'd have to do all that in about two months' time.

I promptly returned to Milwaukee to meet with parents and private school officials. Already, Polly, Larry, and I were functioning effectively as a team. First, they toured me around the three largest nonsectarian private schools, Urban Day and Harambee, which were predominantly black, and Bruce-Guadaloupe, which was mainly Hispanic. The experience was an epiphany. Here were children from low-income families—kids written off in the public school system— who were learning in a modest but safe and orderly learning environment. Parents were volunteering. Unlike some public schools where parents are often considered ignorant and treated as pariahs, here parent participation of some sort was required as a condition of enrollment. But the most palpable difference between the private and public schools was the high standards and expectations: the kids were expected to succeed, and they obviously did.

It also was obvious that much of the success of inner-city private schools is attributable to strong leadership. Harambee's principal, Sister Callista Robinson, and Urban Day's principal, Zakiya Courtney, exhibited firm, tough, and loving control over their schools. I immediately recognized them as heroes to the kids they were serving.

I met with officials from several private schools and explained what was going on. Sure enough, none was willing to sign Grover's forms evidencing agreement with the regulations. Trouble was, the deadline was approaching. Asking them for an act of faith, I suggested that they sign the forms, adding a proviso that they considered themselves bound only to the regulations authorized by state law. That would beg the question of Grover's regulatory authority, but allow the program to get started. With trepidation, they agreed. It was their mission to educate those kids, and they were willing to take a risk.

Then we discussed each regulation in turn. I asked the private school officials to give me their bottom line: What can you live with, what can you not? The two big problems were the public school rules, which would eviscerate the schools' disciplinary discretion, and the rules regarding disabled children. The schools were willing to admit any child whose needs they could accommodate, but the rules suggested that they would have to provide special resources for *any* child, regardless of cost—a requirement that public school *districts* must satisfy (in exchange for federal funding), but which individual public schools need not.

Later I attended a meeting with parents. It was a revelation to me and I suppose it would have been to most Americans. The defenders of the status quo have carefully and successfully spun a myth that poor parents don't care about their children's education, and that even if they did, they would be too ignorant to make well-informed school choices for their children.

The meeting with the Milwaukee parents shattered that myth for me. Demographically, they fit the stereotype: poor, overwhelmingly minority, mostly single moms, few high school graduates. The concept of school choice, as it is for most inner-city parents, was alien to them. But they instantly grasped its importance, and were willing to fight for it. Every parent in the room knew two things. First, they understood that the only way their children could escape poverty was to obtain a good education. Second, they all knew where a good school was in their neighborhood, and it was usually private.

I explained as best I could what was going on in the legal arena. I told them that we needed a few parents to represent them as parties to the litigation. I tried to translate the legal issues into plain English, and told them that it was an uphill battle against powerful and determined adversaries. But it was crucial, I emphasized, that their interests be represented in the courtroom. I told them to focus on what was most important—their children's education—and to ignore as much as they could the legal turmoil that would be swirling around them.

One of the people in attendance was Mikel Holt, publisher of the *Milwaukee Community Journal*, the city's largest African-American newspaper. He would subsequently describe my performance at the meeting in very generous terms;[3] but in fact, I really had only the vaguest notion of what I was doing. Ironically, though, the strategies we deployed in the Milwaukee battle would stay in place all the way through the U.S. Supreme Court.

On that same trip, I paid a visit to the Bradley Foundation. Bradley and its visionary president, Michael Joyce, had played a critical role in developing the program. Joyce considered school choice a "silver bullet" issue: the type of program that could destroy a key pillar of the welfare state. (Not coincidentally, the reform-minded Gov. Tommy Thompson was pursuing pathbreaking welfare reform at the same time.) Joyce and his colleagues, Dan Schmidt and Hillel Fradkin, were totally committed to winning the battle for school choice. They were wary of Polly Williams (as she was of them), but understood the necessity of their temporary alliance. They were also pleased to have our involvement in the litigation, not willing to trust politicians to safeguard the program in court.

They arranged a visit for me with Thompson and his education and legal advisers. I found Thompson to be cheerfully bombastic and a quick study. Unlike most Republicans, who were cautious about school choice, he recognized that it offered huge potential for a Republican to make inroads into urban minority communities. (Indeed, Thompson would go on to carry Milwaukee County in his re-election bid.) His advisers were equally committed, but pessimistic about the legal prospects. With the lawsuit in Madison, they warned, the odds were against us, because every judge in the city was liberal. They considered the program particularly vulnerable on "private or local bill" grounds. Moreover, although the attorney general would defend the program's constitutionality, he also would

---

[3]See Mikel Holt, *Not Yet "Free at Last"*: The Unfinished Business of the Civil Rights Movement (Oakland, Calif.: Institute for Contemporary Studies, 2000).

be bound to defend the regulations. (Technically, the attorney general represented Grover, not the governor.) Although Thompson was optimistic—actually, he didn't exactly predict a victory, he *demanded* one—his aides were resigned to the program not starting in September.

I considered it absolutely critical, if there was any possible way to do it, to get the program up and running. First, it seemed to me that it would be much tougher for a court to strike down an ongoing program and to wrench children out of good schools than to invalidate a program that hadn't started yet. Second, I believed the program was much more vulnerable in the abstract, for it could be subjected to all manner of the sky-is-falling attacks. Only a functioning program would allow us effectively to rebut the parade of horribles.

Back in Washington, I set myself to the task. I managed to find a local counsel in Madison: Anne Sulton, a flamboyant but committed black attorney who was the lawyer for the Madison chapter of the NAACP. That was a fortuitous occurrence because it helped negate the impact of having the NAACP's Chaney as the lead plaintiff. I selected several parents as clients, and interviewed them so I could present their stories through affidavits. I chose as our lead plaintiff Lonzetta Davis, one of the parents who I thought would make a particularly strong impression in the media.

We filed our complaint against the regulations along with a motion to intervene in the union's lawsuit as defendants. (Interveners become a party with all of the rights that go along with that status.) One of the first tactical decisions related to the judge who was assigned to the case, Susan Steingass. I asked Anne Sulton and the governor's counsel about her, and learned she was considered a bright, fair-minded, but liberal judge. Moreover, she was a social friend of Bert Grover's. I had the option to automatically recuse one judge and return to the pool for another random assignment, and I agonized over it, asking about the other possible judges. All of them were liberal, I was assured; the only real choice was between one who was bright and conscientious, or one who was less so. It was a nerve-wracking decision, but I decided to stick with Judge Steingass.

The judge acted quickly to schedule the matters for cross-motions for summary judgment, meaning that she would decide the case on the briefs and arguments, without trial. Because of time constraints, she scheduled the argument for a Saturday morning just weeks before the school year would start—an extraordinary action (indeed, the only weekend argument I've ever seen in 20 years of litigation), but one that indicated that Judge Steingass recognized the importance of the case.

I began researching the law in earnest. That was long before we could afford computerized legal research, so I made repeated forays into the musty shelves of the George Mason University Law School library in Arlington. Many law students consider constitutional law to be glamorous, and in some ways it is; but most of the time those few of us who get to practice it on a regular basis end up researching arcane rules of law. Most of the relevant cases on the issues raised by the union dated back to the early part of the 20th century. Some of the law books didn't appear to have been used for decades.

It was tough getting a conceptual handle on the causes of action. The uniformity clause seemed the easiest: the state constitution guaranteed a "uniform" public education; to me, that seemed to create a floor, not a ceiling. Certainly, it shouldn't mean that all children needed to be subjected to a uniformly *bad* education. The cases seemed to support that view. Likewise, the public purpose doctrine only seemed to require that when the state employed private agents to secure a governmental objective, it need only adopt minimal regulatory safeguards in order to make sure that objective would be achieved. It could not mean, as the union argued, that private entities (such as private schools) could *never* be used to achieve public purposes. Though I was confident on both issues, I didn't want to take them for granted because either could nullify the program and establish a precedent for programs in other states that had similar constitutional provisions.

The private or local bill provision, however, totally stumped me. I now understand it to be a fairly libertarian constraint on government power: any legislation relating to a particular person or locality must be adopted as a free-standing bill, lest it be logrolled into a bigger bill (such as the state budget) that will draw majority support even though legislators might otherwise oppose specific provisions. But the precedents interpreting the provision were complex and confusing. Because the school choice program was limited to Milwaukee and passed as part of the budget bill, it would seem to violate the technical proscription of the private or local bill clause. But if the goal of the provision, as some of the cases suggested, was to ensure that bills were passed in the light of day, the program should survive, because it was the focus of extensive debate. Making matters worse, there were two competing precedents, *Brookfield* and *Milwaukee Brewers*, and whichever one the court chose to apply would seem to dictate the outcome. We would have to try to shoehorn the case into one while our opponents would attempt the opposite. By the time we reached the Wisconsin Supreme Court over a year later, I had developed a comprehensive theory of the private or local bill clause of the Wisconsin Constitution that would take two dozen pages to explain fully. In my time-compressed first brief in Dane County Superior Court, however, I could barely muster two pages.

Even more difficult was argument on the regulations. No case law existed to guide the court on the public school regulations, so all I could argue was that the regulations exceeded Grover's authority under the law. I also attached newspaper articles indicating that Grover, whose job was to enforce the law, was overtly hostile to it.

The disability regulations were a different story. They required an assessment of the federal Individuals with Disabilities Education Act, a complicated federal law with volumes of mind-numbing interpretative regulations. There was no way I could wade through and master them in time.

That's when we got a big break. By this point, the school choice program was the talk of conservative policy circles in Washington, and Kate O'Beirne of the Heritage Foundation invited Polly Williams and me to talk about it at a noon lecture. We also were invited to meet with David Kearns, the deputy secretary of the Department of Education, which happens to have administrative authority over the IDEA. At the meeting he asked what he could do to help. I suggested that the Department of Education provide an opinion letter on the issue of whether the private schools would have to provide special services to disabled students under the IDEA. And we needed it in a couple of weeks. I knew we wouldn't have it in time for our brief, but hoped desperately that we'd have it for the oral argument.

I was asking for a lot: literally moving a controversial decision through a huge bureaucracy in record time. Kearns assigned it to the one person capable of pulling it off: Richard D. Komer, the brilliant deputy assistant secretary in the Office of Civil Rights. Dick had been a colleague of mine at the EEOC and was my racquetball partner. I was ecstatic when I heard he was assigned to do it. Still, I knew it wouldn't happen without heavy pressure from outside. Not only did Governor Thompson apply pressure, but Sen. Robert Kasten (R-Wis.) made calls to the Department of Education as well, trying to find out when the opinion would be issued. When I called Dick to schedule our regular racquetball game, he shrieked at me, "If you'd stop having *senators* calling over here, maybe I could play some racquetball!" It brought a smile to my face to know we had some powerful allies; but I knew it would be a herculean task for Dick to get a good opinion letter to us at all, much less in the time we needed it.

Meanwhile, we began work in earnest in the court of public opinion. In Milwaukee, the *Journal-Sentinel* was unrelentingly hostile. But Mikel Holt's *Community Journal* was solidly on our side, castigating Chaney and the Milwaukee NAACP for opposing a program whose primary beneficiaries were black schoolchildren. Chaney explained that school choice had been deployed in the South as a means to evade the mandate of *Brown v. Board of Education.* True, said the *Community Journal*, but times had changed. To back its point, the newspaper polled the Milwaukee black community and found 90 percent support for the program. It would not be the last time the NAACP was hopelessly out of step with its purported constituency over school choice.

I also wanted to step up the pressure on Bert Grover, who was doing everything he could to sabotage the program. I called a friend of mine, John Fund, who recently had started working as an editorial writer for the *Wall Street Journal.* John had been a journalism student at Sacramento State College when I was a law student at the University of California at Davis, and we had become friends in the small local libertarian circle. John seized the opportunity, penning three hard-hitting editorials that savaged Grover as a modern-day Orval Faubus, blocking the schoolhouse doors to minority schoolchildren. For the first time in a major national media outlet, the civil rights banner was unfurled over school choice, and the equitable arguments were made in the most eloquent and powerful terms. The attacks hit their mark: Grover reined in his public criticism of the program and didn't even show up in court.

27

Back in Milwaukee, Polly Williams was still shaking things up. She had learned that most of the Milwaukee Public School teachers, like many urban public school teachers around the nation, sent their own children to private schools. Yet they had the audacity to challenge the school choice program. Fine, said Polly: if the public schools are good enough for *our* kids, they ought to be good enough for *their* kids. So she announced that she would sponsor legislation making it a condition of employment that public school teachers send their own children to public schools. The response was death threats on Polly's home answering machine. Tongue in cheek, I had to advise Polly that her proposal would be unconstitutional—public school teachers, like all Americans, have a constitutional right to send their children to private schools. But the point about the union's hypocrisy was brilliantly made.

I was still working to establish my credibility with our allies in Milwaukee. Larry Harwell called to tell me that a local news station would be contacting me for comment on the case, and that I was not to talk with them because they were deceitful. Not talking to the media ran counter to my every instinct: we *had* to win the battle in the court of public opinion, and failing to appear meant ceding the argument to our adversaries. Wrong, said Larry: appearing on the show would sanction a negative report. He was insistent. When the call came from the news station, I didn't take it.

At the same time, I was managing to alienate one of the schools. I needed affidavits from some of the private schools, but decided two were enough. I didn't want to burden the schools unnecessarily. They had small administrative staffs and were busy preparing for the rapidly approaching school year. So I asked the principals of Urban Day School and Bruce-Guadaloupe, who happily obliged. But then I received a call from Sister Callista at Harambee, and on her end of the phone was one angry nun. Why didn't I ask *them* for an affidavit? Was I playing favorites? Not at all, I just wanted to spare you the burden, I explained. Apologizing profusely for the slight, I agreed to secure one from Harambee as well. The incident underscored the school's commitment to the program—as well as their pride. But it took a long time to make up for my faux pas with Sister Callista.

Unbeknownst to me, controversy of an even more serious form was brewing in Milwaukee. State Sen. Gary George, an influential black Democrat, wanted to take over the defense of the program. Others were criticizing Polly and Larry for choosing a white conservative critic of affirmative action to defend the program. Months later, Larry told me all of that. But true to his word, he told the critics that Polly and he were sticking with their lawyer.

As oral argument approached, I discussed tactics with Bob Woodson. He suggested chartering a bus to take parents and children from Milwaukee to Madison to be in the courtroom for the argument, and offered to pay for the bus. I accepted gratefully. I also designed some red, white, and blue buttons bearing the words "School Choice," for our supporters to wear.

Everything was ready to go, except me. I was a nervous wreck. This was by far the most significant argument of my career so far. So many people, with so much at stake, were counting on me. There was a great deal of law to master, and I had very little courtroom experience upon which to draw. And where was that opinion letter from the Department of Education?

By the eve of the court hearing, I had given up on it. Dick wasn't returning my phone calls. But inside the agency, he was moving heaven and earth—and a little bit of hell. At 5 p.m., the letter arrived. It was the formal opinion of the Department of Education that the state could not assign its responsibilities under the IDEA to private schools. The decision to attend private schools was a "private placement" under the IDEA. Children choosing private schools would remain eligible for "equitable participation" in the school district's IDEA program, but the law did not create substantive obligations for the private schools.

The letter was magnificent. To this day I don't know how Dick managed to get all of the necessary bureaucrats to sign off on it. The legal reasoning was so strong that the Clinton administration, years later in the context of a Florida school choice program for disabled children, applied and extended its conclusions. Best of all, it delivered a huge burst of adrenaline on the eve of the argument. I had my assistant make several copies to distribute the next day in court. What an unexpected jolt it would deliver to the other side!

Bob Woodson and I flew to Milwaukee and rode the bus with Polly, Larry, and dozens of parents and children for the one-and-a-half-hour trip to Madison. Larry regaled me with stories and I walked up and down the aisle of the bus, meeting everyone. It was a blast. But a half hour before reaching Madison, I opened my folder and discovered, to my shock, that the opinion letters not only weren't stapled, they weren't collated! So the parents started a collation brigade. When we reached the courthouse, just in time for the hearing, one of our number went searching for a stapler.

The courtroom was packed, half with white bureaucrats and the other half with black parents and children sporting their school choice buttons. Though the judge had managed to get the courtroom opened for the rare Saturday hearing, the air conditioning was off, and the atmosphere was stifling.

On the other side was a bevy of lawyers for the teachers union. At the table with me was Warren Weinstein, an amiable lawyer from the attorney general's office who had done a conscientious job on the state's brief. His presence, however, was slight comfort: he would have to switch sides halfway through the argument to defend Grover's rules.

Judge Steingass proved to be a pleasant, engaged, obviously intelligent jurist. My nervousness dissipated quickly, and as the arguments started in earnest I began to hit my stride. In fact, I loved it. Judge Steingass was well-prepared and aggressively questioned all of the lawyers. The courtroom was quiet and the kids were well-behaved, but I could hear murmurs of approval from the parents every time I made a key argument: "That's right!" "Amen!" Their approbation fueled my argument and I suddenly understood why black preachers are so eloquent.

The arguments lasted three marathon hours. The heat in the courtroom was oppressive. But for once my exposure to the famed Washington humidity paid off: I think I was the only lawyer in the courtroom who wasn't perspiring. The argument over the program's constitutionality went back and forth, with no clear advantage. But I noticed Judge Steingass repeatedly glancing over at the parents and children.

By the time it was time to argue about Grover's rules, I had the freshly collated and stapled opinion letters in my hand, and announced it with a flourish. The opposing lawyers were visibly upset, but the judge accepted the letter. After all, it was an on-point legal authority, hot off the press. It was a total coup.

Eventually the argument ended and Judge Steingass promised to issue a ruling as soon as possible. It wasn't clear which way she was leaning, but our supporters in the gallery seemed pleased with the argument. We all got together for lunch, and then Bob Woodson and I flew back to Washington from Madison.

I was pensive but felt we had done all we could. Now it was a matter of waiting. That was a skill I had mastered early in my career: you focus on a case, pour your heart and soul into it day and night for weeks on end, all toward the dramatic crescendo of the most eloquent court argument that you can muster—and then wait. Sometimes it's insufferable: recently my colleagues and I had to wait more than five years for a court decision in one of our cases. So though it seemed interminably long at the time, the couple of weeks that it took Judge Steingass to issue an opinion was mercifully short.

In fact, it came so quickly that I wasn't expecting it. One characteristic of a court decision in a multi-issue case is that it's tough to figure out the bottom line unless you read it in its entirety. In my case, I usually cheat, starting at the end to find out the relief granted. In this case it was everything we wanted: the plaintiffs' demand for an injunction was denied, while our request for an injunction against the most offensive regulations was granted. We had won, unequivocally.

The decision, in my view, turned out to be the most important in the history of the school choice movement until the U.S. Supreme Court decision a dozen years later. The spectacle of children from low-income families—even if only several hundred of them— leaving defective public schools for private schools chosen by their parents, was truly a milestone. It was like taking out the first brick from the Berlin Wall—once removed, the previously impregnable barrier was forever penetrated.

Still, we had to resist the plaintiffs' motion for an emergency injunction from the state court of appeals. But now the procedural odds were in our favor, and after a fast and furious exchange of briefs, the court denied the motion. And as the new school year started, several hundred economically disadvantaged youngsters crossed the threshold to a brighter educational future.

I returned to Milwaukee to celebrate with local choice supporters. Even better, I visited some of the schools to see how the kids were doing. They were doing fine, it turned out, blending in fairly seamlessly, and totally oblivious to the legal turmoil swirling around them. To the parents and school administrators, however, I made it clear that a long and uncertain legal road lay ahead.

That proved to be one constant and debilitating feature in the litigation: the chronic uncertainty. No one could ever be certain that the program would continue. For parents it was a source of anxiety: they didn't want to lose the precious educational opportunities they finally had secured for their children. For school administrators, it meant the stress of hiring teachers, buying supplies, and making plans with no certain assurance that the funding stream would continue. And yet everyone involved in the program seemed utterly confident that we would prevail. I wished I could share their confidence.

The next step was the Court of Appeals in Madison. Though the court had turned down an injunction, it still would consider the case on the merits. Happily, the plaintiffs did not appeal their loss on Grover's forms, but the constitutional issues remained.

In the midst of preparation, disaster struck: one of the private schools, the Juanita Virgil Academy, went belly-up. The school's finances were a mess and angry parents demanded action—which unfortunately took the form of shutting down. The other private schools in the program were full, so most of Juanita Virgil's children were forced to return to the public schools.

The closure was a public relations debacle. Critics of the program assailed Juanita Virgil as a fly-by-night school typical of what we would see in a voucher program; and as usual, they asserted, the beleaguered public schools would have to pick up the pieces.

Our side spun the situation as well as possible. The market was working, we argued: in the private sector, defective schools closed, whereas they remained open in the public sector, which was much worse. Moreover, the main schools in the program—Urban Day, Harambee, Bruce-Guadaloupe—were well-established pillars of the community. Still, the event stung badly, and surely it would spill over into the litigation.

The Juanita Virgil disaster made us realize how important it was that the program not only be defended but that it also be successful. The participating schools had formed a council to help one another and self-regulate, and its importance was underscored. Henceforth, concerns about an adequate program infrastructure would preoccupy choice supporters and would comprise an important focus of the legal defense effort.

The appeals court proved less hospitable than the trial court. The argument was held in the ornate courtroom of the Wisconsin

Supreme Court in the state capitol. As I walked into the courtroom, one of the union's lawyers was chatting amicably with a pleasant middle-aged woman. The lawyer introduced her as Justice Shirley Abrahamson of the Wisconsin Supreme Court. Uh-oh, I thought. Their chummy chat was not a very good harbinger for the battle ahead.

But the bigger obstacle for the moment was the Court of Appeals. The judges seemed unfazed by equity arguments, and focused on the minutiae of the complex tests concocted to determine whether legislation was an impermissible private or local bill. It was a scenario that would repeat itself dozens of times as we argued school choice cases around the country: the more the other side succeeded in shifting the focus from the remedial purposes of the program and mired the argument in constitutional esoterica, the worse our odds. This time they succeeded, painfully well.

When an argument goes that badly, it's difficult to face friends and supporters who put so much faith in you. The well-wishers in the gallery conveyed comforting sentiments, but I knew they sized up the situation the same way I did. For some reason, I walked over to a little second-grader named James, who had been sitting alongside Polly Williams in the gallery, quietly coloring throughout the argument. His serious demeanor made him all the more adorable, and we shook hands earnestly as he looked at me appraisingly. "You did good," he told me. "I like you."

The little guy's words at that moment were worth more than a million bucks to me. I didn't think anyone could bring a smile to my face, but he did. I never again saw him after that, but I've often wondered how he's doing; hopefully, James is a high school graduate by now. Something tells me he's doing fine.

But the Court of Appeals decision was every bit as bad as predicted. The court unanimously struck down the program as an unconstitutional private or local bill. The decision came in the middle of the school year, so the program was allowed to continue until the end of the year. Our only recourse to keep the program going beyond that was the Wisconsin Supreme Court. Because there were no federal issues in the lawsuit, the state's highest court would be the last resort.

Unfortunately, as we prepared for the Supreme Court, our financial circumstances at Landmark were worsening. Our small staff were missing paychecks, and bills were unpaid. At one point, my assistant had to drape herself over her computer in the middle of a brief and beg the men who came to repossess the equipment to leave it. The situation was so dire that I couldn't sleep.

Ever since my mom told me when I was a little kid that it was rude to ask my grandmother for money, I've been averse to fund-raising. But I asked some friends to help us through the winter of 1990. Former Delaware governor Pete DuPont, a school choice stalwart whose short-lived presidential campaign I had supported in 1988, contributed ten thousand dollars.[4] David Keating of the National Taxpayers Union did likewise. I didn't want to broadcast the situation, but confided in some close friends, including Jeanne Allen, who headed the Heritage Foundation's education program, and Ed Crane, president of the Cato Institute. Ed took enormous pressure off my shoulders by offering to bring me and my cases to Cato if necessary. I'll eternally forgive Ed all the home runs he's hit off the Institute for Justice teams in softball over the years for his incredibly generous gesture in that time of need.

It turned out a longer-term solution was in the offing. My former boss Chip Mellor and I had wanted to open our own public-interest law firm since our days together in Denver. It would be an explicitly libertarian law firm, with funding attracted by our commitment to a principled, long-term litigation strategy, rather than litigation following funding. At the time, Chip was heading Pacific Research Institute in San Francisco. Together with leading libertarian legal scholars, we had developed litigation blueprints in the areas of economic liberty, civil rights, private property rights, and the First Amendment. My experience at Landmark seemed to demonstrate that huge untapped potential existed for a creative, empowerment-oriented litigation program.

The challenge was funding: neither of us wanted to approach supporters of our existing organizations. Landmark's president, Jerry Hill, was well aware of my discomfort over the organization's finances, and I told him that Chip and I were trying to start a new firm.

---

[4] On the national stage, Pete DuPont and former education secretaries Bill Bennett and Lamar Alexander have constantly provided generous support for the school choice movement.

Finally, we received an offer of seed funding from foundations supported by libertarian businessmen Charles and David Koch. We targeted a start-up for our new Institute for Justice in early fall.

Landmark and I agreed that I would argue the Milwaukee case under Landmark's auspices even though I would join IJ before then. Thereafter, Landmark would represent Polly Williams in any subsequent litigation.[5]

On September 3, 1991, Chip and I opened IJ with a staff of seven in subleased offices at the corner of 10th and Pennsylvania. For both of us, it was a dream come true: a chance to practice public-interest law the way we always believed it should be practiced. Chip and I are well-suited as partners. We balance each other's shortcomings and boost each other's spirits. The sum of the whole is greater than the parts. Chip is an excellent lawyer and a good manager. We see the world in much the same way (except for our baseball allegiances—I root for the Yankees while Chip is a long-suffering Red Sox fan), and we're both passionately committed to IJ's mission and clients. It works well.

And from the very first day, we vowed to defend *every* school choice program until the constitutional cloud was removed. We adapted a motto from the late-night television commercial: If you have a choice program, you have a lawyer!

At the moment, there was one case and it received my rapt attention. Sizing up the seven-member Wisconsin Supreme Court, the odds did not seem very favorable. Chief Justice Heffernan was liberal, as were two associate justices, William Bablitch, a former Democratic state legislator, and Shirley Abrahamson, a nationally renowned activist judge. On our side, we were confident only of one justice, Louis Ceci. Three justices seemed in play—and we needed all of them to win.

The Court recently had rejected, by a four-to-three vote, a "tax equity" lawsuit that sought to have the state's school funding system declared unconstitutional. Tracing back to lawsuits filed in New Jersey and California in the late 1960s, the lawsuits are a favorite

---

[5]Under the more recent leadership of Mark Levin and Pete Hutchison, Landmark Legal Foundation has been a significant and effective player in education policy litigation, acting as a constant thorn to the National Education Association by holding it accountable for various misdeeds.

tool of left-wing public-interest groups. The lawsuits have been successful in more than one dozen states, but the remedies—higher taxes and more funding for failing school districts—have utterly failed to boost student achievement. Intuitively, one might predict that judges who were receptive to tax equity claims also would be receptive to school choice. In fact, the correlation is almost perfect— in reverse. That gave us some hope for success in the Wisconsin Supreme Court, whose majority had admonished advocates to look to the legislature rather than to the courts for educational equity. And in enacting the Milwaukee Parental Choice Program, the Wisconsin Legislature had done exactly that.

That formulation guided the structure of our brief. At this level we had 50 pages, and I was determined to use them to full advantage. Our challenge at the outset was to neutralize the inherent advantage that plaintiffs enjoy: framing the terms of the debate. That is an advantage that my colleagues and I, who usually represent plaintiffs, appreciate enormously. But here, it was the unions who were able to choose the field of battle.

Defense lawyers typically merely negative the plaintiffs' assertions—if they say "X," we say "Not-X"—but there is no rule that you have to do it that way. So instead of instantly responding to the union's legal assertions, I started our brief with "background principles" that in our view should inform the Court's deliberations. I started with the cherished principle of parental autonomy, recognized by the U.S. Supreme Court in *Pierce v. Society of Sisters*, and followed by the Wisconsin Supreme Court in other cases. Then I set forth the sacred constitutional promise of equal educational opportunities, articulated in *Brown v. Board of Education* and embraced by the Wisconsin Supreme Court under the state constitution. Both of those principles, I argued, were vindicated by the Milwaukee Parental Choice Program. Finally, I argued for judicial restraint and deference to the legislature—a "presumption of constitutionality" that IJ usually has to overcome in its attacks on government regulation, but a useful doctrine when defending pathbreaking reform. The Court should begin its review of the program by consulting all three of those principles, I argued, before it even turned to the plaintiffs' assertions.

By now, our arguments on the substantive issues were stronger and a bit more sophisticated. After all the research and agonizing over obtuse provisions and doctrines of the Wisconsin Constitution, I felt like I had been present at the founding, or at least at the debates over the dreaded "private or local bill" clause. As to the plaintiffs' other arguments, we argued that their legal theories would arrest any meaningful education reform—no doubt, exactly what they wanted to accomplish. Distressingly, the American Civil Liberties Union had opted to file an amicus brief supporting the union, arguing that the diversion of funds to private schools undermined the state's commitment to public schools. This was an absurd position for the ACLU to take, given the number of times it has sued public schools, leading to a huge "diversion" of funds from public schools. I could understand why the ACLU would oppose school choice that included religious schools due to the organization's extreme views on separation of church and state—but the program we were litigating was limited to nonsectarian schools. I called my friend Nadine Strossen, national ACLU president, to protest. She agreed that the ACLU had no business challenging a nonsectarian school choice program, and denied that the ACLU would ever do such a thing—but there it was, in black and white.

We needed decisively to rebut their arguments, because a precedent of this sort could stymie school choice elsewhere. We argued that (1) the uniformity clause applied on its face only to "district" schools, whereas these were private schools enlisted to help fulfill the objectives of public education; (2) the provision provided a floor, not a ceiling, for state action in support of public education; and (3) the program in fact advanced the goals of public education by extending opportunities to children who desperately needed them. Again, that argument would create a recurring theme, namely that school choice serves the true goals of public education.

But there were still holes, particularly the absence of legislative intent for the program. So we developed some of our own, presenting data on poor student performance in the Milwaukee Public Schools and drawing on affidavits from Polly Williams, parents, and school officials. We also discussed at length the findings of John Chubb and Terry Moe in *Politics, Markets & America's Schools*, which established an academic rationale for school choice.

Another tactic, subtle but important, was rhetoric. The union constantly abbreviated the program's name (MPCP) and referred to it as a "voucher" program. We always spelled out the full name of the Milwaukee Parental Choice Program and used the terms "school choice" or "parental choice." Throughout our brief, we emphasized the David versus Goliath nature of the case and its real-world human impact. It was a close case on the law, but we had the equities solidly on our side.

Those elements of our school choice brief in the Wisconsin Supreme Court would remain constant in the subsequent dozens of briefs in other school choice cases. We would always endeavor to improve on the original, and to constantly test the underlying premises, but the initial framework proved enduring and effective.

Meanwhile, the battle raged in the court of public opinion. I made numerous trips to Wisconsin to shore up support. On one trip to Madison to debate at the University of Wisconsin Federalist Society, I was greeted at the airport with an urgent message to stop by the Capitol to see Governor Thompson. It turned out he had heard I was in town and just wanted to get together. I was already a fan. Thompson was a true visionary, an apostle of "compassionate conservatism" before George W. Bush was first elected to public service—and an unrelenting advocate for ideas he championed. After a few minutes of chitchat, he asked me, "How about an impromptu news conference?" And within minutes, the two of us were facing a torrent of questions from the entire Wisconsin Capitol press corps. It was a great experience, underscoring the importance of being prepared for the unexpected.

And the curve balls continued to come. A couple of months before the Supreme Court argument, a state senator phoned Polly and told her that he had secret information that would win the lawsuit—but he would share it only if she allowed him to argue the case instead of me. Share the information if you want, Polly retorted, but we're sticking with our lawyer. I was grateful for the vote of confidence but wondered about the secret information. It turns out there wasn't any. In fact, the state senator ultimately asked us to draft an amicus brief for him. It wasn't the last time that some who cast themselves as our "friends" gave us as much anxiety as our adversaries.

But our adversaries were dishing it out too. Superintendent Bert Grover's final revenge against the program was visited in the form of the official first-year state evaluation by University of Wisconsin professor John Witte, whom Grover had handpicked. Given the lofty hopes for the program, the report was troublesome: despite a high degree of parental satisfaction, students in the school choice program scored no better on standardized tests than their Milwaukee Public Schools counterparts. Still, Witte urged that the program continue with further study.

Despite its suspect pedigree and its mild endorsement, the report was devastating. It was also difficult to rebut convincingly, because Witte refused to release the underlying data. After years of legal wrangling, he finally did. It turned out that Witte had compared students in the choice program not with children who applied for the program and who had been turned away by random selection— the ideal "control group"—but with a subset of Milwaukee Public School students that Witte concocted. That subset comprised much fewer minority and much more affluent schoolchildren than the choice program students. But we couldn't know that at the time.

The Witte study sounded a useful cautionary note to school choice advocates: We must not overpromise academic improvements. After all, many inner-city, low-income minority schoolchildren are on a *downward* academic trajectory. It is an accomplishment if that trajectory can be halted or even slowed. Indeed, subsequent school choice studies have fairly consistently shown little academic progress for program participants in the first two years, but significant gains starting in the third, and accelerating in the fourth year of the program.

The study also underscored the importance of humanizing the issue. Our side scored a huge breakthrough when *60 Minutes* reporter Mike Wallace and producer Richard Bonin visited Milwaukee. They liked what they found, and the ensuing broadcast was amazing. It featured Polly Williams arguing that the goals of the civil rights establishment were mixed up: Education should come first, she argued, and integration would follow. Urban Day School principal Zakiyah Courtney talked about a student who had arrived from MPS with horrendous disciplinary reports that she had tucked away in her drawer so as not to alarm the teacher—and the child had become a model student at her school. The telecast featured officials from the union and the NAACP, straight out of central casting. I'll never forget the NAACP official mixing her metaphors and proclaiming the program "a sleeping pill for disaster." It ended with a young black youngster at a private middle school, tearful because he was being held back but vowing to earn the grades the following year to prove he was capable. The program illustrated the tough love of the private schools in the program; and importantly, it began to debunk the pernicious liberal myth that poor minority children are incapable of learning.

And it gave our side enormous credibility. The *60 Minutes* coup taught us an important lesson: if we could get reporters to actually see the program in action, walk the hallways of the schools, and talk to the parents and children, we would have more converts. Throughout the history of the modern school choice movement, our worst enemy has been the straw man. Our opponents constantly have raised every conceivable sky-is-falling hypothetical. School choice means the demise of public schools, they contend. School choice skims the cream, increases racial segregation, benefits mainly wealthy kids. Now with the Milwaukee program, we were able for the first time to answer hypothetical assertions with reality. It was our job, as advocates, to infuse that reality into the court of public opinion, into our briefs, and into our court arguments.

With the Wisconsin Supreme Court argument approaching, Polly Williams and the schools agreed to send a bus of parents and children to Madison. This time, I flew directly to Madison so I could prepare. I would share argument time with the state's lawyer, Warren Weinstein, and intended to hit hard on the equities.

The argument was held on a clear fall day in October 1991. I arrived early to take my place at counsel table alongside our local counsel, Anne Sulton. Polly and Larry were in the gallery, as were Dan Schmidt and Hillel Fradkin from the Bradley Foundation, my partner Chip, my old colleagues from Landmark Legal Foundation, and other well-wishers. But the parents and children from Milwaukee hadn't yet arrived, and the seats were filling rapidly. Unbeknown to me, the bus had broken down en route.

Weinstein rose to argue and was instantly interrupted by questions from all sides, particularly hostile queries from Justices Bablitch and Abrahamson. My adrenaline was pumping. Though I had been an insecure advocate earlier in my career, I had come to absolutely love oral argument, and I couldn't wait for my turn.

Finally it came. As I walked to the podium, I glanced back to the rear of the courtroom, and saw that the children had arrived. But there were no seats left in the courtroom. So instead they were outside of the courtroom doors, a sea of tiny noses pressed against the glass doors. I smiled and thought to myself: what a metaphor, those kids on the outside looking in. The image was the most potent incentive imaginable.

In my argument, I attempted to blend legal and equitable arguments. What this program was about was a transfer of power from bureaucrats—I gestured to the lawyers at the opposing counsel's table—to parents, gesturing to the back of the room. The plaintiffs, I declared, wanted to wrench low-income children out of the only good schools they had ever known; and nothing in the Wisconsin Constitution—which itself, after all, guaranteed equal educational opportunities–would compel such an unjust result. Justice Abrahamson wanted to know, was there any principle that would limit the program to the special circumstances in Milwaukee? I replied that the program was created as a tool for addressing the unique problems of large urban school districts, but there was no constitutional limitation. I said that the Constitution obligated the state to provide a uniform system of public schools, but it was free to go beyond that.

Both sides were grilled intensely. While the union lawyers were arguing, the chief justice stopped the argument to admonish opposing lawyers—implicitly Anne Sulton and me—to stop making facial expressions. I was mortified: that was the first time I realized how much I editorialize with my face and that I should never, ever play poker. Anne and I subsequently behaved ourselves.

We left the courtroom without knowing how the decision would go. I mingled with the parents and children, talked with reporters, and made my way back to Washington. I felt that our side had done its best. But the fear gnawed at me, as it always has at crucial moments in litigation: What if our best wasn't good enough?

The wait was agonizing; but past cases had taught me that the best tonic was to plunge into other work, of which there was plenty. Finally, after a mercifully few short months, in March 1992, the decision arrived in *Davis v. Grover*: by a four-to-three vote, we won.

Though the vote was close, the substance of the decision was a resounding triumph. The decision by Justice William Callow methodically repudiated all of the plaintiffs' arguments. It began with a recitation of the need for the program, turning to Chubb and Moe to supply the underlying rationale of empowering low-income parents and introducing a measure of choice and competition into the education system. The program had not been enacted as a "private or

41

local bill" because by its terms it could be extended to other large cities, and it had been passed in the light of day. Nor did it violate the educational uniformity clause because it was a supplement to, not an abandonment of, the public school system. The state's supervision of the program was adequate to ensure its public purpose. Here the Court made a telling observation:

> Control is also fashioned in the MPCP in the form of parental choice. The program allows participating parents to choose a school with an environment that matches their child's interest and needs, and with a location that is convenient. If the school does not meet the parents' expectations, the parents may remove the child from the school and go elsewhere. In this way, parental choice preserves accountability for the best interests of the children.[6]

It was nearly as eloquent an exposition of the virtues of school choice as Milton Friedman's!

The dissenters, Chief Justice Heffernan and Justices Abrahamson and Bablitch, parroted the union line, finding that the program violated both the private or local bill clause and the uniformity clause. As Justice Abrahamson wrote, "I conclude that the constitution prohibits the legislature from diverting state support for the district schools to a duplicate, competitive private system of schools."[7] Moreover, she asserted, the program was not uniform. Those would be recurrent themes in state court litigation elsewhere as well.

Passionate as both the majority and dissenting opinions were, the strongest words were employed by Justice Ceci, who concurred in the majority opinion:

> Literally thousands of school children in the Milwaukee public school system have been doomed because of those in government who insist upon maintaining the status quo. . . . The Wisconsin legislature, attuned and attentive to the seemingly insurmountable problems confronting socioeconomically deprived children, has attempted to throw a life preserver to those Milwaukee children caught in the cruel riptide of a school system floundering upon the shoals of poverty, status-quo thinking, and despair.

Justice Ceci beseeched his colleagues, "Let's give choice a chance!"[8]

---

[6] *Davis v. Grover*, 480 N.W.2d 460, 476 (1992).

[7] Ibid., p. 482 (Abrahamson, J., dissenting).

[8] Ibid., p. 477 (Ceci, J., concurring).

And that is exactly what the Wisconsin Supreme Court did. Its decision not only gave firm jurisprudential support to the concept of school choice—at least involving nonsectarian schools—but also demonstrated that despite the odds, David could slay Goliath. Our ragtag bunch somehow had managed to overcome a determined opposition and huge resource disparities to keep the program alive and, also, to preserve a shining, real-world example of the potential of school choice.

3. False Starts

As we emerged from the victory in Milwaukee, the question instantly arose: How do we keep the momentum going? The opposition's strategy was clear: isolate the Milwaukee program, subject it to constant bureaucratic and legislative attacks, and spread disinformation about it. That, they hoped, would inoculate the rest of the country from the dreaded voucher virus.

Our challenge was to replicate our success somewhere else. The problem was that school choice was not yet a national movement. Not a single national organization was focused on fomenting or coordinating school choice. The Heritage Foundation and the Cato Institute were producing sound policy arguments, but there was no one to implement them. Indigenous efforts began to spring up in pockets throughout the country, but it was difficult to evaluate their prospects for success.

Fortunately, our allies in Milwaukee—particularly the Bradley Foundation and the Metropolitan Milwaukee Association of Commerce, an enlightened local business group that was strongly supportive of school choice—had a plan. Part of their understanding was that even a small initial program would engender demand for a larger one. The initial program, limited to one thousand students whose choices in turn were restricted to nonsectarian private schools, was quickly oversubscribed. In response, local advocates created a nonprofit organization, Partners Advancing Values in Education, which would provide scholarships to low-income families to send their children to private schools—including religious schools. That program, in turn, would ratchet support for expanding the publicly funded choice program. The efforts drew support from Mayor Norquist and MPS Superintendent Howard Fuller. Unfortunately, they precipitated a chasm with Polly Williams, who was suspicious of the motives of whites, conservatives, the business community, and Catholics. Any effort to seriously expand the program would have to proceed without the active support of the most visible champion of school choice.

The local advocates also understood that the school choice program had to succeed in order for it to serve as a national model. They poured resources into program coordination and information. As a result, there was no recurrence of the Juanita Virgil debacle of the program's first year. They also supported efforts to dislodge data from the state's official program evaluator, John Witte, and to encourage credible academic studies of the program. Equally important, they provided strong and visible support for *public* school reform, demonstrating that school choice and public school reform were not antagonistic but in fact two mutually reinforcing sides of the same coin.

Those early structural efforts of the Milwaukee-based school choice advocates would prove invaluable not only in future expansion of the Milwaukee program but also in creating a true and stellar national school choice model. The Milwaukee experience underscored the imperative of a sound and sophisticated local infrastructure to support school choice.

At the national level, we at IJ decided that we would have to invest significant resources to counsel any local choice advocates who sought our help, precisely because we could not determine in advance which proposals might bloom into reality. Over the years, we would end up spending much more time on failed initiatives than successful ones, literally traveling to the outermost reaches of the nation from Puerto Rico to the Commonwealth of the Northern Mariana Islands in the distant Pacific (inspiring a new IJ motto: We'll go to the ends of the Earth for school choice). Shortly after the Wisconsin victory, I made my first trip to Florida to meet with Jeb Bush—then a public policy nerd with aspirations to run for governor—and other school choice supporters such as Patrick Heffernan. At the time the legislative prospects in Florida were absolutely nil, with Gov. Lawton Chiles safely in the pocket of the teachers unions. But we hoped that we were laying the groundwork for future success. It was a process that repeated itself (and continues today) in state after state.

The potential for school choice in Milwaukee and elsewhere would be limited until religious schools were added to the range of options. For my colleagues and me, and for the reformers in Milwaukee, it was not a matter of desiring a religious influence, but rather of providing as many alternatives as possible. The reality is that religious schools predominate among private schools in the inner cities precisely because they usually are the only options that are economically accessible to families of modest economic means. They incur enormous financial sacrifices to meet that need. But including religious schools would raise a new host of legal issues. We needed to confront them if the school choice movement had any hope of achieving its great potential.

The big legal issue was one that we had not yet had to squarely confront: religious establishment. If school choice was going to be meaningful, it would have to include religious schools. The jurisprudential framework had been established by *Nyquist* in 1973, which had struck down parochiaid programs, and by *Mueller* in 1983, which had upheld tuition tax credits in Minnesota. Fortunately, the Court had subsequently decided other cases that seemed to suggest that *Mueller* provided the rule and *Nyquist* the exception.

In 1986, the Supreme Court unanimously upheld the use of college aid by Larry Witters, a blind student studying for the ministry at a school of divinity. It would be difficult to get any more religious than that! The Court's opinion, authored by the liberal Justice Thurgood Marshall, emphasized the two points that had formed the core of *Mueller*: neutrality, in the sense that Witters was choosing from a wide variety of educational options, and individual choice. Justice Marshall observed that most of the educational institutions were nonsectarian, and that few would pursue the course chosen by Witters. Justice Lewis F. Powell, who had authored the majority opinion in *Nyquist*, wrote a concurring opinion supported by five justices that went further than Marshall's opinion. Justice Powell focused less on numbers and more on the program's evenhandedness, declaring that "state programs that are wholly neutral in offering educational assistance to a class defined without reference to religion do not violate" the primary effect test under the Establishment Clause.[1] Justice Powell's opinion created a clear, workable standard by which school choice programs could be drafted.

Seven years later, the Court upheld, by a five-to-four vote, a program that provided a publicly funded interpreter for a deaf student attending a Catholic high school.[2] The majority again applied the two

[1] *Witters v. Washington Dep't of Services for the Blind*, 474 U.S. 481, 490–91 (Powell, J., concurring).

[2] *Zobrest v. Catalina Foothills School Dist.*, 509 U.S. 1 (1993).

Mueller criteria, neutrality and indirect aid. Notably, the interpreter signed both secular and religious subjects, which meant that the Court was not drawing a bright-line distinction that would forbid religious schools from using government funds only for secular instruction—a line that most religious schools, which intertwine religious and secular instruction, could not abide.

The aid would not confer an imprimatur of state endorsement of religion in that context, the majority emphasized, because the interpreter would be present in a religious school only if the parents had chosen to enroll their child there. Two of the dissenting justices focused on the symbolism of having a government employee interpreting teachings in a religious school, and stated that they would be less troubled if the state was transmitting funds to the parents instead.

Together, the cases suggested a favorable trend and a framework within which we could dispense advice to school choice advocates. Unlike our other areas of litigation at IJ, in which we were attempting to develop the law, here our goal was to preserve a reform program, so our advice would be very cautious and conservative. Also, learning from Milwaukee, we concluded that the actual contours of the program should be dictated by local realities. So as to vouchers versus tax credits or other design features, we would be emphatically agnostic—and equally enthusiastic. The need to establish a constitutional precedent congenial to school choice would be our overriding goal. But we needed choice programs to defend in order to create legal precedents that would resolve the issues once and for all.

One such program, in fact, already was up and running in the tiny town of Epsom, New Hampshire. It was developed by Jack Kelleher, a town selectman who had become a devotee of the philosopher Ayn Rand while reading voraciously on flights around the world as a government courier. He cashed in his government pension, built a house with his own hands, and aspired to live as a hermit. But the local government was constantly interfering with him in one way or another, which prompted him to run for local office. There he discovered that education was by far the town's largest expense: tiny Epsom had no schools of its own, so it had to pay ever-escalating tuition to an adjacent district. It was a true instance of taxation without representation.

So Kelleher offered an alternative: any taxpayers who relieved the town of the expense of public school tuition by enrolling their children in private schools would receive a rebate on a portion of their property taxes. It was, as economists might say, *Pareto optimality*: the taxpayers as a whole benefited from lower tuition costs; the parents benefited from lower taxes; and the students benefited from increased educational choices.

Of course, the teachers union and the ACLU didn't agree. And so, unbeknownst to me, Jack Kelleher had driven all through the night to meet me at my Landmark Center for Civil Rights office and present me with a challenge: we will pass the tax abatement law if *you* agree to defend it.

It was an offer I could not refuse. Even though the town was small, the precedent could be big: with the number of children increasing around the nation, pressure to build costly new schools was intense. If local governments could enlist private schools to absorb part of the burden, they could save costs—and expand school choice at the same time.

I flew up to New Hampshire to meet with the principals. Because the town's only restaurant burned down some time ago, we dined on tuna fish sandwiches at Jack's rustic home. I spoke at an authentic town meeting, which lasted until the wee hours. Every townsperson had his or her say—and sentiments were divided, though tilted in favor of the plan. I outlined our offer of legal representation—"free" seemed to be the biggest selling point—and answered questions for hours. At the end, the three selectmen voted in favor of the program—and I fell in love with the salt-of-the-earth people in Epsom.

The lawsuit came swiftly. This one had two thrusts: the plaintiffs argued that the program would establish religion because religious schools would benefit from the abatements, and the town lacked the authority under state law to provide tax abatements for educational purposes. The latter argument was especially troublesome. Unlike states, which are considered sovereign entities in our federal system, municipalities are creatures of the state and possess only those powers that are expressly conferred by the state. Again, a fairly libertarian doctrine—but a serious obstacle to the town's rebate policy.

The case gave rise to our first school choice trial, probing the motivations of the selectmen and the effects of the program. Immediately it was clear that I faced a huge disadvantage by being an out-of-state lawyer in New Hampshire. The judge overruled every objection I made, no matter how meritorious, and sustained every objection made by the ACLU lawyer, no matter how frivolous. Eventually I was reduced to making objections just to signal the witness that he was on track, along the lines, "Your honor, counsel is badgering the witness, and it's clear that no matter how many times he asks the question the witness will answer it the same way." But it was painfully clear that we were not going to prevail in that forum. And indeed, we didn't: the court ruled that Epsom lacked authority under state law to provide the rebate.

Under the terms of my separation agreement with Landmark, I had to leave the case when I moved to IJ, which was painful. Landmark appealed to the New Hampshire Supreme Court, which unanimously affirmed the trial court decision. Over the years, other localities approached us at IJ with similar ideas—and we even defended an Epsom-style plan in Northeast Delco, Pennsylvania—but always to the same effect: the courts or other authorities would find that the local government was acting outside of its scope of authority. The lesson for the school choice movement was that except in the most unusual circumstance, school choice would have to be effectuated at the state level rather than at the local level.

The school choice issue did return momentarily to the national stage, albeit in unexpected fashion. In 1993, some new inhabitants occupied the White House, and they brought with them a school-age daughter. As governor of Arkansas and a "new" Democrat, Bill Clinton had written to Polly Williams commending her for the Milwaukee Parental Choice Program. But as the Democratic presidential nominee, Clinton had to appease the national party's most important special-interest constituency—the teachers unions. And that meant categorically opposing school choice.

But as a parent, Clinton saw things differently. After the Clintons moved to town, the District of Columbia created a school choice program, solely for the residents of a single city block, specifically 1600 Pennsylvania Avenue. The district offered the Clintons a choice no other District of Columbia family enjoyed: a choice of any public school in the city. The Clintons examined their options and made the only rational choice that parents of means could make: no public school in the District of Columbia was good enough for their daughter. So they enrolled her in an elite private school.

We weighed carefully whether to affix the scarlet H—for hypocrisy—in branding the Clintons. We decided to do so, and it stuck, deservedly, in a big way. It's one thing for a government official to make a good educational choice for his child. It's another for that same government official self-righteously to insist that he is an apostle of public schools and that school choice would drain public schools of its best students. Polly Williams made the world safe for calling it like it was when she quipped, "The Clintons shouldn't be the only people who live in public housing who get to send their kids to private schools."

But while the buzz of school choice continued in policy circles, all was quiet on the legal and legislative fronts. If something was going to happen, we were going to have to jump-start it.

IJ and Landmark pursued different approaches. Working with Polly Williams, Landmark filed a lawsuit in federal district court in Milwaukee alleging that the choice program violated the First Amendment by excluding religious schools, thereby interfering with free exercise of religion. Given Polly's skepticism about including Catholic schools in the program, it was odd that she pursued such a strategy. But it was also risky: a court could agree with the plaintiffs—and rather than extending the program to include religious schools, it could invalidate the program altogether. It also forced the Democratic attorney general (now governor), James Doyle, to argue against the constitutionality of including religious schools in the program. But the legal theory was sound, in my view, and the lawsuit served the salutary purpose of highlighting the need to expand the program to include religious schools.

At IJ, we developed a different approach. As in other IJ legal strategies, we borrowed from the left: here, its idea of "educational equity" lawsuits. The typical pattern in those cases was for "overburdened" school districts to sue for more money under the state constitutions' education guarantees. It seemed to us that the rights being asserted rightly belonged not to school districts, but to children; and that the proper remedy was not more money for failing school districts, but a pro rata distribution of funds to the children who were deprived of educational opportunities.

At first blush, our proposed remedy seemed radical, but that was only because jurisprudence in the educational area was topsy-turvy. Truly radical and extreme remedies—forced busing, racial quotas,

51

court-ordered tax increases, judicial control of school systems—were considered commonplace. But the most basic judicial remedy—monetary damages—had never been considered.

To the libertarian objection that government shouldn't be in the education business at all, we replied that if government was in that business, it ought to be held accountable. Our theory was, in essence, a "warranty" for the vitally important product of education. If a person bought a car that turned out to be a lemon, a court would not order taxpayer subsidies so the manufacturer could produce a better car—it would order the car company to return the consumer's money. That's exactly what we were seeking.

The remedy we were proposing already had been adopted in another area: the Individuals with Disabilities Act. Under that federal law, every disabled child is guaranteed a "free and appropriate public education." The U.S. Supreme Court ruled unanimously that if a school district defaults on that obligation, it must provide a private school education.[3] For years, the IDEA has been the largest private school opt-out program in the nation—and an amazingly well-kept secret.[4]

But outside of that context, the idea was completely novel. To make it work, we needed to find potentially hospitable state constitutions and poor-performing school districts. And to make a visible case in the court of public opinion, we needed school districts in major media markets. To create a national story, we decided to file two cases simultaneously.

After careful searching, we chose Chicago and Los Angeles. Chicago's school system was corrupt, unwieldy, and notoriously abysmal. Only one high school in the entire system was scoring above the 50th percentile on standardized tests; over half of the city's high schools were in the bottom one percent nationally. At the time, the Chicago Public Schools had about 400,000 students and an administrative bureaucracy of 1,200. By contrast, the Chicago Catholic

---

[3] *School Comm. of Burlington v. Dep't of Educ. of Mass.*, 471 U.S. 359 (1985).

[4] In addition, across the nation, public school districts refer tens of thousands of disabled, "special-needs," "at-risk," and other educationally challenging children to private schools at government expense. So much for the frequently heard argument that public schools are saddled because they must take children that private schools won't. In fact, private schools long have served the role of escape valve for government schools.

Schools educated about 100,000 youngsters with an administrative staff of 40. The public schools, in other words, had four times the students but 30 times as many bureaucrats. That seemed to explain a lot. Meanwhile, the Illinois Constitution guaranteed an "efficient" and "high-quality" public education. We could argue that the schools were failing to fulfill those guarantees no matter how they were defined.

The sprawling Los Angeles Unified School District, and the nearby Compton and Inglewood school districts, likewise were failing to perform at the most minimally acceptable standards for low-income minority students. The California Supreme Court had decreed that education was a "fundamental right," and we would argue that the right was not meaningful unless students could opt out of failing schools.

We needed to beef up at IJ to take on the new cases. Among our hires was Dick Komer, the former Department of Education official who had drafted the opinion letter on the IDEA. Another was serendipitous: Bob Levy, a summer law clerk from George Mason University School of Law. For Bob, law was a second career. Previously, he had operated a very successful economics statistics business.[5] Bob was able to help us crunch some very complex numbers to make our case on the appalling educational state of affairs in Chicago and Los Angeles. We also brought in John Chubb, co-author of *Politics, Markets & America's Schools*, to brainstorm with the staff for a day and help us craft our claims in light of social science findings.

All we lacked were plaintiffs. In Chicago, we were aided by two school choice activists, Patrick Keleher and Joan Ferdinand; and by the Heartland Institute, a Chicago-based libertarian pro–school choice think tank. In Los Angeles, we were assisted by several activists, including Anyam Palmer, director of the Marcus Garvey Academy.

Heeding the lessons of Milwaukee, we arranged parent meetings in low-income neighborhoods in both cities. In Chicago, Chip and I were accompanied by one of our contributors, Heather Richardson (now Higgins), who heads the Randolph Foundation. Heather is a strategic philanthropist who early on provided seed support for our

[5]Bob is now a constitutional scholar at the Cato Institute and a member of IJ's board of directors.

school choice efforts. We met with dozens of parents at Edna's Soul Food Restaurant, and heard the same types of stories I had heard in Milwaukee: desperate parents who knew they had to get their children out of the failing government schools if they had any real hope for survival. Our lead plaintiff would be John Jenkins, a parent who had rescued his daughter from a dangerous, drug-infested public school and now was, illegally, taking her on the subway every morning across town to a better public school on the other side of the city. Jenkins wanted, instead, to send her to a private school in his own neighborhood.

While in Chicago, I visited Holy Angels School, which made a vivid impression upon me. Holy Angels is a Catholic K–8 school in the middle of one of the windy city's most troubled neighborhoods, surrounded by four of the poorest-performing public schools in the city. All of the students were poor and black. At the time, tuition at Holy Angels was nine hundred dollars per year *per family*. Most inner-city private schools welcome visitors (in stark contrast to most inner-city public schools), and I was greeted warmly at Holy Angels and offered a tour of the school. Eighth graders earn the honor of giving tours, and two beaming young men showed me around. We stepped into one kindergarten classroom containing about 40 children, all of them wearing uniforms, sitting at their desks with their hands folded and glancing at me with smiles on their faces. Something about the situation struck me as unusual, and suddenly I realized what it was: no teacher was in the classroom. She had stepped out for a moment. In my sons' suburban public schools, if the teacher left the classroom, it would be a recipe for chaos. But here were 40 inner-city kindergartners from low-income families— kids the system routinely writes off—and they were exercising *self-discipline*. That brief moment filled me with newfound hope and renewed dedication to help more families avail themselves of schools like Holy Angels.

In Los Angeles, I visited Marcus Garvey Academy, an Afro-centric school in the south-central area. Marcus Garvey's academic expectations are soaring, and I watched with amazement as second graders performed advanced mathematics problems on the blackboard and read aloud books well above their grade level. The experience confirmed again that high expectations can be self-fulfilling.

Our lead plaintiff in Los Angeles was Star Parker, a local activist who later would go on to host a radio show and start the Coalition for Urban Renewal and Education. Star had arranged a parents meeting for us in south-central Los Angeles for the early evening of April 29, 1992.

On that fateful trip I was accompanied by Dirk Roggeveen, who had just joined IJ after prosecuting race-hate crimes for the Department of Justice. Dirk and I spent the day meeting with other community activists before our parent organizing meeting. We learned that a jury had just acquitted the police officers who had savagely beaten Rodney King, and we wondered whether there would be trouble. But that prospect seemed unfathomable in the balmy spring evening as we drove toward our meeting in south-central Los Angeles.

As we sat at a red light on our way to the parents meeting, our car was suddenly jolted. I looked across the street and saw several black men throwing rocks at us. The first one had just missed the open window. As I watched in disbelief, one of the men charged the car with a two-by-four. I rolled up the window and he started attacking the car with it. I drove into oncoming traffic—careful not to run over the attacker's foot—then drove through a red light. Dirk and I decided to wait until we arrived at the meeting to call the police. Unbeknown to us, the police already had abandoned the area to the marauders.

When we arrived at the office complex in which the meeting was scheduled, Star had a television on, watching live footage of the trucker Reginald Denny being beaten, only two intersections away. Still, we could not fathom the full horror of the violence engulfing the neighborhood. We decided to proceed with the meeting anyway. After all, the parents had braved danger to be with us. The riot seemed an all-too-appropriate backdrop for what we were discussing.

After the meeting, Star learned that the main highway was barricaded, and she led us on an alternate route to safety. The streets were full of marauders, and I silently composed the ironic obituary— school choice activist and former civil rights lawyer lose their lives in LA riots—that surely would appear if we weren't able to escape. It was only later that Dirk and I learned how close we had come: the shopping center in which our meeting had taken place was burned to the ground that night. That evening from my hotel room I watched the fires raging around the city. I could only imagine the pent-up outrage that would completely break down the rule of law and make people abandon such essential shared values as the importance of human life.

To put it mildly, the Los Angeles riot made a mental mark, giving me a much greater sense of urgency—and militancy—than before. The next day I was supposed to go to Davis to speak at my old law school, but snipers were shooting at airplanes at Los Angeles International Airport, so flights were grounded. Eventually I made it onto a flight to San Francisco, relieved to get out of the inferno.

Or so I thought. Instead, I arrived downtown just in time for the San Francisco riot, and my cab drove right through it as I pondered grimly my dumb luck in managing to get a front seat for a riot tour of the United States. Fortunately, Mayor Frank Jordan had much better control of the situation than his Los Angeles counterpart, and the evening passed without incident.

The next day I spoke at a Hoover Institution conference on education reform. In a voice sapped by laryngitis, I recounted the transformative events of the previous two days. As I looked out on the audience, I was astonished to see the faces of two people I instantly recognized but never had met: Milton and Rose Friedman, the godparents of the school choice movement. I had idolized the Friedmans since college. Oh man, I thought: I must've died in that riot and gone to heaven!

My voice gave out fairly quickly. After the talk, the Friedmans came over to greet me and to voice enthusiasm for my remarks and IJ's work. I swelled with pride but could barely croak out words of thanks. Great job, Clint, I told myself: you finally get to meet your heroes and all you can do is make squeaking noises.

Once back in Washington, my colleagues and I prepared our lawsuits with renewed determination. We lined up two outstanding volunteer lawyers to serve as local counsel: Dan Kubasiak, a well-connected Democratic lawyer in Chicago, and IJ board member Manny Klausner in Los Angeles. Bolstered with statistics gathered by Bob Levy, the complaints painted a grim picture of educational malpractice. The captions of the complaints themselves told a story: we represented dozens of families in both cities, but almost none of the mothers had the same surnames as their children. In a tide of single-parent poverty, education was the beacon.

We launched the cases on consecutive days. In Chicago, the news conference was packed with cameras and reporters. Several parents spoke, and they reminded me why we always place our clients front and center. One parent surprised me by saying, "We already have school choice." Puzzled looks—mine included—greeted him as he continued. "We just have to lie about where we live. We register our children with their aunts or their cousins. We have choice; we just have to break the law." It was powerful testimony to the need for systemic change.

The next morning in Los Angeles, I awoke at 3 A.M. to appear on a national morning talk show. But when the parents and I arrived at a morning news conference to announce the lawsuit, there were no reporters. Trying to comprehend what was going on, I glanced down at our news release, and realized the goof in the headline that had managed to get past multiple pairs of eyes: "School Choice Lawsuits Filed in Chicago and Illinois." Oops! No wonder the interest in California wasn't too intense.

The national media coverage was stupendous. *USA Today* trumpeted in a headline: "Inner-city Parents Put Schools on Trial."[6] An unexpected *Washington Post* editorial captured both the strategy and the changed dynamics of the choice struggle:

> Publicly funded educational vouchers—the murky catchword is "school choice"—have been a staple of the conservative agenda ever since economist Milton Friedman first proposed them in 1972. . . .
>
> [T]his month, . . . two attention-getting lawsuits [were] brought on behalf of low-income parents in Los Angeles and Chicago, challenging the quality of the inner-city schools and demanding voucher remedies. The cases' legal precepts— alleged violations of state laws that guarantee such things as "an efficient system of high-quality educational institutions" and the encouragement of "intellectual improvement"—are less noteworthy than the new ideological coloration of this litigation strategy organized by a nonprofit group calling itself the Institute for Justice. Gone is the purely economic rationale for school choice. . . . The new rationale is embedded in the language of class struggle, and it's decidedly more militant: Only school choice can "liberate" disadvantaged parents and their children from inferior public schools. The buzzword from the plaintiffs and from such reformers as

[6] Dennis Kelly, *USA Today* (June 10, 1992), p. 10.

Polly Williams, the sponsor of the Milwaukee voucher plan, is "empowerment". . . .

It's impossible to counter what these people observe—that the public schools in the inner cities are separate and unequal places. . . . It's also hard to refute the argument that attempted reforms have failed—reforms involving substantial infusions of money.[7]

Ultimately, the *Post* concluded that because it wouldn't help many children and was of doubtful constitutional validity, "choice is not the answer to the gross inequities that prevail among America's schools." But the editorial conferred a strong and unexpected establishment imprimatur on our effort. And only a few years later, the *Post* abandoned its reticence and became one of the nation's most consistent and influential backers of school choice experiments.

The school districts responded to the lawsuits with motions to dismiss for failure to state a cause of action. In California, the first round went well. Superior Court Judge Raymond Cardenas picked up immediately that our lawsuit was based on a "warranty" theory. That seemed reasonable to him, and he declined to dismiss the lawsuit. Unfortunately, that was the high-water mark for our litigation.

In Chicago, we drew a liberal Democratic judge, Aaron Jaffe, a former state legislator overtly hostile to the lawsuit, which he promptly dismissed as failing to raise an issue that the courts could resolve. The Court of Appeals agreed.[8] Meanwhile, in an unpublished opinion, a hostile California Court of Appeals ruled that no cause of action was stated under California law, and that a voucher remedy would violate the California Constitution.

Though the cases failed in the court of law, they played an important role in framing the terms of the debate in the court of public opinion and in bridging the divide between the original Milwaukee school choice program and the next round of school choice legislative activity in 1995. Most important, they helped align the interests of school choice reformers with inner-city minority schoolchildren.

Meanwhile, legislative efforts in the continental United States were going nowhere. But school choice made a breakthrough in 1993 in

[7] "School Choice on Trial," *Washington Post* (June 24, 1992), p. A18.
[8] *Jenkins v. Leininger*, 659 N.E.2d 1366 (Ill. App. 1995).

the Commonwealth of Puerto Rico where the innovative Democratic governor, Pedro J. Rossello, pushed through a trailblazing reform program. Under Rossello's plan, failing public schools would be shut down and reopened as deregulated "community schools." Low-income children were given scholarships to attend private schools if they wished.

It was the first modern school choice program to allow students to use public funds in religious schools, so the case immediately attracted national attention. The program instantly generated a high degree of educational dynamism in the commonwealth. In its first year of operation, more children actually left private schools for the newly reinvigorated community schools than left public for private schools. And for the moment, it was the only school choice show, even if it wasn't exactly in town. So we decided that IJ should intervene on behalf of parents to defend the program.

Talk about logistical challenges! Accustomed to litigating school choice in the frosty climes of Milwaukee, I looked to the tropical island as an idyllic place to litigate. But the illusion faded rapidly. Though Catholics provided strong support for the program—and unlike elsewhere, we calculated in Puerto Rico that it was helpful to have them front and center—the island was bitterly divided along partisan lines. Rossello had a strong popular and legislative mandate, but was engaged in all-out war with the judiciary, and five of the seven members of the Puerto Rico Supreme Court were from the opposition party. Litigating from the mainland was a logistical nightmare. Legal proceedings are conducted in Spanish, so we had to hire a San Juan firm not only to serve as local counsel but also to translate our briefs and conduct the arguments. Philanthropy is not strong in Puerto Rico, so not only did we have to pay full freight for the legal fees—ultimately more than $200,000—we also were unable to generate any significant financial support.

Despite challenges, my colleagues and I made a pass at influencing public opinion. We worked closely with the major English-language newspaper, the *San Juan Star*, to focus attention on the program. I wrote a *Wall Street Journal* op-ed to credit the commonwealth for its far-reaching education reform. We coordinated with local Catholic schools to identify parents and children who could put a human face on the case. We even translated our school choice buttons into "Libre Seleccion," for supporters to wear inside the courtroom. But in this situation, our efforts in the court of public opinion had little impact in the courtroom.

The case unveiled a strategy that would be replicated by our opponents in subsequent cases. Instead of focusing on the First Amendment—where choice opponents knew they were vulnerable—they focused on the religious establishment provisions of the state (or in this case commonwealth) constitution. Often those provisions are more explicit and restrictive than the language of the First Amendment, prohibiting "aid" for the "benefit" of religious schools. Many of the provisions were part of the anti-Catholic campaign led at the turn of the 20th century by Sen. James G. Blaine (R-Maine). More recent constitutions like Puerto Rico's also incorporate the Blaine amendment.

Another advantage the opponents had in emphasizing state constitutional arguments is that decisions by state courts interpreting them are unreviewable by the U.S. Supreme Court, unless some federal issue is presented. The other side could read the precedents as well as we could, and we suspected they would prefer to avoid a showdown in the U.S. Supreme Court until a change in its composition.

Our state constitutional argument paralleled the federal: the scholarship program was neither aid to, nor for the benefit of, religious schools. It was aid to children, for their benefit. The interpretation of the Blaine amendment varies widely from state to state, and there was no strong precedent on point in Puerto Rico. So ultimately we were entirely at the mercy of the Puerto Rico Supreme Court in this first Blaine amendment test case.

The lawsuit was a disaster, the results preordained by the unfavorable partisan split in the courts. We lost in the trial court, then the case was appealed directly to the Puerto Rico Supreme Court. The argument took place just after Memorial Day. Over the holiday weekend, I attended a conference in Portugal, and flew to San Juan via New York. I suspected my luggage wouldn't keep up with that unusual travel itinerary, and sure enough it didn't. With no stores open, I faced the prospect of appearing in court the next morning in casual clothes or a borrowed suit.

My luggage arrived in the middle of the night, but I needn't have worried: lawyers are required to wear robes in the Puerto Rico Supreme Court. It felt like the glee club, but the proceedings were anything but gleeful. The Solicitor General had insisted on beginning the argument for our side, so that he could demonstrate the Rossello administration's commitment to the program. I appreciated the gesture—though I doubted that the anti-Rossello Court would—but worried that the Solicitor General wasn't prepared for all the complex issues presented by the lawsuit. Not to worry, he assured me, because he would only speak for a few minutes, then turn it over to the commonwealth's principal lawyer on the case.

The Court had other ideas, and kept him up there for 45 minutes. By the time the other lawyers on our side finally rose to argue, the case was pretty much lost. Adding to the agony for me was having to listen through a translator whispering words into my ear. The argument turned out to be a very long three hours. And the result, once the decision came down, was all too predictable: by a five-to-two party-line vote, the Court invalidated the program as a violation of the religious establishment provision of the Puerto Rico Constitution. The only consolation was that the decision was in Spanish and of very limited precedential value on the mainland. But it was painful nonetheless: for the first time, the teachers unions were successful in wrenching children out of private schools and forcing them back into the inferior government schools.

It would have been consoling to know then that it also would be the last time, never to recur in an ongoing program in the 50 states. But then the sting of losing would not have been such a powerful motivation.

Meanwhile, Landmark was faring no better in its federal lawsuit in Milwaukee. The judge ruled against Landmark, holding that it would violate the First Amendment to add religious schools to the choice program. The ruling was head-spinning in its implications, for it essentially meant that the efforts of local advocates to expand the program to include religious schools had already been declared unconstitutional even before such an expansion was enacted, making their campaign a decidedly tough sell in the legislature.

Compounding the litigation defeats and the dearth of legislative activity around the nation was a continued lack of unity and direction in the choice movement. The movement continued to be divided among those advocating vouchers, which were direct and tangible but subject to all manner of complications, and tax credits, which were immune from government regulation but not immediately helpful to the people most in need. Another divide was between those who supported universal and others who favored means-tested vouchers, with strong pragmatic and equitable arguments supporting each side. A constant stream of experts came forward to present "model" school choice programs, creating the ironic spectacle of a movement devoted to competition and choice being preached to by central planners.

Whenever I was asked whether I preferred vouchers or tax credits, or universal versus means-tested vouchers, my answer was "yes." In my view, we were not (and still are not) at the point as a movement where we could pick and choose. That is why our attitude at IJ was so ecumenical: we would help everyone and anyone who had a viable choice program, regardless of its contours. When we considered how tough the battle was to establish the baseline principle that it was permissible to empower parents to choose their children's schools—or that government could include private schools among the range of educational options at all—I didn't feel that we could afford the luxury of intrafamilial squabbles over design features of school choice programs. Our opposition was powerful and united; we were not powerful and simply could not afford to be divided.

That perspective affected my attitude toward charter schools—decentralized, largely autonomous public schools—that were arising around the country. At first, I was skeptical, viewing them as the education establishment's effort to construct a program of *perestroika* to forestall the *glasnost* of school choice. And maybe initially, or in some states, they were. But when I looked to see who were the adversaries of charter schools, I recognized they were the same as ours. And in some states, charter schools seemed generally designed to achieve a long-overdue deregulation of government schools, making them in essence quasi-private. It seemed to me a step in the right direction.

I had no qualms about the question of priorities, however. Though in theory I favored universal school choice, my experience in inner cities radicalized me to the point that I ardently supported means-tested choice as a movement priority. The need, of course, was desperate. But more than that, the system was inequitable. One could argue, of course, that wealthy people already have the choice to send their children to private schools, and poor parents should have that same choice. It's a powerful rhetorical argument; and in a nation dedicated to equal educational opportunities, it carries moral salience. But there are lots of things the rich can purchase that the poor can't, a point that liberals like to make to tweak conservatives. Walter Dellinger, U.S. Solicitor General under Bill Clinton, quipped to me that he favored school choice because it is a form of income redistribution that conservatives actually support; and there's some truth in that perspective.

But the public school system and tax policy are skewed in profoundly inequitable ways that require choice as an alternative. A wealthy family can move to the suburbs and spend huge amounts of tax dollars to create a good public school system—a form of school choice. Their choice is backed by generous tax deductions both for their mortgage payments and local taxes. Poor families, of course, receive no such tax breaks, and in essence can be seen as paying more for inferior schools. It seems inherently fair to extend the transportability of benefits that accrue to wealthy families in the form of tax deductions to poor parents in the form of vouchers. In that sense, we really were seeking for poor parents something approaching the measure of choices available to wealthier ones.

While I pondered—and debated, seemingly endlessly—philosophical questions like that, what really mattered to me was getting kids out of bad schools and into good ones. Because for me, and for many of my colleagues, the battle had become personal. It was about specific families, and specific kids, whom we had grown to care about deeply. It was that passion that fueled our determination, even in the lean times.

Another fissure running through our movement was distrust between minority advocates of school choice and conservatives. My own efforts throughout the 1990s to curb racial preferences[9] were used by choice opponents to sow suspicions about me among minority school choice advocates. I viewed racial preferences as a zero-sum game: minority students with the greatest advantages and strongest credentials were leapfrogged above nonminority students, while the underlying problems of educational inequalities were not being addressed. Indeed, as social scientists Stephan and Abigail Thernstrom found in their pathbreaking study on race, the gap in academic performance between black and white high school students actually

[9]See, for example, Clint Bolick, *The Affirmative Action Fraud: Can We Restore the American Civil Rights Vision?* (Washington: Cato Institute, 1996).

widened in the early 1990s.[10] To me, school choice *was* affirmative action, in its highest and truest sense, targeting tangible aid to students who need it so that they can compete effectively. Generally speaking, such issues rarely arose among school choice activists, but instead were invoked by anti–school choice liberals to cast aspersions on the nontraditional school choice alliance.

All in all, the grassroots litigation efforts between 1992 and 1995 were pretty much a debacle. Still, the period was a formative one, with developments quietly occurring around the nation that would provide a foundation and give rise to a new and promising burst of activity starting in 1995.

In Milwaukee, the choice program was bursting at the seams, with a long waiting list of students, a cap expanded to a still-too-limited 1,500 students, and too few nonsectarian private schools to accommodate them. The PAVE private scholarship program was sending scores of low-income children to private religious schools, but the scholarships paid only half of the tuition, and that program had a waiting list as well.

Another problem was that no high schools of significance were participating in the choice program, with the consequence that youngsters in the program would have to return to MPS for high school. Brother Bob Smith, principal of Messmer High School, decided to try to get his school into the program. Messmer was formerly a Catholic school that was targeted to be shut down by the diocese. The school community rescued it and transformed it into an independent Catholic school, serving an overwhelmingly poor and minority student population.

Like so many inner-city private school principals, Brother Bob is an impressive person. Possessing a disarming quick wit and a warm sense of humor, the Capuchin brother has total control of his school and the complete respect of his students. His mantra is "no excuses." All students are held to the highest disciplinary and academic standards. And despite the odds, they succeed. Test scores are above the state average and nearly all of the students graduate.

---

[10] Stephan and Abigail Thernstrom, *America in Black and White: One Nation, Indivisible* (New York: Simon & Schuster, 1997), pp. 355–59. Abigail Thernstrom is a member of IJ's board of directors.

Messmer applied for admission to the program, but could not fit into the definition of "nonsectarian." The best hope to provide a high-quality high school for students of the program was turned away. The program would have to be expanded. And the groundwork was being laid to do just that.

At the same time, other choice activity around the nation was being abetted by a growing school choice movement. Jeanne Allen had left the Heritage Foundation to form the Center for Education Reform, a national clearinghouse for school reform information. Patrick Rooney of Golden Rule Life Insurance Company created a private scholarship program in Indianapolis that would serve as a model for dozens of others around the nation. A group of business leaders started the American Education Reform Foundation to promote school choice efforts. Key philanthropists such as John Walton, Lovett "Pete" Peters, Jerry Hume, James Leininger, Roger Hertog, Virginia Manheim, Bruce Kovner, John Bryan, John Kirtley, Bill Oberndorf, and Peter Flanagan were backing the movement.

At IJ, we were beefing up our staff in ways that would prove crucial to our future school choice efforts. We hired Nina Shokraii (now Rees) as our outreach coordinator. Nina had worked for Grover Norquist, the consummate conservative grassroots activist, at Americans for Tax Reform. She would help organize communities to support school choice litigation.

We also hired a new communications director, John Kramer, who came to us from a public relations firm. I was worried at first that he was too serious to work in the irreverent and lighthearted atmosphere at the Institute for Justice. Boy, was I wrong. "Kramer" turned out to be not only a world-class prankster but one of the finest communications professionals in the conservative and libertarian movement. He introduced IJ to two key media relations concepts: "pounding the phones" to follow up on media releases, and preparing extensive and well-documented background materials to help make reporters' jobs easier. Kramer also began providing training to parents and activists to help the school choice movement effectively communicate its message.

We certainly didn't realize it at the time, particularly in the face of seemingly constant setbacks, but through the years of false starts, we were sowing seeds that would soon bear sweet fruit. And, imperceptively, perhaps, the movement was growing more sophisticated, learning from its defeats and its triumphs. It was getting ready for the big time.

It was a good thing, too, because from our adversaries we had seen nothing yet. The beast was only now awakening.

4. And Then There Were Five

The period of quietude for school choice ended abruptly in 1995. Once again, the catalyst was Milwaukee. The target of school choice supporters was to expand the program in two critical ways: to increase the number of eligible students tenfold from 1,500 to 15,000 and to increase capacity in the program markedly by adding religious schools to the range of options.

The school choice supporters had assembled a remarkable coalition. The expansion was supported at the top political levels by Governor Thompson and Mayor Norquist. Both men were becoming important figures nationally in the burgeoning school choice movement. Thompson was giving flesh to the concept of empowerment for Republicans. Norquist, a Democrat, helped give school choice bipartisan support. His support was unwavering and his vision radical: he favored a citywide program and advocated it on the grounds that Milwaukee could not hope to retain a vibrant business community unless it produced highly skilled graduates of its educational system.

Backing school choice expansion in the legislature were numerous Republicans and a few key Democrats. Assemblyman Scott Jensen, a brilliant legislative strategist, was particularly dedicated and adept at guiding the legislation.

But by far the most important part of the coalition was on the ground. Although most businesses tend to shy away from anything that could get them into trouble with the public school establishment—hence the business community almost never leads the way on school choice—the situation was markedly different in Milwaukee. The Metropolitan Milwaukee Association of Commerce adopted expansion of school choice as its top legislative priority. MMAC's president, Tim Sheehy, is passionately devoted to school choice. And his top lobbyist at the time, Mary Jo Pacque (now Baas), was totally dedicated to the cause as well as persistent and skillful in navigating the legislative arena.

Parents were organized like never before. Here, the guiding force was Parents Advancing Values in Education, the private scholarship program that was helping thousands of economically disadvantaged children attend private schools. But PAVE's backers, including the Bradley Foundation, made it clear that their financial support was not open-ended: the goal ultimately was to convince the legislature that it should expand school choice. As a result, parents were highly motivated to become advocates of expansion to safeguard their children's educational opportunities. An outgrowth of the PAVE program was Parents for School Choice, which was created to organize families to support an expanded program. Heading PSC was Zakiyah Courtney, the dynamic former principal of Urban Day School. The religious school community, including Brother Bob Smith of Messmer High School, contributed substantial organizing muscle. And local activists including newspaper publisher Mikel Holt and Howard Fuller, who had resigned as MPS superintendent over the slow pace of reform, added their weight and credibility to the effort.

The Milwaukee effort was the first to strategically link privately funded scholarships with public policy. The coalition that was assembled was truly remarkable and possibly unique in the history of American politics, uniting the low-income community, the business community, a Republican governor, a Democratic mayor, civil rights activists, and the religious school community.

The glue holding it all together was two remarkable activists, George and Susan Mitchell. Former reporters for the *Wall Street Journal*, the Mitchells were longtime community activists who had forged a close relationship with Howard Fuller, MMAC, and the Bradley Foundation. Now they were tasked with making the expansion happen—a daunting task in light of the ferocious opposition of the powerful teachers union, the state's largest newspaper, and most of the Democratic establishment.

Because the expanded program would raise new constitutional risks by encompassing religious schools, I was involved in the legislative effort from the very beginning. It was a role we were aggressively cultivating at IJ, urging school choice advocates to take pains to legally bulletproof their proposals, under both the state and federal constitutions, as best they could in anticipation of the inevitable legal challenge. It required us to invest heavily in counseling activists whose proposals had little chance of enactment, but we felt we had to make the investment because every proposal could potentially be the one to resolve the federal constitutional issue in the U.S. Supreme Court. Our legal advice is delivered with a light touch—we avoid providing advice on policy issues or political strategy, preferring to defer to local activists—but we try to provide the constitutional parameters within which the policy decisions can be made with relative safety.

It was clear that the Milwaukee expansion had a high prospect for success, so I made several trips to Wisconsin to meet with the key players, including Mike Joyce at Bradley, Tim Sheehy and Mary Jo Pacque at MMAC, Scott Jensen, and Governor Thompson's education and legal advisers. I also met with George and Susan Mitchell, who are two of the finest people I've ever known. They make an amazing couple, with different but complementary skills. Susan is the consummate strategist and organizer. She has an amazing ability to see the big picture and to submerge her own ego to bring and hold coalitions together. She also sweats the details, creating layers of fail-safe structures to make sure that anything that needs to happen does. George, by contrast, is the quintessential researcher and persuader. He masters the minutiae and provides meticulous documentation of everything he advocates. And through earnestness and sheer persistence, he wears people down until they concede that his position has merit. I credit George with crucially changing the editorial posture of the *Milwaukee Journal-Sentinel* from knee-jerk opposition to grudging admiration for the school choice program. It is a joy to watch George and Susan in action, and I am thankful that I never have encountered anyone remotely in their league on the other side.

During one of my early forays, I spoke at a parent training session. I observed for an hour or so and was enormously impressed. Parents for School Choice had recruited a number of parent organizers who would mobilize families for rallies and legislative hearings. Two of them were Pilar Gonzalez (now Gomez) and Janine Knox, who would become leaders of the Milwaukee school choice community and IJ clients in the defense of the expanded program. (Though a Democrat, Pilar addressed the 2000 Republican National Convention on school choice.)

One of the lead trainers was John Gardner, who was a labor organizer and at one time had worked for Cesar Chavez. I'm not sure two people more different from each other have ever been introduced. We eyed each other warily: I was wondering what on earth this union organizer was doing in our midst; John was trying to figure out who this right-wing Washington lawyer was and what he wanted. It took a while for our suspicions to dissolve; and despite the fact that we disagree on almost every issue other than school choice, we developed a rich friendship and an excellent working relationship. John is indeed left-wing, so much that he truly believes in power to the people, whether through union organizing or through smashing union monopolization of public schooling. Over the years he has taught me a great deal about political tactics, and even more about the potency of cross-ideological alignments.

I worked closely with the governor's and Scott Jensen's staffs on the mechanics of the legislation. Once again, the bill would be included in the budget. That gave me predictable anxiety after what we had been through in the first litigation, but at least this time we had a favorable precedent on which to build. Paramount, of course, were concerns over the inclusion of religious schools. I argued for the broadest possible range of educational choices, suggesting that suburban public schools be added to the mix. I characterized that option as purchasing constitutional "insurance," especially on the neutrality side of the ledger. But adding suburban public schools was not politically viable; and as a practical matter, inner-city youngsters already could attend suburban public schools under the "Chapter 220" voluntary desegregation program.

More attention was focused on two other provisions of the bill. One provided that choice students could opt out of religious activities. I was worried that such a provision would alienate religious schools, but it turned out that most Milwaukee religious schools (many of whose students, as in most large cities, are not members of the religious institution that sponsors the schools) already had such policies, but few pupils availed themselves of the opt-out. The second feature created a payment mechanism whereby checks would be sent to the parent in care of the chosen school, and signed over to the school. I opined that neither provision was constitutionally necessary, but both would be symbolically helpful: the first in demonstrating that the program was not intended to establish religion, the second in illustrating that the funds were expended as the result of individual parental choices.

One other issue arose. In most cities, religious schools subsidize the cost of tuition. That would mean that if the state aid was limited to the amount of tuition, the program could have the perverse consequence of forcing religious schools to raise the difference between the amount of the voucher and the actual cost of education. But if the state provided more money—say, a flat $5,000 voucher to a school whose tuition was $3,500—the extra amount could be perceived as an impermissible subsidy to religion. We solved the conundrum by capping reimbursement at the amount of the school's tuition or actual per-pupil operating expenses, whichever was greater.[1]

When the bill was crafted, I thought the sum product was constitutionally defensible. But it was a tough sell in the legislature because of the federal court ruling in the Landmark lawsuit. I returned to Wisconsin repeatedly to testify in legislative committees trying to defuse the decision's impact. Fortunately, Susan Mitchell's focus on organization helped immeasurably: at every hearing, there was a strong presence of parents and community leaders to testify in favor of the bill. It was enormously important to present a human face, and the coalition was able to do so in exemplary fashion.

Meanwhile, George Mitchell, John Kramer, and I launched a media blitz, doing a road trip to meet with editorial boards across the state. Our goal was to convince editors, regardless of their positions on the policy merits of school choice, that it was constitutional. It was fun to watch George and Kramer in action. They are both total bulldogs, and rarely back down. They argue like cats and dogs about sports—oddly, Kramer is a Green Bay Packers fan while George, like me, is a San Francisco 49ers fan—but the two of them together are an unbeatable team. No question is left unanswered, no issue unresearched. At each meeting, I calmly explained that the expansion was drafted to comport with applicable U.S. Supreme Court precedents, as well as decisions by the Wisconsin Supreme Court interpreting the state's religious establishment clause. It was the first time we had taken the show on the road with respect to a school choice program that included religious options, and the reception was encouraging.

[1] The maximum voucher amount was about $5,000, roughly representing the state's per-pupil contribution to MPS students.

Despite the ruling in Landmark's case, I believed we were in fairly good shape, at least on federal law. Our confidence was bolstered in June by a decision of the U.S. Supreme Court upholding funding for a religious publication at the University of Virginia.[2] The university had taken the same position as had the State of Wisconsin in the Landmark lawsuit—that it would be unconstitutional to fund the religious publication, even though it funded nonreligious activities. The Court in a (typical) five-to-four decision disagreed. The "guarantee of neutrality," wrote Justice Anthony Kennedy for the majority, "is respected, not offended, when the government, following neutral criteria and evenhanded policies, extends benefits to recipients whose ideologies and viewpoints, are broad and diverse."[3] Not only that, it would be constitutionally *impermissible* under the First Amendment as a form of viewpoint discrimination to exclude the religious publication.

Even the dissent by Justice David Souter gave us optimism, for it focused on the distinction between direct and indirect aid. "*Witters*, *Mueller*, and *Zobrest* . . . turned on the fact that the choice to benefit religion was made by a non-religious third party standing between the government and a religious institution," he wrote. "Here there is no third party standing between the government and the ultimate religious beneficiary to break the circuit by its independent discretion to put state money to religious use."[4] In the expanded Milwaukee program, of course, the parent would provide the necessary "circuit breaker."

The decision made us confident that we would prevail in the U.S. Supreme Court, with two important caveats: *if* the Court honored its previous precedents, and *if* the composition of the Court did not change. The latter was a serious concern given that the margin on the Court was a precarious single vote (in the person of the always unpredictable Justice Sandra Day O'Connor), and Bill Clinton would fill any vacancies. Two of the justices who had voted on our side in religious establishment cases, Chief Justice William H. Rehnquist and Justice O'Connor, were the subject of constant retirement

---

[2] *Rosenberger v. Rector and Visitors of Univ. of Va.*, 515 U.S. 819 (1995).
[3] Ibid., p. 839.
[4] Ibid., p. 886 (Souter, J., dissenting).

rumors, so the pressure was great to get a case to the U.S. Supreme Court as quickly as possible.

Meanwhile, action also was brewing in Ohio. The Cleveland Public Schools were such an unmitigated disaster that a federal district court, citing appalling mismanagement by local school officials, transferred control over the school system to the State of Ohio. The numbers 1 in 14 will forever haunt my memory: a student in the Cleveland city public schools had a slightly *less* than a 1 in 14 chance of graduating on time with senior-level proficiency; the same student had a slightly *greater* than a 1 in 14 chance of being a victim of crime, inside the schools, each year. It blew me away that in light of such a debacle, anyone would depict any proposed reform as too radical, rather than as not radical enough.

Though Ohio has rarely been known for policy innovation, the political stars were in alignment. Gov. George Voinovich caught the school choice bug from a prominent Republican contributor, David Brennan, a tough-minded and mercurial businessman who single-handedly had rescued the city of Akron from economic malaise. Now Brennan wanted to get into the business of education, and school choice provided a vehicle.

Unlike Milwaukee, the school choice supporters did little to create a grassroots or bipartisan coalition (which would prove a constant source of frustration during the subsequent litigation), relying on party discipline in the legislature. But grassroots support came anyway in the person of Fannie Lewis, the long-time City Council representative of the impoverished Hough neighborhood. A renegade Democrat with Polly Williams's irrepressible spirit but none of her racial hostility, the elderly Lewis organized several bus-loads of parents to make the three-hour trek from Cleveland to Columbus to lobby for school choice.

Sensing a Milwaukee-like political dynamic, I traveled to Columbus and Cleveland to assess the terrain. In Cleveland, I met first with Fannie Lewis, who organized a group of parents from whom we would draw our clients if the program passed. Driving around the Hough neighborhood was an amazing experience: it still bore the scars of race riots during the 1960s, yet evidenced unmistakable signs of progress. Lewis had pushed through a program to sell vacant lots to urban homesteaders, pursuing a vision of private property rights (rather than government-sponsored "urban renewal" schemes) as the basis for neighborhood revitalization. I was equally impressed at the reverence in which Lewis's constituents held her. Fannie Lewis pledged her complete support to her "Washington lawyer"; and in the seven years of litigation that followed, she never once failed to deliver.

While I was in Cleveland, I visited St. Adalbert School, a Catholic private school that two of Fannie Lewis's grandchildren attended. More than 60 percent of the children came from families below the poverty line. Of the school's 213 students, 212 were black. Only 21 were Catholic. It was bursting to the seams, and precisely the type of environment in which the public school apologists insist that learning cannot take place. And yet the school was orderly, the teachers were dedicated, and the children excelling. It's the type of school that would become available to Cleveland schoolchildren if school choice were to exist. Once again, a visit to a school provided a visual image that would inspire me throughout the litigation.

That night I had dinner with David Brennan, who was impressive in different ways. A huge man topped off with a trademark cowboy hat, Brennan was trained as a lawyer and possesses a quick and incisive mind, and he expresses his thoughts perhaps more bluntly than anyone I have ever met. Over dinner he grilled me on legal theories and strategies, and assured me that he and his allies would get the job done in the legislature. Brennan also was in the process of creating nonsectarian Hope Academies in Cleveland to participate in the program. Like Fannie Lewis, Brennan did not disappoint.

Later I met with Tom Needles, the governor's well-seasoned education adviser. The Cleveland scholarship program contained one feature that was an improvement over Milwaukee: it would invite public suburban schools to participate, undergirding the program's neutrality. It also created tutorial assistance grants for students remaining in the Cleveland Public Schools. But the amount of the scholarship was only $2,250, capped at a school's tuition. Students would have to contribute 10 percent ($250) on their own. Moreover, up to half of the program's participants could already be enrolled at private schools, which could lead to charges that the program was subsidizing private schools or wealthier parents rather than facilitating school choice for poor families. In fact, many children in the inner city are in private schools only in the most precarious of economic circumstances, so it makes sense to help them stay there. But that is a subtlety that often gets lost in a debate.

I was ambivalent about those features. On the one hand, even $250 could be a lot of money for poor parents to pay; but on the other hand, requiring parents to pay something might increase the degree of commitment to the school and the program. Likewise, it was important to rescue kids trapped in failing government schools, but at the same time it was important to help parents who already were making a financial sacrifice to send their children to private schools. The amount of the scholarship was problematic, however. Although it would cover tuition in virtually all of the city's private schools, it would not create an incentive for new schools to start, and capping the scholarship at the amount of tuition would require participating private schools to come up with massive subsidies because the tuition in inner-city private schools almost never covers actual costs.

Much more worrisome was the governor's intent to create the program through the state budget. Talk about alarm bells! I researched Ohio law and found that such a strategy could be problematic, and I implored the governor to try to enact the program as a separate piece of legislation, but to no avail.

One huge advantage in Ohio compared with Wisconsin was the media: the state's three most prominent newspapers, the *Cleveland Plain-Dealer*, *Columbus Post-Dispatch*, and *Cincinnati Enquirer*, all are avowedly pro–school choice. Most of the state's judges are Republican as well. So the lay of the land seemed favorable.

But we would have to create our own support infrastructure. Working with Fannie Lewis, Nina Shokraii and I trekked to Cleveland to visit several schools. Ever since the Los Angeles riots, we made sure to arrange for a car and driver to accompany us whenever we visited the inner city, especially because it is easier to get into the inner city than to get out.[5] In this instance, we were expecting a town car, and were shocked when we were picked up by a garish stretch limousine—precisely the ostentatious image we didn't want to convey. At each school, kids ran up to the car expecting someone like Michael Jordan or Shaquille O'Neal to emerge—only to bear looks of absolute puzzlement when two white people who definitely were not celebrities or basketball players got out. (Navigating a

[5] My colleague Chip Mellor challenged the Denver taxicab monopoly in part because of the difficulty encountered by inner-city residents in obtaining taxicab service.

stretch limousine through a McDonald's drive-through was especially memorable.) As in Milwaukee and elsewhere, the schools were characterized by heavily minority and low-income student bodies, large classrooms, and inadequate facilities—yet still boasted high academic standards, high expectations, and remarkable achievements.

Ultimately, the program was adopted by a strict party-line vote as part of the governor's budget bill. Unlike the Milwaukee program, which was due to expand that fall, the Cleveland program would not commence until a year later, in fall 1996. So although we were expecting an imminent challenge in Wisconsin, we had no idea when we would face a challenge in Ohio. But we had to be prepared for it.

Meanwhile, three other lawsuits appeared on the horizon, although it would be some time before they were filed. In Arizona the previous year, two principled and dynamic state legislators, Rep. Lisa Graham (now Keegan) and Sen. Tom Patterson, had come within a few votes of enacting the nation's first statewide voucher program. In the end, they "settled" for the nation's most far-reaching charter school program. Lisa then ran successfully for Arizona Superintendent of Public Instruction, in part to make sure the legislation they fashioned would not be watered down in the bureaucracy.

But even with the defeat of school vouchers, the school choice community in Arizona wasn't finished. A former legislator (now U.S. representative), Trent Franks, came up with the idea (apparently in the shower) of a scholarship tax credit. The idea was brilliant. The shortcoming of most tax deduction or credit programs is that they do not benefit the people who need help the most: low-income families. But this proposal would transfer funding from wealthier taxpayers to less-fortunate families: taxpayers would receive a dollar-for-dollar state income tax credit of up to $500 for individuals and $625 for couples for contributions to private scholarship funds. The scholarships could not be used for the taxpayer's own children.

By now, national groups such as the Children's Educational Opportunities America (later renamed Children First America) and the Children's Scholarship Fund, backed by visionary philanthropists such as John Walton and Ted Forstmann, were up and running in dozens of cities. In Arizona, Jack and Isabelle McVaugh had pioneered the concept, launching the Arizona School Choice Trust in 1992. Because the tax credits would refund the full cost of contributions, they would provide a huge boost to the scholarship funds.

As a result, the credits operated as a de facto voucher program. Best of all, from a libertarian standpoint, the credits would not likely expose private schools to additional regulations. But they were just as likely as vouchers to evoke a legal challenge from the teachers unions—even though they were a bit less vulnerable at least at the federal level—because the U.S. Supreme Court had validated tax deductions nearly two decades earlier in *Mueller*.

Meanwhile, litigation storm clouds were brewing in Vermont and Maine. Unbeknownst to most people, those two New England states have the oldest voucher programs in the country, dating back to the 1800s. Several rural communities decided it was too expensive to build public schools, so the states came up with the idea of "tuitioning": in communities that lacked public schools, the locality would pay tuition to attend a public school in an adjacent district or a private school. At different times, the states included religious schools among the range of options; but by the 1990s they were excluded, not because of a policy decision but because the states had concluded that it would be unconstitutional under the First Amendment to include them—essentially, the same view that was expressed by the federal district court in Milwaukee.

The situation in Vermont was odd. In the 1960s, the Vermont Supreme Court had ruled that tuitioning to religious schools violated the First Amendment. But in 1994, citing the evolution of U.S. Supreme Court jurisprudence, the Court reversed itself, holding that reimbursement of religious school tuition was constitutionally permissible.[6] Yet the state did not interpret that decision to allow for the pre-payment of tuition, as the program provided. The state's position was tenuous, to put it mildly. Because of the tuitioning program's overt neutrality—indeed, most of the children chose to attend public schools—it would seem ideally suited to meet the U.S. Supreme Court's standards.

The tuitioning programs provided a response to a question I hear frequently in public forums: How can school choice help families in rural areas in which there may be only a public school and no private one? First of all, the market responds. If demand exists—in the form of families who have funds at their disposal to choose private schools—supply will follow. It might consist of a school

---

[6] *Campbell v. Manchester Board of School Directors*, 641 A.2d 352 (Vt. 1992).

formed in a church basement, or one formed by several families congregating together, or even distance-learning over the Internet. School choice facilitates all that. It also reduces the pressure—which was intensifying nationally because of the exploding school-age population—to build costly new public schools.

Given the choice, parents vote with their feet. Reportedly, in Vermont and Maine, the population was growing faster in tuitioning towns than in cities with public schools. The phenomenon created a new twist to the adage that people move to communities because of their public schools, so that now people were moving to communities because there are *no* public schools. In 1996, the tiny town of Chittenden decided to take matters into its own hands, extending tuitioning to religious schools. Not only was it a matter of educational equity, it was also sound fiscal policy because religious school tuition was less costly to the taxpayers. The three-member Chittenden school board asked IJ to represent it, and we agreed.

Meanwhile, parents in Maine who wanted to send their children to religious schools approached the Institute for Justice to challenge the discriminatory tuitioning policy. Recognizing that such action would be important in overcoming state-imposed barriers to school choice even if we won the constitutional battle in the U.S. Supreme Court, we agreed to take on that case as well. So within two years of the expansion of the Milwaukee school choice program, we would have five school cases proceeding simultaneously.

It almost was six. School choice activity was raging around the nation. Backed by Gov. Tom Ridge, Pennsylvania came within a few votes of passing a school choice program, and other states produced viable legislative programs as well. But the one other venue in which school choice did pass, unexpectedly, was in Congress.

With the election of a Republican congressional majority, House Speaker Newt Gingrich made school choice for the District of Columbia a top legislative priority. The public schools in the capital city were a national disgrace. The District could not even determine for certain within several thousand the number of pupils in the system. Test scores were abysmal, and physical plants were crumbling, despite ever-escalating federal contributions. Of course, the city's politicians, most notoriously Delegate Eleanor Holmes Norton (D-D.C.), were dead set against school choice. But economically disadvantaged families wanted it desperately.

Gingrich tasked Rep. Steve Gunderson (R-Wis.) with developing a plan. We worked closely with Gunderson and with aides to Gingrich, Rep. Dick Armey (R-Tex.), and Rep. Tom DeLay (R-Tex.) on the proposal. Support came mostly from Republicans, but several Democrats joined our ranks, particularly Sen. Joseph Lieberman (D-Conn.), a school choice stalwart. Wanting badly to get a case to the U.S. Supreme Court, we included a provision that would provide fast-track review.

Frustratingly, and not for the last time, the major anxiety came not from our adversaries but from our friends. We had worked hard to make the proposal as lightly regulated as possible, obligating the schools only to general nondiscrimination requirements and financial and academic reporting obligations. But the U.S. Catholic Conference, the national lobbying arm of the Catholic Church, took the position that the full panoply of federal civil rights regulations should apply, which would result in most private schools declining to participate in the program. The Catholic Conference lobbyists contended that their position was rooted in concerns over equity, and indeed the Conference is considerably more liberal than the church as a whole. But the more cynical view was that because Catholic schools already were obligated to comply with certain federal regulations because of their participation in the federal school lunch program, they wanted to extend the same obligations to other private schools to create a competitive advantage. Either way, the position was far out of step with most Catholic dioceses, and we alerted as many as possible to put pressure on the Catholic Conference. In the end, the bill retained light regulations; but the clash with the Catholic Conference subsequently would recur, maddeningly, every time there was federal legislation.

On November 2, after considerable arm-twisting by Gingrich, the House of Representatives voted 241–177 to enact school choice for the District of Columbia. Eventually the Senate passed it, too, sending the bill to President Clinton, who promptly vetoed it. Whatever the scope of Clinton's misdeeds in office, vetoing school choice for children in the District of Columbia for children who desperately needed it—while his own daughter was thriving in a posh private school in northwest Washington—surely ranks among the worst.

It did make for a good opening joke in some of my speeches, though. I would ask audiences if they knew that the District of

Columbia had a school choice program for residents of public housing. It was limited to one square block in the inner city—specifically the 1600 block of Pennsylvania Avenue, Northwest. The residents of that block, alone among District of Columbia residents, were offered the choice of any public school in the city. But being good parents, they decided none of the public schools were good enough, so used taxpayer funds to choose a private school. Limited as it was, the program proved an unqualified success: 100 percent of the students in the program graduated and went on to Stanford.

Of course, I wish the program in the nation's capital was a bit larger than that, and it would have been a pleasure to defend it against legal challenge. Still, five school choice cases were a lot to litigate. Ultimately, I took the lead in Wisconsin, Ohio, and Arizona, and assigned Dick Komer to head up the pioneering cases in Vermont and Maine. As we prepared over the summer of 1995 for the litigation barrage, we assembled a remarkable litigation team. In addition to our staff attorneys and our media and outreach gurus, John Kramer and Nina Shokraii, we brought aboard a Yale law student, Matthew Berry, who was so intelligent and precocious that most people thought he was already an attorney. That summer, I paused to reflect that we had assembled, in typical IJ fashion, what surely was the most religiously ecumenical litigation team ever: a Catholic, a Jew, a Protestant, a Muslim, and two atheists.

We weren't sure when the Ohio case would be filed, but we had to be ready in any event. A Milwaukee lawsuit, we knew, was imminent. So we had to prepare simultaneously on multiple fronts. The intensity was palpable throughout IJ: any one of these cases could be the big one. With so many in play, one was sure to reach the U.S. Supreme Court.

Despite gearing up for the immediate litigation, we also maintained a long-range perspective. In most of our IJ cases, we represent the plaintiffs (and indeed, our mind-set is very plaintiff-oriented— I often joke that Chip and I could be rich if we were personal injury lawyers). The school choice cases placed us in a decidedly different posture. In those cases, not only were we defendants' lawyers, we weren't even the *lead* defendants' lawyers. That role was played, for better or worse, by the state. So it mattered a great deal who the state's lawyers were. Not just in the short term but in the long run: as lawyers not for the main parties but for interveners, we could present argument at every stage *except* the U.S. Supreme Court, where typically only one advocate per side gets to argue.

Those considerations led me to contact Mike Joyce of the Bradley Foundation to ask him to convene a strategy meeting. What concerned me was that, left to its own devices, Wisconsin would be represented by the office of its attorney general, Jim Doyle. Doyle is a centrist Democrat, and I had no reason to think his staff would not conscientiously defend the law. But the Landmark suit had cast him in a difficult posture: he had been forced to argue that it would be unconstitutional to expand the program to include religious schools. In my view, that created a hopeless conflict as well as the stark and painful possibility that his briefs in the Landmark lawsuit would be cited against us in our case. But I realized we were walking into a difficult political thicket with the Republican governor and the Democratic attorney general.

Joyce promptly convened a meeting in Milwaukee. Governor Thompson participated, along with his aides. Joyce also invited William Kristol, the Republican pundit and editor of the *Weekly Standard*; and former federal judge and U.S. Solicitor General, Ken Starr. I had known both Bill and Ken slightly for several years, and I was delighted that the governor was considering Starr as special counsel if Doyle was replaced. I also had worked with Jay Lefkowitz, Starr's colleague at the Washington, D.C., law firm of Kirkland & Ellis, when he was a rising young star working on regulatory issues in the first Bush administration.

Befitting the challenge ahead, Joyce had assembled a top-notch team. Ken Starr, in particular, was an inspired choice. Ken is one of the most talented lawyers I've ever met. But there are lots of brilliant lawyers in Washington, D.C. What sets Ken apart is his warmth, charm, and sincerity. I don't think Ken has ever met anyone in his whole life whose name he's forgotten. He's amazingly self-deprecating and deferential whenever someone has more expertise on a particular matter. He's a quick-study and a superb negotiator. But he is also a total bulldog. Though he never loses his charm, he is absolutely dogged and keeps his eye on the ball every single second. I have no idea of his hourly rate, but whatever it is, Ken is worth it.

We talked for several hours over dinner and beyond. I presented a two-pronged strategy: the governor should move to appoint special counsel because of Doyle's conflict, and we should pressure Doyle to move to have the decision in the Landmark lawsuit vacated because the expanded program had rendered the lawsuit moot on appeal. We diverged into other subjects, particularly the substantive arguments of the case ahead. I favored a cautious, narrow approach, while Ken preferred a more expansive argument that would help straighten out the U.S. Supreme Court's muddled First Amendment jurisprudence, but we agreed on the basic points. Shortly after the meeting, our Wisconsin friends persuaded Doyle to move to have the district court decision vacated, which rendered it useless as a precedent in our case. And Thompson agreed to hire Starr to take over the defense of the program, with Bradley footing the bill.

The other side was upping the ante, too, bringing in its first team. No longer would state union affiliates take the lead in the litigation. Instead, they brought in the high-powered Washington, D.C., team, led by Robert Chanin, a partner at Bredhoff & Kaiser and the National Education Association's general counsel. Over the years, I would grow to know Chanin well. To put it mildly, first impressions were, for me, off-putting. Chanin is the quintessential obnoxious labor lawyer, replete with a thick New York accent and a sarcastic, argumentative demeanor. He wags his finger at the court and refers to judges as "Yawanna." He also, oddly, used to keep a colored toothpick in his mouth at all times, even at counsel table, removing it only when it came time to argue. But he is also a masterful orator who makes every second count, wielding total command of his subject matter. Over six years of litigation and myriad encounters, I grew to admire him, despite myself. The guy is good. He's an ethical lawyer who is interested in cutting to the chase. And he represents his clients with zeal.

The supporting cast was colorful as well. There was Barry Lynn from Americans United for Separation of Church and State, a sharp-tongued former ACLU lawyer and an ordained minister who for some reason is full of venom toward school choice. Steve Green, a law professor and a pleasant enough guy who works for the same group, came to be known in school choice circles as the "grim reaper," because he seemed to show up with his metaphorical scythe everywhere school choice arose. And then there was Eliot Mincberg, who works for the ill-named People for the American Way. I've spent more time debating Eliot over the years than just about everyone else combined, so it's good that he's a decent if misguided guy. His organization, though, is profoundly left-wing, and coaxed the NAACP into an unholy alliance against school choice. Revealingly, neither Kweisi Mfume, who heads the NAACP, nor anyone else of prominence in that organization, is willing to debate school choice.

We didn't have to wait long for the lawsuit—or rather, lawsuits. As would be the norm, two separate lawsuits were filed by the rival teachers unions, the NEA and the American Federation of Teachers. The NEA's lawsuit was joined by a host of lawyers from anti–school choice groups, including the ACLU, the NAACP, Americans United for Separation of Church and State, and People for the American Way. It especially rankled me to see the NEA co-opt the ACLU and NAACP. IJ would never subordinate itself to someone else's agenda. But it was a potent combination all the same. And we hoped we were ready for it.

The lawsuits, which were consolidated into a single action, contained no surprises. Once again, the plaintiffs challenged the program under the Wisconsin Constitution's private or local bill clause, uniformity clause, and public purpose doctrine. Added, however, were challenges under Wisconsin's Blaine Amendment, which forbade the appropriation of state funds in "aid" or "support" of nonpublic education, and under the First Amendment.

I was most concerned about the religion provision of the Wisconsin Constitution. As in many states, the Wisconsin Supreme Court had interpreted state constitutional provisions independently of, and in many instances more broadly than, the First Amendment. It had not done so in the context of the religion clause, but the plaintiffs were pushing the court to do so. In this and other cases, they would emphasize the full range of state constitutional issues, recognizing that if a state supreme court struck down a program on state constitutional grounds, it would preclude review by the U.S. Supreme Court. Their strategy confirmed that they were reading the tea leaves the same way we were: that our side would win in the U.S. Supreme Court. So our strategy was to litigate the cases as swiftly as possible, given the possibility that President Clinton could alter the composition on the Supreme Court before we got there. (If I had known it would take us more than six more years, it would have depressed and worried the hell out of me.)

The state religion clause forced us to tread delicately. We did not want to offend the court by suggesting that it *must* interpret its

Constitution in conformity with the First Amendment. Instead, we would argue that an independent interpretation of the state provision would lead to the same result. After all, the First Amendment, too, though written in more generic language, would prohibit appropriations in aid or support of religious schools. But this aid was to *students*, not schools. Not a single dollar of government funds would cross the threshold of a private school unless a parent chose such a school in preference to other educational options.

That fact also helped us on our First Amendment argument with respect to the criterion of independent choice. But we faced difficulty on the neutrality prong, because the program, by its express terms, was limited to private schools. Here, we set forth the full range of educational options available to Milwaukee students, only a tiny fraction of which were private. We also fleshed out the argument that in Wisconsin, student aid was transportable, so that it followed the students regardless of their educational choices. We would argue that the expansion of the parental choice program merely would add religious schools to a preexisting array of choice options.

I tasked our summer clerk, Matthew Berry, with developing the factual predicate for those arguments. He was aided by George Mitchell, who in his usual meticulous manner had managed to fathom the state's complex student aid formula, and John Gardner, who had gotten himself elected as a reform insurgent to the Milwaukee school board and now served as its finance committee chairman. We had to prepare rapidly because, once again, the issue initially would be decided over the course of the summer. (Anyone who litigates school choice cases rarely gets to enjoy summer vacations.) When the lawsuit was filed, Milwaukee lawyer Michael Dean, working pro bono, raced to Madison to file our intervention papers.

Meanwhile, Governor Thompson had hired Ken Starr's firm, and when the first hearing was held, two sets of lawyers showed up purporting to represent the state. They argued over whether the governor or attorney general should be allowed to proceed.

The governor's team outflanked the attorney general. Reasoning that the Wisconsin Supreme Court would be more favorable than a Madison trial court, the governor filed a petition for original action in the Supreme Court, which would allow us to bypass the trial court. I liked the strategy because it could accelerate the case for review in the U.S. Supreme Court. The court acted swiftly, assuming jurisdiction and granting the governor's motion to take over representation of the state. To his credit, Attorney General Doyle remained supportive throughout the litigation.

The court issued an accelerated briefing schedule and ordered oral argument on the question of whether the program should be enjoined. We worked frenziedly not only to put the brief together but also to produce an array of affidavits that would present the parents' voices and the statistics we had been developing in support of the program. As the hours ticked down, I overheard Matthew Berry patiently explaining the intricacies of the education budget to the state auditor so we could include an affidavit from him. It brought a smile to my face: this young fellow already was a central part of our legal team yet he was only a first-year law student. The intensity of the litigation and our shared passion for the program brought out the best in the entire team.

The court had undergone two personnel changes since the 1992 decision, each side having lost one vote, leaving three who had voted for us and two (our old friends, Justices Shirley Abrahamson and William Bablitch) who had voted against. The two new justices were Anne Walsh Bradley and Jon Wilcox, both of whose views on these issues were unknown. Justice Bradley immediately recused herself for undisclosed reasons, leaving the number of justices at six.

I worked closely with Ken Starr and Jay Lefkowitz in the weeks leading up to the argument. Starr was an amazing quick-study with a deft oratorical touch. We decided to divide the issues: Ken would argue the religion clauses under both constitutions, and I would take the remaining state issues. The division made sense: I knew the state issues from the previous litigation, and a decision against the program on one of those grounds would prove disastrous.

Once again, the courtroom was filled beyond capacity, this time with plenty of parents and children inside the courtroom. As I waited my turn, I watched two masters in action. The silver-haired Chanin presented an eloquent constitutional critique of the program. Starr's substance was equally strong, but his style was much more deferential to the court. By this time, I felt that the program was my baby, in the legal sense, but watching Ken's masterful argument made me feel that the religion issues were in exceptionally good hands. Arguing the remaining state constitutional issues gave me a chance to emphasize the equities. All eyes were on the presumed swing vote, Justice Wilcox, whose questions seemed favorable to our side. We left the courtroom feeling cautiously optimistic.

Meanwhile, we were fighting the clock. Back in Milwaukee, thousands of children and dozens of schools—mostly Catholic and Lutheran, but also evangelical and Jewish—were joining the program and trying to make plans under the cloud of litigation. The schools in particular were in a tough position, having to hire teachers and purchase supplies with no certain assurance that the program would expand. The cloud hovered omnipresently over each program, and it amazed me that the people involved could go about their business amid all the uncertainty. It also intensified our own determination to keep the program afloat. So much depended on it.

As the days drew on with no court decision, I asked Matthew to determine when the first private schools would open under the program. The purpose of an injunction was to preserve the status quo, and we reasoned that once the schools opened, the status quo would shift from the previous program to the expanding one, hence an injunction would be legally inappropriate.

Sure enough, several of the private schools were slated to open the last week of August, a week or so before the public schools. I learned this news when Matthew Berry burst excitedly into my office and exclaimed what surely were the oddest words ever spoken at the Institute for Justice: *"We are the status quo!"*

We filed a supplemental submission with the court explaining that development. By now, it was hard to believe that the court would enjoin the program, which inevitably would plunge the entire system into chaos.

We were wrong. In the first week of September, the court issued its decision. It had deadlocked three-to-three. We won Justice Wilcox's vote, but inexplicably had lost Chief Justice Day. In a very brief order, three justices concluded that the program was unconstitutional, three justices did not. The court agreed, however, that the expansion should be enjoined, and remanded the matter to the Dane County Circuit Court. Not only was the expanded program halted before it started, but we would have to start the entire legal process from scratch.

We were in shock. The phone calls to our clients were among the toughest my colleagues and I would ever make. Pilar Gonzalez cried when she heard the news, and there were dozens if not hundreds of others who reacted with similar grief. For parents who had been given the opportunity to hope for the first time, it was like the end of the world.

And yet, as unbelievable as it would have seemed at the time, the darkest days were yet to come.

5. Valley Forge

If Susan Mitchell were to adapt a phrase from James Carville, surely it would be, "It's the infrastructure, stupid!"

Never was the value of infrastructure more apparent than in the aftermath of the Wisconsin Supreme Court's injunction in September 1995. The private schools, which had constructed a network to share information and confront common problems, instantly sent out word that they should proceed with their plans for the new school year: students should proceed to attend their chosen private schools, notwithstanding the injunction. Meanwhile, the Bradley Foundation, PAVE, and MMAC sprang into action, offering half-tuition scholarships to all families who newly were planning to enroll in private schools in anticipation of publicly funded vouchers. The schools scrambled to make up the difference in tuition. Some families decided that the uncertainty was too much and sent their children back to public schools; but remarkably, the vast majority were able to stay with their chosen schools, thanks to the outpouring of philanthropic support.

On the legal front, we were starting afresh in the Dane County Circuit Court. We decided that we would take the offensive, so that before the plaintiffs could seek judgment on the merits, we would ask for an evidentiary hearing to have the injunction dissolved. That would enable us to frame the terms of the debate and to put on something of a show trial to demonstrate the efficacy of school choice. Moreover, it would give us a strong record on the inevitable appeal and, as it turned out, a strong record from which to draw on in subsequent cases as well. The state's lawyers agreed it was strategically and symbolically appropriate for the parents to take the lead in trying to remove the injunction.

The case was assigned to a newly appointed judge, Paul Higginbotham. The judge had no track record, and we knew nothing about him, except that he was African-American, bright, and educated in private schools. That seemed encouraging, but we wanted to leave nothing to chance. So we set out finding a local counsel who could lend us some credibility and expertise in the local courts.

I learned that Susan Steingass, the judge in the first case five years before, had retired from the bench and returned to private practice. She was my first call. I asked whether she remembered the case. She sure did. We chatted amiably about it for several minutes. It turned out she previously had been a public schoolteacher—a fact that, had I known it at the time of the earlier case, probably would have induced me to exercise our discretion to have another judge named. It was a good thing I didn't know it. She told me that seeing all of the parents and children in the courtroom made an impression, and that her perspective as a former teacher made her receptive to the equitable case of securing high-quality educational opportunities for economically disadvantaged schoolchildren. Her comments put a huge grin on my face: it was enormously gratifying to have a judge validate an approach that emphasized the vitally important human dimension.

I asked Steingass if she could serve as local counsel, but understandably she felt her prior ruling would create a conflict. But she was happy to recommend a lawyer she considered the finest trial counsel in Dane County: Steve Hurley.

I contacted Steve and he was receptive, though he didn't know where he stood on school choice. Frankly, I didn't care: to have a fighting chance, we needed the most savvy local counsel we could find.

I went to visit Steve and we hit it off instantly. Steve's notoriety as an attorney had come primarily from criminal cases, including one particular high-profile case in which Steve managed to get a death sentence overturned. But my eye immediately was drawn to several awards and Hollywood paraphernalia on display in Steve's office. It turned out that Steve had authored several scripts for the television show *Picket Fences* and coauthored the script for one of my favorite movies, *Primal Fear*, which starred Richard Gere as a criminal defense lawyer and debuted Edward Norton as his client accused of murdering a priest. Steve told me that he had used one of his favorite lines in the movie. When Gere's character is asked by a reporter whether he ever wanted to be a judge, he replies, "Why would I want to umpire when I can still play ball?" As an aspiring novelist (I swear that after this, my fifth nonfiction book, I finally will finish my novel), I instantly felt a bond with Steve Hurley. And eventually, he became a strong supporter of school choice as well.

Like most Madison lawyers, Steve has liberal political tendencies, but like Steingass he identified with the equities on our side. He knew Judge Higginbotham and felt that although he was a liberal judge, he was fair and intelligent, and that we couldn't do much better. So we decided to stick with Higginbotham; and together, Steve Hurley and I started putting together a game-plan.

Meanwhile, the unions had filed a lawsuit in Cleveland. Once again, the local NEA and AFT affiliates filed separate lawsuits, which were immediately consolidated. The NEA lawsuit was joined by lawyers for the American Civil Liberties Union, Americans United for Separation of Church and State, People for the American Way, and other naysayers. Unlike in Milwaukee, the local NAACP affiliate did not join the litigation. The lawsuits were filed in Columbus, the state capital, and alleged both state and federal religious establishment claims along with—as I had warned—a claim that the program had been unlawfully enacted as a private or local bill as part of the state budget.[1]

The plaintiffs had waited so long to file the lawsuits that a good deal of activity already had taken place to get the program started. In so many ways, the program and its operation were different than in Milwaukee, and my colleagues and I were having to learn to navigate widely divergent political and logistical terrains wherever we went. Unlike in Wisconsin, where the foxes were in charge of the henhouse, in Ohio the state had hired a passionate pro–school choice advocate, Bert Holt, to administer the program. We were able to work closely with her to obtain key data about the program.

Unlike Milwaukee, neither the schools nor the parents were organized. The local business community, working closely with David Brennan, had put together a school choice committee under the leadership of conservative activist David Zanotti, but it viewed its role primarily as political and saw little value in creating grassroots

---

[1]Confusingly, in Ohio this provision is referred to as the "uniformity clause," whereas in other states such as Wisconsin, the uniformity clause refers to educational uniformity.

support. Complicating matters, Fannie Lewis distrusted both Brennan and Zanotti and vice versa. We considered it imperative to work with both sides.

Brennan had opened two large nonsectarian schools, called the Hope Academies, to participate in the program, and they enrolled hundreds of kids. Their participation in the program was crucial, especially in terms of perception, because nearly all of the remaining schools were religiously affiliated. So approximately 83 percent of the children were enrolled in religious schools in the program's first year.

Pointedly, despite the fact that they would receive about $6,000 per student under the program (compared with $2,500 for private schools), not a single public school district opted into the program. The reason was obvious: many of the families in the suburban public schools had escaped the inner city, and they didn't want the "problems"—that is, poor minority schoolchildren—following them. So the doors to suburban public schools remained closed to children in the scholarship program.

That dynamic between the cities and the suburbs vexes the school choice movement everywhere in the nation. Even many suburban parents who incur private school tuition often oppose vouchers because they don't want to open their schools to undesirable newcomers. It is a disturbing reality that creates a very difficult political challenge. The irony is that inner-city parents don't want their children to go to those schools either. They want to send their children to good schools in their own neighborhoods. But in Cleveland, the practical consequence of the "not in my backyard" phenomenon had the practical consequence of skewing a facially neutral program heavily in favor of religious school enrollment.

Our approach was to emphasize the nonsectarian aspect of the program. We decided to represent a group called Hope for Cleveland's Children, the umbrella group for the Hope schools, along with several families using scholarships in either religious or nonsectarian schools. We promptly moved to intervene in the lawsuits. Another school, the nonsectarian Hanna Perkins Academy, moved to intervene, represented by local attorney David Young, who also represents the local Catholic archdiocese.

The state's lawyer was Ohio Solicitor General Jeffrey Sutton. Unlike his boss, Ohio Attorney General Betty Montgomery, Jeff was a philosophical conservative who is strongly committed to school choice.[2] Though only in his 30s, Jeff already was an experienced U.S. Supreme Court advocate. We met and immediately developed a good rapport. At the same time, I toured editorial boards around the state. John Kramer and I developed excellent relationships with the three main newspapers in the state, which came through for us with supportive editorials at every crucial juncture in the litigation.

We were fairly optimistic about our chances. Even though the enrollment data were not completely favorable, the program was neutral on its face. Although the Ohio Constitution contains a religious establishment clause, it does not have a Blaine amendment. To the contrary, Ohio was part of the Northwest Territory, in which public education largely was provided in religious schools, a fact reflected in the favorable tone of the constitutional provision. Moreover, Ohio traditionally had supported religious schools with textbooks and transportation. But the Ohio Supreme Court recently had struck down the state education finance system, which typically correlates negatively with school choice and was unpredictable. And the local or private bill problem continued to concern me.

Although only the first stop in what could be a long legal journey, the trial court would be enormously important, because its decision likely would determine whether the program would open in the fall. Unlike Wisconsin, the judges in the state capital are mostly Republican. The case initially was assigned to Judge Deborah Cook, but she was nominated by Governor Voinovich to the Ohio Supreme Court. So the case was transferred to Judge Lisa Sadler, a recent Republican appointee.

The unions' opening briefs set a new standard for stridency. The NEA brief characterized the scholarship program as a "money laundering scheme" to funnel government funds into religious schools. The AFT picked up the theme, referring to school choice parents as "inconsequential conduits" in the transmission of aid to religion. Those were fighting words, and they inflamed the parents—and their lawyers. We would not soon forget the disdain with which the unions viewed the parents.

---

[2] Jeffrey Sutton subsequently was nominated by President George W. Bush in early 2001 to serve on the U.S. Court of Appeals for the Sixth Circuit. As of this writing, the nomination has been stalled by Senate Democrats and liberal special-interest groups for well over a year.

We hit hard on the equities in our brief. We described the background of the program, which was a legislative response to an unprecedented federal court decision transferring control of the Cleveland City School District from the city to the state. The scholarship program was just one of the array of choices made available by the state. And the need was dire: we cited the 1-in-14 statistic and set forth several headlines from local newspapers chronicling the academic crisis and state of criminal siege taking place in the Cleveland public schools. The program, we argued, was crafted precisely to state and federal constitutional precedents. We supplemented the legal arguments with affidavits from parents and school officials and with data from the Cleveland school district.

The trip from Cleveland to Columbus takes about three hours—twice the distance of the trek from Milwaukee from Madison—but we determined to bring parents for the opening courtroom battle. Oddly, we encountered resistance to the idea from some of the local activists. I learned only later that Attorney General (now state auditor) Montgomery, an intensely ambitious politician, did not want to share the legal limelight, and exerted pressure on the local activists to resist our ideas for a rally at every turn. (Jeff Sutton dutifully recounted the party line, "That's not the way we do things in Ohio.") But Brennan finally agreed to orchestrate the trip, and chartered some buses and arranged for box lunches. Fannie Lewis also organized a few dozen parents. I rode along with them.

Parents and children wearing red, white, and blue school choice buttons predominated in the courtroom. The opposition was there in full force, with Chanin making his usual arguments for the NEA, focusing on the pervasively sectarian nature of the schools, the supposedly controlling *Nyquist* decision, and the contention that we didn't even need to reach federal issues because the state claims were dispositive. Joining Chanin was Marvin Frankel, an elderly former federal judge, who was arguing for the AFT. Though he commanded respect—it's always unnerving when one of the lawyers on the other side is addressed as "judge"—his arguments were largely incoherent, and I could tell that Chanin was not pleased to have to share time with him.

On our side, Jeff Sutton presented a solid and passionate argument for the state. Dave Young's approach worried me a bit: he focused on the quality of the Catholic schools, which I agreed was important but which I worried would play into our opponents' hands by highlighting the religious nature of the schools. I sought to balance it out by stressing that the program was a secular legislative response to a serious educational problem. I attacked the AFT for characterizing the parents as "inconsequential conduits." "How dare they!" I exclaimed. "With this program, for the first time, the parents are *not* inconsequential."

Usually courts pepper lawyers with questions, especially in controversial cases, and the lawyer's main task is to respond fully while making all of the important points. But I've learned that sometimes judges don't ask any questions at all, so you have to be prepared to make a complete presentation. That's what happened here: Judge Sadler did not ask any questions, and displayed a poker face throughout. Still, we took that as a hopeful sign: a judge usually will not strike down an important state law without at least asking some questions. Our optimism pervaded the rally held afterward on the steps of the state capitol.

Sure enough, Judge Sadler ruled quickly with a thorough and well-reasoned opinion. The 50-page ruling focused primarily on the federal Constitution, noting that cases after *Nyquist* had created a constitutional framework that was hospitable to school choice. The state constitution, she ruled, was not more restrictive than the First Amendment with regard to religious establishment.

The plaintiffs filed an emergency motion for an injunction in the Court of Appeals, but at that point the odds were against them. Both sides filed extensive briefs. The court promptly denied the motion, opening the door to the nation's second urban voucher program. Thereafter the case would proceed on a normal course of appeal of the ruling on the merits, and we could catch our breath for a bit in Ohio.

Good thing, because battles were heating up elsewhere. The state of Vermont had cut off funds to the town of Chittenden for its policy of paying religious school tuition, and we had agreed to represent the school board in a legal challenge to the state. As Dick Komer worked feverishly to get the case ready for trial court, New York philanthropist Peter Flanagan came to the rescue of students who had enrolled in Catholic schools.

And we needed to prepare for the hearing to dissolve the injunction in Milwaukee, which was scheduled for August 15. Milwaukee had become the Mecca of the school choice movement. A new group called the American Education Reform Foundation, headed at that time by Kevin Teasley and supported by businessmen John Walton, Patrick Rooney, Bill Oberndorf, John Kirtley, and others, was organizing trips for activists, politicians, and journalists from around the country to visit the schools and meet with people on both sides of the issue. The visits were enormously important in reinvigorating those who already supported school choice and in encouraging skeptics to view school choice in a new light. So it was imperative to keep the program going and, if possible, to lift the specter of unconstitutionality.

Judge Higginbotham set aside a day for the case, earmarking four hours for an evidentiary hearing and three-and-a-half more for oral arguments. We had two goals. The first was to get the injunction dissolved in its entirety, allowing the expanded program to begin in the 1996–97 school year. The back-up goal was to at least allow the expansion to occur with respect to nonsectarian schools. That meant we had to present evidence on both the religion and nonreligion issues in the case. And the limited time would force us to choose our witnesses carefully.

First we began compiling the evidence. It was critical, I believed, for us to characterize the program as one piece of a broader education reform effort. In that regard, we could rely largely on Howard Fuller, whose record as a civil rights activist and as a supporter of public schools was beyond reproach. But by now we had additional evidence at our disposal because it was clear that the public schools now were responding favorably to the impetus of competition. And for that evidence we turned to John Gardner.

Apart from my nephew and niece who were raised in San Francisco and, much to their uncle's dismay, have become socialists, there is no leftist of whom I am fonder than John Gardner. Gardner crafted an affidavit, mainly in response to the uniformity argument, that the program was not an "abandonment" of public education as the plaintiffs contended. Indeed, because choice students took only the state portion of their student aid and left the local portion within MPS, Gardner pointed out that for each choice student, the amount of per-pupil spending actually *rose* in MPS. Moreover, Gardner pointed out that the dichotomy depicted by the unions between school choice and public school spending was a false one: in both absolute terms and as a share of MPS spending, state aid had increased substantially since the choice program was enacted in 1990. That was a policy point over which school choice advocates disagreed. Howard Fuller, for instance, believes strongly that there should be a financial consequence for public schools that lose students to private schools in choice programs to provide a greater incentive for reform and improvement. But the fact that Wisconsin had in fact substantially increased its financial support to Milwaukee's public schools at the same time as it created school choice was very helpful to our legal argument. Further, there was no question that the program had forced the previously recalcitrant MPS to adopt consumer-oriented reforms such as creating additional choices, including charter schools, and giving the superintendent the power to fire poor-performing teachers and shut down failing schools.

For several days in advance of the hearing, the Bradley Foundation provided an apartment for me to prepare witnesses. Knowing that we had time to call only two parents, George and Susan Mitchell interviewed about two dozen to determine which would make the best fit. We ended up choosing Pilar Gomez, whose involvement with the program made her particularly knowledgeable and passionate, and Val Johnson. Though Val was a Protestant, she sent all of her children to Catholic schools, where they had performed very well.

I planned also to call Howard Fuller, John Gardner, and Zakiyah Courtney. A lawyer is not allowed to instruct witnesses on the substance of their testimony, but can go over questions and answers. I always prepare by constructing parallel columns on which I write the questions on one side and the answers I expect to receive on the other, so that if a witness forgets something I can ask a follow-up question to elicit the response I'm seeking. By the time I finished preparing with the five witnesses, it was down to a very good rhythm.

Then on the eve of the argument, new evidence turned up in the form of a pathbreaking study by Paul Peterson, a social scientist at the John F. Kennedy School of Government at Harvard University. Talk about an unexpected source! It turned out that Milwaukee activists had succeeded in freeing up the test-score data that previously had been available only to the state's official researcher, John Witte. While Witte had compared choice students with a dissimilar sub-set of MPS students and found few if any academic gains,

Peterson compared students who applied for the program with those who applied and didn't get in, and who remained in MPS. Though the numbers were small, the comparison was probative. In the first two years, Peterson found little academic difference; but starting in the third year and accelerating in the fourth, he found substantial gains. So much, in fact, that over four years the academic gap between black students in the program and white students in MPS declined by between one-third and one-half.

Those findings were amazing and of enormous importance. As Stephan and Abigail Thernstrom had found in *America in Black and White*, despite all manner of public investment and affirmative action programs, the academic gap between blacks and whites actually had widened over the previous decade so that black high school seniors lagged in academic performance by the equivalent of four school years behind their white counterparts. If the Milwaukee program could be shown to help erase that gap, it would mark a major breakthrough in efforts to deliver on the promise of equal educational opportunity.

I called Peterson at Harvard and he instantly agreed to come to Madison to testify. It was a risk, because he would be flying in as the hearing was starting and I wouldn't even have a chance to meet him. It also meant I would have to rely on John Gardner's affidavit rather than his live testimony, which I know would have been excellent. But this new evidence was enormously helpful, and the source was likely to be considered highly credible in liberal Madison.

Despite our intense preparation, I cautioned our allies that the odds against dissolving an injunction ordered by the Wisconsin Supreme Court were daunting. But I was confident at least that we would create an outstanding record that would serve us well on appeal.

The hearing was packed. A pool camera had been installed to share footage with an array of local television stations. I had a huge knot in my stomach. Though I've argued dozens of times in court and love it, I'm much less experienced in evidentiary hearings, and try to make up for my lack of experience through preparation. But it doesn't make me less nervous when the time comes.

Judge Higginbotham entered the courtroom. He turned out to be quite young, but serious in demeanor. We began going over preliminary matters, and Steve Hurley leaned over to me and whispered, "Crack a joke."

"What?" I asked.

"The judge is nervous," he explained. "This is a very big case. You need to break the tension. Crack a joke." It never would have occurred to me that a *judge* might be nervous; but given all the media attention, I realized Steve might be right.

So I did. I can't remember what I said, but throughout the hearing, I tried to inject self-deprecating humor into the proceedings, which wasn't tough to do given my propensity to engage in procedural faux pas. The judge seemed visibly to relax, just as Steve had suggested. And that made me more relaxed as well.

From the judge's demeanor and comments at the outset, it was clear he was skeptical about the program, which confirmed our instinct about having the odds against us. The first big skirmish was over the admissibility of Paul Peterson's testimony. The other side complained that they had known nothing about it until the eve of the trial. I replied that the study was hot off the press and was extremely probative of the issues before the court. The judge ruled that the testimony was proper. Though I was pleased at the outcome, lawyers know that sometimes rulings of that nature are negative harbingers, because judges often will bend over backward to be fair to the side they plan to rule against.

I began our case with Howard Fuller. He walked through the history of failed public school reforms in Milwaukee and his own resignation as MPS superintendent because of his frustration over the intransigence of the system. Then he described the school choice program and its positive effect on MPS reform efforts. Moreover, he testified, the focus of education needed to be on the kids, many of whom were poorly served by MPS. The purpose of public education, he testified, was not to promote the system as an end in itself but as a means of accomplishing the goal of educating every child. The more options the system provides, the better. The reason for expanding of the program to include religious schools could be explained in one word: capacity. There were too many kids who wanted to attend private schools and not enough seats in the nonsectarian schools. Finally I asked him the ultimate legal question, though I instructed him to answer it in real-world terms: What was the program's "primary effect"? It was, he responded, to expand educational opportunities to children who desperately needed them, and to give low-income parents some measure of the control over their children's education that wealthier parents enjoyed.

Dr. Fuller's testimony was a tour de force. I knew that his reputation preceded him, but it was amplified by his confident, earnest demeanor. Here was not some wild-eyed radical trying to dismantle public schools, but a calm expert testifying that school choice was essential to *save* public schools and to fulfill the goals of public education. It was clear that Fuller's testimony made a positive impression on the judge.

Next was Zakiyah Courtney, who also made an outstanding witness. I asked her if she had heard about the Harvard study. Yes, she replied, but it only confirmed what everyone who knew anything about the program already understood: that it might take a while for children to adjust to a new environment, but over time the effect of sound basics and high expectations was to improve educational outcomes. Courtney described the chaos created by the injunction and the continuing anxiety and uncertainty that pervaded the parents and the schools.

Courtney was followed by Pilar Gomez and Val Johnson, who testified eloquently about the soaring hopes created by the program—and the crushing blow delivered by the injunction. Pilar testified that she would sacrifice everything, even food on the table, to keep her children in private schools. I asked Val if enrolling her children in Catholic school had influenced their religious beliefs. She laughed and said no. Judge Higginbotham interjected, "You'd better hope the pope doesn't find out." The courtroom erupted in laughter. But the point was an important one. Val Johnson testified that she chose Catholic schools not for their religious content but because of the strong educational program and the values that the school promoted. That is the reason why roughly half of the children in urban Catholic schools are not Catholic.

We finished with Paul Peterson. He testified in strong, clear, yet academic terms, which he was able to translate into plain English. I thought the findings he presented were gripping. But something about his demeanor didn't click with the judge. Unlike the other witnesses, the union lawyers cross-examined Peterson relentlessly about his methodology and the small sample of students. At the end, I thought we had scored net points with Peterson's testimony, depending on how the judge viewed Peterson. But the other four witnesses each had hit a home run.

The other side countered first with Robert Jasna, the MPS superintendent. He came across as an earnest bureaucrat, and there wasn't much value in his testimony, which centered on the efforts that MPS was making to deliver a high-quality education. In cross-examination, he conceded that the school choice program was a catalyst for positive reform—the very point we were making. I asked him if it were true that the superintendent now had greater power to fire poorly performing teachers and to close failing schools. That was true, he answered. But were those reforms the subject of litigation? Yes they were, he replied. Who was challenging those reforms? The teachers unions, he answered.

The other side finished with an "expert," Alex Molnar of the University of Wisconsin (now relocated to Arizona State University). Molnar personifies the stereotypical left-wing ivory-tower academic: smug, self-righteous, and condescending. But Molnar makes an engaging witness, and to my horror, I could tell that Judge Higginbotham was captivated by his easygoing manner and his glib assertions. The school choice program was snake oil, he testified. It accomplished nothing for the students enrolled in it. Attrition was high, and private schools were unaccountable. The money could be better spent on programs in the woefully underfunded government schools that had a proven track record of success. Unlike Peterson, Molnar pointed to nothing to back up his claims, and yet they seemed to make a better impression on the judge.

I cross-examined Molnar with what I am sure was undisguised contempt. Had he watched the parents testify about their experience with the program? Yes. What did he think about that? We had done a remarkable job in finding articulate parents, he responded. Were they mistaken in their judgment of the impact of the program on their children? Yes, he replied, the advantages were illusory. Had he ever once visited any of the schools in the program? No. Had he ever studied the program? No.

I hoped that the cross-examination undercut Molnar's credibility. The judge declared a brief recess, during which I stayed in the courtroom to collect my thoughts, and George Mitchell thoughtfully brought me a sandwich to quiet my rumbling stomach. Minutes later, we proceeded to closing arguments. I recounted the real-world and expert testimony of the effects of the program on both the children in the program and the public schools, and the devastating effects of the injunction, which had not only disrupted the private schools and their students but impaired reform efforts in MPS.

Superintendent Jasna, I argued, actually had bolstered our testimony, and Molnar's opinions were utterly without foundation. Placing the facts in the legal context, I argued that the "primary effect" of the program was not to advance religion, but to expand educational opportunities.

Steve Hurley whispered to me that he felt we had moved the judge: his hostility toward the program had dissipated over the course of the day. Although it was clear that he remained troubled by the presence of religious schools in the program—which he seemed reflexively to perceive as a violation of church and state—he now was referring to the overall program as one that advanced laudable educational goals.

Sure enough, Judge Higginbotham agreed to dissolve the injunction with regard to expansion in nonsectarian private schools, while retaining it for religiously affiliated schools. The practical effect of the judge's ruling was to allow about 150 additional students to attend private schools the following year—only a small fraction of the children who wanted to join the program, but a significant victory nonetheless. All things considered, the summer of 1996 was a successful one: we began with one functioning urban school choice program enrolling about 1,500 students and ended it with two programs and about 3,800 students.

But the partial victory in Milwaukee would be our last for quite some time. Judge Higginbotham retained jurisdiction over the merits of the case, so we faced four more months of briefing and arguments with a result that appeared preordained. Then it was on to the Court of Appeals, the only level at which we lost in the last Wisconsin litigation, and which still loomed as hostile territory. The Court of Appeals in Ohio was uncertain terrain, as were the courts in the other states in which we were contemplating litigation. I warned my partner Chip that we could be in for a string of losses, and we quietly put out the word to our supporters that things could get much worse before they got better.

Even as we girded for further battle in Judge Higginbotham's court, we were casting an anxious eye at the Wisconsin Supreme Court. If we lost, as expected, in the Court of Appeals, then another three-to-three split in the Wisconsin Supreme Court would affirm that decision. And if an adverse decision turned on state law issues, as it surely would, then it would preclude further appeal to the U.S.

Supreme Court. The expansion would be defeated. So we either had to win in the Court of Appeals—a nearly impossible task—or somehow get a fourth vote in the Wisconsin Supreme Court.

The latter prospect became possible with the retirement of Chief Justice Day, who was replaced by a new Tommy Thompson appointee, Patrick Crooks. We did not know Justice Crooks's views, but even if he voted with us, if we lost in the Court of Appeals we would need to retain the three votes we had. The complication in that regard was that Justice Jon Wilcox, who had voted with us, faced a November retention election against Walt Kelly, a candidate backed ardently by the teachers union. Because the earlier three-to-three deadlock had provided a snapshot of where the justices stood, it was a rare instance in which we knew the judicial candidates' likely votes on a crucial case before the election. It was imperative to the school choice movement for Wilcox to win re-election.[3]

IJ faced unprecedented challenges gearing up for school choice litigation in multiple venues, while expanding its docket in its other core areas. We added a new attorney, Nicole Garnett, primarily to help with school choice cases. Nicole had graduated from Yale Law School and clerked in the U.S. Court of Appeals for the Eighth Circuit for an outstanding judge, Morris "Buzz" Arnold. Her energy and enthusiasm were contagious and a huge help.[4]

Chip Mellor and the IJ development team worked overtime to make sure we had the resources to get the job done. In addition to the growing philanthropic interest in the issue generally, we learned that a major new player would enter the arena. We met with Gordon St. Angelo, who previously headed the Lilly Endowment, and learned that Milton and Rose Friedman had asked him to take the helm of a new foundation, created largely from their personal funds,

[3]Conservatives and libertarians in recent decades have focused heavily on federal judicial nominations, and not nearly enough on state judicial appointments and elections. That is troubling, because state courts predominate on many important issues, from tort law to criminal law to family law, and of course they have exclusive domain over state constitution interpretation.

In the Wilcox race, school choice supporters weighed in heavily—unfortunately, some with too much zeal. The Wilcox campaign was sanctioned for impermissibly coordinating independent expenditures with an outside group. Justice Wilcox personally was cleared of any impropriety.

[4]Nicole now teaches at Notre Dame Law School along with her husband, Rick Garnett, who has authored a number of amicus briefs in support of school choice.

devoted exclusively to school choice. It was tough for me to admire the Friedmans more than I already did, but this tangible manifestation of their devotion to school choice was remarkable.

Meanwhile, we were working more closely than ever with our sister organizations, especially AERF, Children First America, and the Center for Education Reform. CER played a key role in each lawsuit by coordinating amici. A growing number of groups around the country were interested in supporting the legal effort, and initially the result was more cacophony than harmony. Jeanne Allen agreed to coordinate the groups, enlisting star lawyers to draft "umbrella" amicus briefs that multiple groups could join. At the same time, academics such as Paul Peterson and Jay Greene were studying privately funded school choice programs and finding positive results. And think tanks such as the Heritage Foundation, Cato Institute, Heartland Foundation (and its superb publication, *School Reform News*), Manhattan Institute, Hoover Institution, Pacific Research Institute, National Center for Policy Analysis, Empower America, Goldwater Institute, Evergreen Freedom Foundation, the Mackinac Center, and others around the nation were pumping out policy analyses and spreading the news about the benefits of school choice.

A related and significant development was the launch of the Black Alliance for Educational Options by Howard Fuller. Increasingly, school choice was viewed as a conservative movement, and Fuller considered it vital to the integrity of the issue to establish an independent voice for black Americans interested in school choice. BAEO supports all forms of school choice that are targeted toward fulfilling the aspirations of low-income and minority schoolchildren. The group supports both vouchers and charters, but is cooler toward tax credits unless they are targeted toward low-income beneficiaries. With Fuller's credibility in civil rights circles, and day-to-day leadership provided by a dynamic young activist, Kaleem Caire, BAEO quickly attracted widespread national support from independent-minded, mostly liberal black public officials and leaders. The group began organizing chapters in large cities around the nation to organize at the community level. Its creation and rapid growth demonstrated the broad base and growing popular support for school choice.

In sum, the movement was maturing, and working cohesively as a movement should. Anytime we needed something to support the litigation—whether scholarship assistance for a client's child, help in organizing parents, or whatever—a group like AERF, Children First America, or the Friedman Foundation invariably would come to our aid. Likewise, we were always willing to lend a hand, not only on the legal front but with outreach or media. The movement approached every challenge with a can-do mentality that became self-fulfilling.

In Wisconsin, we were buoyed by the decisive election victory of Justice Wilcox, which made us feel that we had a decent shot in the state Supreme Court. But first we had to get there. Judge Higginbotham scheduled oral argument on the program's constitutionality for December 24 in Madison. I could have asked to appear by telephone, but I always prefer to be in court. Usually I leave nothing to chance, but this time, not wanting to leave if I was going to get marooned in Wisconsin for Christmas, I took the last possible flight, connecting in Milwaukee. Everything went like clockwork until the propeller airplane tried to land in Madison and was forced by fog to return to Milwaukee. Sensing my anxiety, a passenger near me, who turned out to be a Midwest Express pilot trying to get home to Madison for the holidays, offered to drive me. We rented the last available car at the airport and made a mad dash through the thick fog to Madison. When the pilot found out what I was doing there, he drove even faster and dropped me off at the courthouse with minutes to spare.

The atmosphere inside the courtroom was worse than the weather outside. The empathy toward the program that Judge Higginbotham had displayed four months earlier had disappeared, replaced with an obvious hostility. I wasn't sure whether the judge had succumbed to pressure for having partially lifted the injunction or whether he just wasn't in the Christmas spirit. Either way, the arguments did not go well, and I returned home for Christmas worried that we would lose even the small progress we had made over the summer.

My fears were justified. On January 22, 1997, Judge Higginbotham struck down the expansion in its entirety. Audaciously, the judge thumbed his nose at the U.S. Supreme Court, declaring that "[i]t can hardly be said that th[e expanded program] does not constitute direct aid to the sectarian schools. Although the U.S. Supreme Court has chosen to turn its head and ignore the real impact of such aid, this court refuses to accept that myth." He went on to conclude that the program's "primary beneficiaries" are religious schools, although "parents of students attending those schools will certainly gain a benefit." He made no mention of the real beneficiaries: children. The judge cleverly attempted to insulate his opinion against review by the court he had criticized by grounding it solely on the religious establishment provisions of the Wisconsin Constitution.

Remarkably, the judge also concluded that because the program no longer was "experimental," its passage as part of the state budget violated the private or local bill provision of the Wisconsin Constitution. That meant the nonsectarian school expansion was unconstitutional as well. The one silver lining in the opinion was that the judge found no violation of the educational uniformity clause.

We barely had time to lick our wounds in Wisconsin when we had to travel to Columbus on February 13 to argue the Cleveland case in the Ohio Court of Appeals. Jeff Sutton, Dave Young, and I took turns arguing before the three-judge panel. When Dave had finished, the chief judge remarked, "Now we'll hear from Mr. Bolick, who has looked the entire time like he wants to jump out of his seat." That comment drew spirited laughter from the gallery, and of course the judge was correct. Distressingly, however, the panel seemed unmoved by equitable arguments, and troubled by various aspects of the program. I returned to the airport in a gloomy mood, which was exacerbated when I discovered that my seat-mate on the flight home was none other than Bob Chanin. Ordinarily, I would have struck up a conversation with my constant foe, but the trip passed in silence.

The news from the U.S. Supreme Court seemed more optimistic. The Court had granted review in a case called *Agostini v. Felton*, which involved the provision of remedial educational services to students in religious schools receiving federal Title I compensatory education funds. As a result of a *Nyquist*-era decision, *Aguilar v. Felton*,[5] religious school students were entitled to receive such services from public school teachers, but not on religious school premises. As a result, religious schools often had to purchase trailers and put them outside on their playgrounds so their students could receive remedial instruction while segregated from religious school

[5] 473 U.S. 402 (1985).

activities. The spectacle was absurd, and we were pleased that the Court took a case that would allow it to reconsider *Aguilar*.

Helpfully, the Clinton administration filed a brief urging the Court to allow religious school teachers to provide services on site, though it carefully avoided any insinuation that the analysis should apply to school choice. I knew that U.S. Solicitor General Walter Dellinger thought the current programs were constitutional, and was glad that he was weighing in even with a narrow argument.

We also filed a brief. Because the case involved direct aid, we asked the Court to set forth a clear analytical framework that carefully contrasted direct and indirect aid programs. Given how thin IJ's staff was stretched, we asked Mark Snyderman, a private-sector lawyer who previously had clerked for Justice O'Connor, to draft our brief. The resulting brief put the school choice issue squarely before the Court, and we hoped that the decision would provide the guidance that the lower courts needed.

That day couldn't come soon enough. On May 1, the Ohio Court of Appeals issued its decision overturning the lower court decision and striking down the Cleveland program. The court viewed the federal and state religious establishment provisions as coextensive—a useful finding that would allow U.S. Supreme Court review—but concluded that religious schools were the only real choice available. The court also found that the program violated the private or local bill provision of the state constitution. The practical ramifications of the court's decision were tremendous: unless we were able to convince the Ohio Supreme Court to grant a stay—an unlikely scenario—the Cleveland program would not continue into its second year.

The decision came near the end of the workday, and even though I was expecting bad news, the effect was devastating. I knew from years of public interest work that the battle goes on until there are no further possible appeals—and this case still had a long way to go. But I couldn't bear the fact that kids might have to leave their schools, and I didn't have the heart to break the news to the parents. Also, I couldn't face the prospect of having to spin yet another loss in the media, or to read gleeful quotes from the likes of Barry Lynn and Bob Chanin. The losses were beginning to pile up. The prospect of losing both Milwaukee and Cleveland, the twin pillars of urban school choice, now was a real possibility. The implications were overwhelming.

That night was the Cato Institute's 20th anniversary, a gala event I had looked forward to for a long time, but I didn't want to infect anyone else with my bleak mood. Instead, I bade my colleagues a good night and sat alone in my office, wondering for the first time if we were wrong about all of this and whether the legal campaign we were leading was headed ultimately to crushing defeat.

6. One in the Bank

As 1997 rolled in and the litigation tempo picked up, and with the specter of the U.S. Supreme Court on the horizon, my colleagues and I decided that we needed to regroup for the coming battle. We scheduled for April a strategy meeting that would bring in some of the top scholars on the constitutional issues of school choice. The purposes were two. We wanted the scholars to scour our briefs to tell us whether we needed to modify our approach in some way. At IJ, we always try to pause periodically to recheck our premises, and this seemed an appropriate time to do so in the school choice context. We also wanted to begin crafting a strategy geared specifically to the Supreme Court. With the Wisconsin case providing a potential vehicle, we weren't sure we'd have a chance to do so later.

The meeting included most of our side's top legal luminaries on establishment clause issues. Professor Michael McConnell of the University of Utah had argued religious establishment and free exercise issues about a dozen times before the U.S. Supreme Court, winning every time—except in *Aguilar*, which was being reconsidered as we met.[1] Professors Douglas Kmiec, now dean at Catholic University law school, Eugene Volokh of the University of California–Los Angeles, and Michael Heise, now at Case Western, are all religious establishment scholars. Phil Murrin was Bill Ball's law partner and had litigated a number of religious establishment and free exercise cases. Mark Snyderman, a private-sector lawyer who had clerked for Justice O'Connor, rounded out the group.

The conference was held at the Jefferson Hotel, which turned out to be located across the street from the behemoth headquarters of the National Education Association. Hence we dubbed the conclave "Shadow of the Beast."

---

[1] Despite splendid qualifications and strong bipartisan support, as of this writing, Michael McConnell's nomination to serve on the U.S. Court of Appeals for the Tenth Circuit has been stalled by the U.S. Senate since 2001.

Chip and I chaired the meeting, setting forth our strategy of defending all school choice programs as intervener-defendants. The participants made comments on the legal presentations in our briefs and, with some suggestions, agreed that it was essential for IJ to be in court as a party separate from the states, and that we were making the best possible arguments. So most of the session was dedicated to Supreme Court strategy, and here we made some essential decisions that would guide us for the next five years.

First, the group agreed that we should try to get a case to the Supreme Court as quickly as possible. The Court, at best, was aligned toward us by a five-to-four margin, but a new Clinton appointment could throw the balance against us. That signaled a critical approach: we should support Supreme Court review even if we *won* in the highest court below, an unusual tactic but acceptable when a legal issue will remain unresolved until a Supreme Court decision. Such an approach might juxtapose us against the state, which institutionally would incline toward defending the decision of its highest court, but that was an added benefit of acting as an independent party.

Second, the swing justice obviously was Justice O'Connor. Everyone agreed that she was especially sensitive to the equities. The participants noted that the luxury of having two or more parties defending a program meant that they did not have to repeat each other's arguments; in fact, it would be a waste to do so. So we should assume that the state competently would make the major legal arguments, and make our brief primarily a "Brandeis brief." The concept hearkened back to the late Justice Louis Brandeis, who as an advocate introduced economic and sociological data in his Supreme Court briefs. So should we, in order to make the case as compelling as possible.

This approach was amenable to IJ's style. Every year we provide a three-day seminar in public interest law to three dozen or so top law students from around the country. Over the years we've graduated several hundred students, and it provides us with a cadre of well-trained and enthusiastic pro bono lawyers. Not only have many of our alumni gone on to prestigious judicial clerkships, academic appointments, and private practice, but the process forces my colleagues and me to distill how it is that we do what we do. In my sessions on public interest litigation tactics, I teach that there are two purposes of a public interest brief: providing the judge with a strong legal basis to rule in our favor, and helping make the judge *want* to rule in our favor. That is what we refer to as the equities. But it also involves telling a compelling story (I use Stephen King, rather than prominent lawyers, as a model for an effective brief-writing style) and bringing in corroborating facts from a variety of sources, including client affidavits and social science. It is an approach that is counterintuitive to many lawyers—indeed, offensive to some, especially government lawyers, who hate to hear about equities—but it is an important part of the American legal tradition. And in this context, the group agreed it might prove crucial to our success.

A third tactic was strategic amicus briefs. Such briefs are often a dime a dozen, especially if they merely repeat the arguments of the parties. We came up with two ideas that would be difficult to pull off, but which could attract serious attention from the Court if we were able to. The first was a brief by big-city mayors, who would not necessarily take a strong position on the constitutionality of school choice, but would urge the Court to preserve it as an essential policy option for large urban school districts facing catastrophic educational conditions. The second would be a brief from a broad array of constitutional law professors, representing diverse philosophical perspectives. Although policy differences over school choice separated most liberal and conservative academics, we were noticing that as a constitutional matter, there seemed to be a growing academic consensus that a properly crafted school choice program should survive First Amendment scrutiny. Not only Walter Dellinger but prominent liberal academics such as Laurence Tribe at Harvard, Akhil Amar at Yale, Jesse Choper at Berkeley, Samuel Estreicher at New York University, and Jeffrey Rosen at George Washington University had publicly expressed that view. If we could get some of them to join a brief, it could demonstrate to the Court that our position was solidly within the constitutional mainstream.

The group also endorsed a strong campaign in the court of public opinion. Like everyone else, judges read newspapers and watch television. Our goal in this regard was twofold: to create a favorable climate for school choice through positive news features, and to seek respectable treatment from highly respected legal commentators such as Nina Totenberg of National Public Radio, Linda Greenhouse of the *New York Times*, David Savage of the *Los Angeles Times*, and

Jeffrey Rosen, who doubled as the legal correspondent for the *New Republic*.

Finally, the group agreed that it was imperative that when a test case finally reached the U.S. Supreme Court, we needed the best possible advocate to argue the case. As interveners, we were entitled to argue at each stage until the Supreme Court. But at the Supreme Court, typically each side is limited to a single advocate. I knew that a state would not likely choose another party's counsel to argue its case. So at that early stage we began considering who might be the best candidate to argue the case—and how we could convince the state to agree.

The Shadow of the Beast conference recharged our batteries and gave us a renewed sense of optimism. But then it was back to the here and now, where the picture looked much grimmer. We badly needed a win. In debates and media appearances, our opponents were bludgeoning us with the assertion that no court anywhere had upheld school choice that included religious schools. I retorted that the Court that mattered most—the U.S. Supreme Court—had done so twice, in *Mueller* upholding tax credits and in *Witters* upholding postsecondary aid. But as far as voucher programs were concerned, we had few other precedents to which we could point. The media generally parroted the unions' line that we were on a serious losing streak, and that of course undercut our credibility across the board.

Trouble was, there was no likely victory on the horizon anytime soon. By this time, we were writing regular memoranda to school choice allies to keep them informed of legal developments. In May, Chip and I sent out a memo discussing the recent Ohio Court of Appeals decision, and forecasting that the legal situation might very well get worse before it got better.

It turned out we were a bit better at forecasting than most meteorologists. In June, the trial court in Vermont struck down the town of Chittenden's policy of reimbursing families for religious school tuition. Curiously, the court disagreed with the Vermont Supreme Court's 1994 *Campbell* decision that had upheld payment of religious school tuition, and instead ruled that the First Amendment prohibited it. Because there is no intermediate appellate court in Vermont, we would appeal directly to the Vermont Supreme Court. Meanwhile, we girded for battle over the Milwaukee program in the Wisconsin Court of Appeals.

Other developments were much more positive. In Ohio, with David Brennan working his usual legislative magic, the state legislature renewed the Cleveland program for two more years, expanding the program by two grades. That bolstered our resolve to seek a stay of the Court of Appeals decision from the Ohio Supreme Court, a difficult proposition but the only way that the program would continue into the coming school year.

The best news came, once again, from the U.S. Supreme Court, which ruled in *Agostini v. Felton*[2] that public school teachers could provide remedial instruction to eligible students on religious school premises. To us, *Agostini* presented a tougher constitutional question than vouchers, because it involved public school employees teaching in religious schools at government expense. That seemed to raise concerns of symbolism—the impermissible commingling of church and state—that had troubled several justices, including Justice O'Connor, in other contexts. School vouchers, by contrast, involved indirect aid that would create no visible public perception of religious "endorsement." By sustaining this aid, it would be difficult conceptually for the Court to strike down less-direct aid. But of course, vouchers are a much more difficult political issue—making it in reality a much more difficult legal issue as well.

Still, everything about the opinion gave us hope. To underscore that *Agostini* was a tougher case than school choice, we had presented a "neutral" brief, supporting neither side. Because that approach was unusual, it had the added benefit of drawing attention to it. We asked the Court to speak clearly in presenting a broadly applicable analytical framework, and it did. The decision was written by Justice O'Connor—an encouraging sign because she was the swing vote— and joined by the other four conservative justices. Instead of a divided rationale, the majority agreed on a unified principle— indeed, the very principle of neutrality on which we were staking our case. The Court expressly overturned the contrary *Aguilar* decision, and noted that in the years since that decision (and, by extension, since the *Nyquist* decision), it had altered its analytical framework, even upholding direct aid to religious institutions under certain circumstances.

[2] 521 U.S. 203 (1997).

The Court articulated a clear standard, declaring that aid programs do not violate the establishment clause "where the aid is allocated on the basis of neutral, secular criteria that neither favor nor disfavor religion, and is made available to both religious and secular beneficiaries on a nondiscriminatory basis."[3] That was a standard that all school choice programs readily would satisfy. Even more, the Court introduced a subtle, yet potentially significant, shift in its definition of neutrality, emphasizing neutrality between religious and secular beneficiaries, rather than between public and nonpublic. If intentional on the part of the Court, that shift could help us with programs like Milwaukee, which on its face created only a private school option. Equally significant, as the Court previously had done in *Mueller*, it rejected any rigid mathematical formula for determining a program's constitutionality. It was the program's neutrality, rather than the independent decisions of beneficiaries about where to use their aid, that mattered from a constitutional perspective.

So *Agostini* was very good news. Now we just had to get a case up to the Supreme Court before the Court's composition changed.

Agostini also provided solid momentum for the Wisconsin Court of Appeals argument, although of course the case presented weighty state constitutional issues as well as the First Amendment. By that time, Ken Starr was involved in other pursuits, so the state's lead lawyer now was Jay Lefkowitz. Ordinarily, Jay and I divided the issues with his arguing the First Amendment and my presenting the state constitutional issues, but on that occasion Jay had a conflict and couldn't make it out to Wisconsin. So another state lawyer handled the state issues and the switch-hitting Bolick took on the First Amendment.

I flew out early and brought along my eldest son, Evan, who was on summer vacation. The trip was a whirlwind, consisting of meetings with parents, PAVE, and MMAC, along with a flurry of media interviews. The night before the argument, Steve Hurley and I took Evan out for his first gourmet dining experience at a terrific French restaurant in Madison. (This was a serious tactical mistake as a parent. Now Evan insists on his own foie gras appetizer any time we go out to a pricey restaurant.)

---

[3] Ibid., p. 231.

As usual, Susan Mitchell, Zakiya Courtney, and Dan McKinley provided logistical support, bringing dozens of parents and children to occupy the courtroom in the state Supreme Court. The argument was intense and spirited, and Chanin was his usual annoying and eloquent self. When I rose for my rebuttal, I finished by noting that when the unions' lawyers had talked at length about the program's "primary beneficiaries," they had overlooked someone. The gallery quietly murmured my final words in unison with me: "the children." It was a stirring and dramatic moment.

Following the argument, the parents and lawyers for our side were greeted warmly and enthusiastically at a reception hosted by the governor. As always, as I spoke to those assembled, I admonished everyone to take the long view: regardless of how the Court of Appeals ruled, we still had one—or possibly two—more steps to go.

Wearing his school choice button (a dangerous choice of apparel considering that his mom is a public school teacher), my son Evan was pumped up. It's tough to explain to my sons what on earth I do for a living. I once asked my middle son, Todd, who had announced at age four that he wanted to be a lawyer, "What exactly does a lawyer do all day?" He thought about that for a moment, then replied, "He goes on TV!" So this was a nice opportunity to show one of them, at least, that there's a bit more to it than that. We capped off the trip with our flight home on Midwest Express (Evan is an aficionado of their chocolate chip cookies as well). After we boarded, Chanin and his minions came on, and Evan whispered, "Dad, he's still got the toothpick in his mouth!" This movement and its adversaries truly include some colorful characters.

We wouldn't have to wait long for a decision from the Court of Appeals, which had agreed to expedite the case so we would get a decision before the start of the new school year. While we waited, we received good news from two sources. In a wonderful development, the Ohio Supreme Court granted our motion to stay the Ohio Court of Appeals decision striking down the program. That meant the program could continue—and expand by another grade—in the coming year. And Judge Higginbotham granted our request to stay the portion of his opinion striking down the expansion of the Milwaukee program in nonsectarian private schools. Those developments made me realize how badly I had violated my own advice about taking the long-term view when I had reacted so strongly to the adverse decision by the Ohio Court of Appeals. Because of the state Supreme Court's stay, the appeals court ruling had no practical effect. But I was glad I had gotten my emotional overreaction out of my system. I and the people around me would need steel nerves for the duration.

Among the people now on the IJ team was our new outreach coordinator, Maureen Blum, who had taken the position of the irreplaceable Nina Shokraii, who had left IJ to head up education policy at the Heritage Foundation. Though very different from Nina in many ways, flamboyant Maureen has the same take-charge attitude and is a consummate organizer and cheerleader. There are probably very few lawyers in America for whom media is the left hand and outreach the right hand, but the combination would serve us well as the battles spread and intensified.

The summer of 1997 ended with an adverse two-to-one ruling from the Wisconsin Court of Appeals. The majority ruled exclusively on the state's Blaine Amendment, although it found *Nyquist* to be the controlling federal precedent. The dissenting opinion was longer and far more incisive than the majority, however, which helped tee up the case nicely for the Wisconsin Supreme Court. But the loss was particularly momentous: we now would need the votes of four out of the six justices in order to prevail. If the Wisconsin Supreme Court deadlocked three-to-three, the result would affirm the Court of Appeals decision. And because it was based on state law grounds, we could not appeal it to the U.S. Supreme Court. The stakes were amazingly high.

Meanwhile, we were working intensely with Rep. Dick Armey (R-Tex.) and Sen. Daniel Coats (R-Ind.) on a new school choice bill for the District of Columbia. Before the bill could even get out of the starting gate, it was attacked like the last one by the U.S. Catholic Conference, which again wanted the full array of federal civil rights regulations to apply to private schools under the legislation. Once again, Dick Komer and I rushed to Capitol Hill to do battle with our "friends." We were incredulous that representatives of Catholic schools would argue for such regulations, particularly when we knew from our experiences in the real world that the schools themselves did not. The Catholic Conference's freelance political activities must drive rank-and-file Catholics crazy. The long and bizarre debate finally ended when Sen. Coats's talented aide, Townsend

Lange (now McNabb), exclaimed, "This is all fine and good, but there is no way on earth we are going to load up this bill with all sorts of regulations." In the end, the bill contained only a general nondiscrimination requirement that mirrors existing private school obligations. But the episode was a painful reminder that sometimes our friends can be more obstructionist than our enemies.

As we prepared to do battle in the Wisconsin, Ohio, and Vermont Supreme Courts, two new battlegrounds opened up. In Maine, we filed a lawsuit challenging the exclusion of religious schools from the state's tuitioning program. As in Vermont, the state defended the discrimination as a requirement of the First Amendment's establishment clause. And in Arizona, the teachers union and its allies filed an original action in the Arizona Supreme Court challenging on state and federal constitutional grounds the state's tax credit for private school scholarships. In addition to several families, we represented Lisa Graham Keegan, the superintendent of public instruction; Trent Franks, the former legislator who authored the tax credit; and Jeff Flake, executive director of the Goldwater Institute (and now a congressman).

It was not clear which of the five cases would move most quickly toward the U.S. Supreme Court. I was quietly pulling for Milwaukee. Though Milwaukee did not expressly include government schools among the options—a potential flaw—it was the best developed of the programs. Dick Komer preferred Vermont because it did include government schools, but in my view it lacked the same equitable appeal as the programs targeted toward low-income kids. But we all agreed that we needed to get a case up there as quickly as possible, and we weren't going to be fussy about which one.

The pressure for productivity was on us like never before. In one single-month span between October and November, we had major briefs due in Wisconsin, Arizona, Ohio, and Vermont. It also meant juggling media and infrastructure in all five states and at the national level. We worked independently but met regularly as a team, and used conference calls and e-mails to make sure we were synchronized with our national and local allies.

All of the school choice activity, of course, was in addition to the other work which we were engaged in at the Institute for Justice. Several of my colleagues were focused entirely on cases outside of the school choice area, particularly economic liberty and property rights. As litigation director, it was my job to keep it all coordinated, along with Chip, an excellent litigation supervisor (as well as a terrific litigator in his own right). Throughout the school choice litigation, I also always had at least one case in some other area in litigation, mainly to maintain a fresh focus. During the major litigation crunch, I was litigating what turned out to be a successful challenge in San Diego to California's ridiculous cosmetology licensing regime on behalf of African hairstylists. I found our work in the school choice and economic liberty areas mutually reinforcing, two sides of the empowerment coin.

But school choice occupied most of my attention, and the demands were heavy. During intense litigation periods, I often visualize football images that help get me through. It will surprise no one who is familiar with my size and remarkable klutziness that I have never played football, other than the two-hand touch variety. But I often imagine myself as a running back, grinding out yardage. It only takes three-and-a-half yards on each carry to retain possession of the ball. And if you keep your eyes on the hash marks and grind out enough three-and-a-half yard carries—being careful not to fumble the ball—eventually you'll cross the goal line. That's exactly what my colleagues and I had to do.

It turned out that the first case scheduled for oral argument was Arizona on December 16. (Jeff Flake always jokes that I had an uncanny ability to have Arizona events scheduled in the winter. But I figured that the frequent winter excursions to Wisconsin and Ohio balanced that out.) In many regards the state is enormously hospitable. It still is, to some extent, the land of Barry Goldwater–style individualism. It had come close to adopting a full-scale voucher program, and boasted the nation's largest and most deregulated charter school program, along with open public school enrollment. The concept of "choice" was firmly established in the popular lexicon.

But the state Supreme Court was another matter. For years, the five-member court had been dominated by Justice Stanley Feldman, Arizona's version of Shirley Abrahamson and a leading proponent of liberal state court activism. His nemesis, Justice Frederick Martone, provided a counterbalance, but the court tilted to the left. In a recent school equity decision, the Court had struck down the state's school construction funding formula on educational equity grounds. Moreover, the state has a strong Blaine amendment, which provides that "[n]o tax shall be laid or appropriation of money made in aid of any church, or private or sectarian school. . . ."

I coordinated carefully with the lead lawyers for the state, Tom McGovern and Patrick Irvine. We decided to take our first stand on the nature of tax credits, which in our view were not "public funds" at all, because the money belonged to the taxpayers and never came under the state's control. It was a long-shot argument, but if successful it would establish an enormously useful precedent. Next, we argued as we did in other Blaine amendment states that the credits were advanced not in aid of private or sectarian schools, but students. Once we reached the First Amendment—*if* we got that far— we had a strong case because the *Mueller* decision already sanctioned tax deductions. But here, the credits were not available for public school tuition, for the simple reason that the state already provided open and tuition-free public school enrollment. So once again we would argue that the tax credit merely added new choices to a wide array of pre-existing educational options. We also made one argument that the State didn't, wrapping ourselves in the Arizona Supreme Court's tax equity decision and arguing that tax credits were one means by which the state was fulfilling its constitutional mandate of equal educational opportunities.

The state's lawyers and I engaged in extensive moot court participation. They agreed that because of my experience, especially with First Amendment issues, I should take about half of the argument time. Trouble is, in the Arizona Supreme Court, parties have to manage their own time, and if one advocate goes over it will be charged against cocounsel's time. As a result, although I was expecting to have seven minutes, I also prepared arguments of six, five, four, three, and two minutes—just in case.

My experience in courts around the country has made me pretty adaptable to whatever judicial environment in which I find myself, but I was astonished to learn that unlike the green, yellow, and red lights that most supreme courts use to help advocates keep track of time, the Arizona Supreme Court places a digital clock in front of the advocates, ticking off the seconds like a sporting event. Bob Chanin got up first and was true to his usual form, sparring gamely with Justice Martone. When Tom McGovern got up, he said he wanted to reserve seven minutes for me. The questions were fast and furious. It appeared that Justices Feldman, Thomas Zlaket, and

Charles Jones—the latter ordinarily a conservative—were hostile, while Justices Martone and James Moeller seemed sympathetic. About eight minutes into his argument, McGovern tried to extricate himself, but to no avail. The Court kept firing questions as I watched the seconds ticking preciously away. Finally McGovern was able to sit down—with 2:49 remaining on the clock. I pulled out my notes and did my best imitation of Joe Montana's two-minute drill, talking faster than I've ever talked in my life, supplementing McGovern's answers where I thought a different perspective might work and emphasizing the educational equities.

Afterward, Lisa Keegan, Trent Franks, and several parents seemed very pleased with the argument. But I was glum, counting the vote as three-to-two. It would really hurt if we lost our first state Supreme Court showdown; and because independent state grounds existed to invalidate the program, we likely would not have occasion to appeal to the U.S. Supreme Court.

But I didn't have much time to worry about it because the Wisconsin and Vermont Supreme Courts scheduled oral arguments for the following March. Both sides had marshaled strong amicus support. In addition to an excellent brief by Jeanne Allen's Center for Education Reform on behalf of numerous pro-school groups, Susan Mitchell coordinated a pathbreaking brief in the Milwaukee case signed by three members of the Milwaukee school board along with Mayor Norquist and Howard Fuller. Co-authored by the mayor's brilliant aide David Riemer and Milwaukee lawyer Michael Dean, the brief presented a broad range of educational and financial data for the court to consider. The bipartisan approach on behalf of highly credible public servants was one that we wanted to replicate if we ever got a case to the U.S. Supreme Court.

Susan and the rest of the Milwaukee support team also made preparations for a rally on the steps of the state capitol, which housed the Wisconsin Supreme Court, in advance of the afternoon argument. Along with our respective teams, Jay Lefkowitz and I worked together to prepare, with Jay focusing on the First Amendment issues and my focusing on state constitutional issues. With so much on the line, the tension was palpable.

Chip and I flew to Madison the day before the argument. March 4 was a cold day, but clear. We were expecting several bus loads of parents and children from Milwaukee, but our jaws dropped when we saw a caravan of *16* buses, depositing over 600 enthusiastic rally participants at the steps of the majestic capitol. Everyone was equipped with buttons, signs, or both. The sight of it replaced the knot in my stomach with pure adrenaline.

The rally kicked off with a private school choir leading the crowd in inspirational gospel songs, including "We Shall Overcome." Zaki-yah Courtney and Brother Bob Smith excited the crowd with passionate speeches reminiscent of the Rev. Martin Luther King. The spirit was intense.

As I stood on the top step surveying the crowd, I noticed a group of people approaching from behind. It was Bob Chanin and his retinue of grim-faced lawyers. I jabbed Chip and we both looked over our shoulders and smiled. Yet another fine metaphor: to get inside the court, the bad guys had to get past the kids.

This time we had reserved plenty of seats inside the courtroom for parents and children, much to the consternation of the teachers union folks who had to stand or watch television monitors outside the courtroom. The atmosphere was electric. Jay Lefkowitz was girded for battle, as were Chanin and his minions, who prowled nearby. This was it, perhaps the penultimate argument.

It was a bit disconcerting to see Justice Abrahamson occupying the center chair, having been elevated to the position of chief justice. But it was comforting to still have Justice Jon Wilcox on the bench. While Jay argued, thrusting and parrying with Chief Justice Abrahamson and Justice Bablitch, my eyes were riveted on the newest justice and presumed swing vote, Patrick Crooks.

When it was my turn, the chief justice welcomed me back to Madison with a warm smile. "It's always great to be here, Chief Justice Abrahamson," I replied, thinking that someday perhaps I'd leave Madison with her vote on some issue—but certainly not that day! I started out by talking about the important and wonderful day on which the court previously had sustained the original Milwaukee School Choice Program, and argued that the expanded program was a logical extension designed to fulfill the program's educational objectives. I worked my way through the state constitutional issues and had a good give and take with the justices. Justice Crooks asked insightful questions but didn't tip his hand.

Then Chanin got up. He started with the state constitutional issues, then worked his way to *Nyquist*. By that time I was sure I could give Chanin's argument for him, and I think that his mantra of *Nyquist* will nag me forever. As Chanin went on, I scribbled suggestions for Jay, who would present rebuttal for our side.

But then a few minutes before the end of the argument, Chanin paused, as if he had concluded. But he hadn't. "A point of personal privilege, your honors," he began.

Jay and I looked at each other expectantly. What was Chanin doing? And what the heck was a point of personal privilege?

"I'm tired of being cast as the man with the black hat," Chanin went on. He and his colleagues had been castigated, unfairly, as enemies of schoolchildren and education reform. And the depiction wasn't true, he insisted. Even though it was entirely beside the point to the argument, Chanin said, he felt compelled to respond. He and his clients cared about kids. They were champions of schoolchildren and public education, and he wanted the record to reflect that.

When Chanin was finished with his remarkable monologue, he sat down.

I glanced back incredulously at Chip, who was seated in the front row. He returned my wide-eyed expression. We had just witnessed something totally unexpected: *Chanin had melted down.* And the best thing about it was that it was the kids who had caused him to do it.

I can barely remember what else happened in the argument, and when we left I had no idea which side had prevailed. But I was giddy over Chanin's meltdown, which had exposed the first crack in his polished and eloquent veneer. When I saw Susan Mitchell, we were beside ourselves, trying to fathom the spectacle we had just witnessed. If ever we had wondered whether the massive effort involved in organizing and transporting parents and children to court arguments was worth it, the question was answered emphatically. What sweet vindication of our strategy.

In a somewhat awkward moment, I had to pose with Chanin in front of the doors to the Supreme Court for a photograph for *Education Week*, which was doing a feature on our ongoing battles. As usual, we had little to say to each other. But I didn't think he felt particularly good about his argument in the most important forum in which we yet had sparred.

Returning to Washington, we had to put the argument out of our minds. Dick Komer was preparing for argument in the Vermont Supreme Court, and we were moving forward on multiple fronts.

Fortunately, Dick had managed to recuse two members of the Vermont Supreme Court who had worked on the case on the other side before joining the court.

A key member of our team, Nicole Garnett, left that summer to clerk for Justice Clarence Thomas, and thereafter to join her husband, Rick, on the faculty of Notre Dame Law School. Fortunately, her shoes were filled by our former summer clerk, Matthew Berry, who had just finished an appellate court clerkship and had developed into an excellent young lawyer.

Though we had five cases going, most of the focus remained on the impending decision in Milwaukee. Speculation was rampant, and the tea leaves seemed to read both ways. But I experienced a personal revelation when the *Education Week* article came out bearing the photo of Chanin and me at the Wisconsin Supreme Court. I looked closely at his expression and then at mine, and said to myself, "My God, we won!" But being a tad superstitious, I kept that thought entirely to myself.

The Wisconsin Supreme Court kept us waiting a mercifully short three months. Stoking the drama, the court announced that it would issue its decision on June 10, 1998, and that it would open early, at 7 A.M., to release the decision.

The time since the argument had passed pretty quickly to that point, but then it slowed to a crawl. I became absolutely neurotic, and I think the entire IJ staff did as well.

We prepared assiduously for the decision. Kramer had me draft two alternate news releases so we could get them out the instant we saw the decision. Maureen would alert our clients. The decision would be released on the court's Web site; but never wanting to leave anything so important to chance, we arranged for Steve Hurley to be at the court to get the decision and phone us instantly.

Pretty much the entire IJ staff was at the office before 8 A.M. in anticipation of the decision, gathered around the computer in Kramer's office. I paced anxiously. Finally the appointed hour arrived—and passed. The tension was exquisite. What was going on?

Unbeknownst to me, Steve Hurley had a family medical emergency and wasn't at the court. And the decision was delayed getting onto the court's Web site.

Finally we dispatched our paralegal, Gretchen Embrey, to call the court. "Just ask them to read the last line of the decision," I instructed.

"Hey, it's coming in!" Kramer exclaimed. The decision was appearing on his computer screen—one painstaking line at a time.

"Oh, no" I said. "The caption alone is two full pages. It'll take forever!"

Then Gretchen returned, a grin on her face. Everyone looked at her. "What's the news?" I asked.

"It's remanded to the trial court!" she replied.

But that told us nothing—the decision would be remanded whether we won or lost. Why hadn't I asked her to get the last *two* lines read to her? "Go call them back!" I urged.

"Okay, here it comes," Kramer said. The caption finally had run its course and the text of the opinion was coming out.

"Scroll down, scroll down," I demanded. I can be a pain in the ass when I'm feeling impatient.

I looked at the screen.

"Opinion by Steinmetz, J.," it read. That was a hopeful sign, but not definite.

And then: "Dissent by Abrahamson, C.J."

"WE WON!!" I screamed, leaping into the air. And then all of us—Kramer, Chip, Matthew, Maureen, pretty much the whole staff—were shouting, hugging, laughing, jumping up and down. It was exciting, fulfilling, amazing, and totally sublime.

We had won the biggest test of the biggest school choice case so far, the first state supreme court ruling of the crucial Establishment Clause issue. The Milwaukee Parental Choice Program—a beacon of hope for countless economically disadvantaged schoolchildren throughout the nation—was going to get a whole lot bigger. And suddenly everything that had come before—the sweat, the tears, the stress, the highs and terrible lows—were so utterly and completely worth it.

7. A Blizzard of Decisions

Sometimes even when an attorney wins a case, the opinion turns out to be disappointing. The quality of a win can be as important as the win itself.

But the Wisconsin Supreme Court decision in *Jackson v. Benson*[1] was absolutely stellar. It gave us a solid precedent on both the First Amendment and the Blaine amendment. And if the U.S. Supreme Court decided to review it, we felt it was a strong decision to defend.

The decision was meticulous and well-reasoned. It did exactly what we hoped it would do: carefully ground the outcome in existing precedent rather than engaging in judicial adventurism. The court did not suggest that *Nyquist* was no longer good law—which would have been an unnecessary provocation of the Supreme Court, in our view—but rather that the broader body of jurisprudence of which *Nyquist* was one part was congenial to the Milwaukee program. "A State's decision to defray the cost of educational expenses incurred by parents—regardless of the type of schools their children attend—evidences a purpose that is both secular and understandable."[2] The court applied the two standards that had evolved in the U.S. Supreme Court's jurisprudence—"neutrality" and "indirection," meaning that the choice of where to spend education dollars is made by the parents among a wide array of choices. On the latter point, the court made a very important finding from our argument that deeply gratified my colleagues and me:

> [T]he State's system of per-pupil school financing, in which public funds follow each child, now encompasses a wide range of school choices—mainly public, but some private or religious. . . . Qualifying public school students may choose from among the Milwaukee public district schools, magnet schools, charter schools, suburban public schools, trade

[1] 578 N.W.2d 602 (Wis. 1998).
[2] Ibid., p. 857.

schools, schools developed for students with exceptional needs, and now sectarian or nonsectarian private schools participating in the [school choice program]. In each case, the programs let state funds follow the students to the districts and schools their parents have chosen.[3]

In sum, the court concluded that the program "places on equal footing options of public and private school choice, and vests power in the hands of parents to choose where to direct the funds allocated for their children's benefit."[4] That finding placed the program on firm jurisprudential ground on the issue of neutrality. But it also recognized the conceptual breakthrough of student-based funding—the idea of dollars following the student rather than going as an entitlement to a school—that could provide the basis for systemic education reform.

The court applied the same framework to its analysis of the Blaine amendment, providing an analysis that could prove helpful in other contexts. And mercifully, it finally put to rest—in Wisconsin at least—the nagging concern about private or local bills.

What remained was the crucial strategic decision of what posture we would take in response to the unions' petition for writ of certiorari[5] in the U.S. Supreme Court. Ordinarily, a party winning a case opposes vigorously Supreme Court review. But we faced the prospect of a fleeting Supreme Court majority, so it might make sense to place our biggest victory at risk, which was the direction that our academic experts had urged at the Shadow of the Beast conference.

But first it was time for celebration, hosted by Brother Bob Smith at Messmer High School, which now would have the opportunity to participate in the choice program. Seeing again what that school has been able to do for kids who were written off by the government school system made me realize all over again what the battle was all about. Several hundred people gathered for a candlelight celebration in the gymnasium where we sang songs, cheered, and shed tears of joy. I can't remember ever hugging so many people.

[3] Ibid., p. 870, n.16.

[4] Ibid., p. 873.

[5] This cumbersome Latin term is the mechanism for appeal of a decision to the U.S. Supreme Court. Review is entirely discretionary, and the Court accepts only a tiny fraction of cases that are presented—usually only when a conflict of authority exists in the lower courts on a particular issue.

That evening, Chip and I had dinner with George and Susan Mitchell at their home. George decided that it was time to uncork a bottle of wine he had won in a bet with Justice Bablitch some time previously. We poured the wine and toasted the dissenting justice— and then discovered the wine had virtually turned to vinegar. "Bablitch's revenge!" George exclaimed to a round of laughter.

Before the school choice case, I had never been to Milwaukee; now I consider it almost a home away from home. If the first school choice program could have happened anywhere, I'm glad it happened there. The people are good, hard-working, salt-of-the-earth types. Even in the coldest of winters, they impart warmth. And they've done it right, getting a school choice program established that is a model for the nation. The spirit and unity that sustained the remarkable coalition through the darkest days was never so evident as during the celebration over the Wisconsin Supreme Court victory.

But then it was back to work. I asked our Milwaukee allies to put together the largest group of interested people they could assemble. The meeting room was filled with activists, parents, and school officials. I set forth the options. We could put the decision in the bank and oppose review. Or we could gamble and support review, which was such an unusual posture that it might increase the odds for review. What were the odds, people wanted to know. Not terribly high, I replied, because this was the first case to be decided and there were others in the pipeline. If the Court didn't accept this case, would an adverse decision in a subsequent case possibly put the Milwaukee program at risk? Yes. Which case would I most like to go up to the Supreme Court? I grinned at that one, and hemmed and hawed a bit before I replied, "Milwaukee."

The consensus was strong and complete: we should support review. I think that the recommendation came not only from the information I gave them but also from the enormous pride that had developed among the activists, parents, and school officials. This was their program. It was the first, and the best. And if a case was going up to the U.S. Supreme Court, they wanted it to be *their* case.

The state, understandably, took the opposite position—it could not very well thumb its nose at its own Supreme Court, which had handed it such a sweeping triumph. But I could tell that Jay Lefkowitz would not be disappointed if the U.S. Supreme Court granted review.

127

We filed our brief urging review, arguing that the issue was an urgent one, not just in resolving the burgeoning litigation surrounding school choice, but in providing guidance to policymakers eagerly seeking ways to solve the urban education crisis. Our position had the added benefit of giving us greater credibility when we said we were confident that the Court would rule in our favor. After all, if we weren't confident, we never would put the Wisconsin decision at risk. Truth was, we *were* fairly confident, but even more confident that our chances then would be better than after a change in the Court's composition. As usual, rumors of health problems and impending retirements swirled around the capital city, wearing away my stomach lining. At school choice conferences when asked what people could do to aid the effort, I would quip, "Pray for the health of five members of the U.S. Supreme Court."

But if I was anxious, the Court wasn't, and it denied review, with only Justice Stephen Breyer dissenting. Rumors abounded—and they could just as easily have emanated from logic as from inside information from the highly secretive court—that neither side was certain of Justice O'Connor's vote. So we would have to wait awhile longer for a Supreme Court decision.

Possibilities remained for review, most notably the Cleveland case, if we could survive in the Ohio Supreme Court. Distressingly, two justices on that court we had counted on recused themselves, one due to a social relationship with David Brennan. That would have killed our chances for sure, except that the Ohio Supreme Court, unlike Wisconsin, replaces justices who recuse themselves by elevating appeals court judges for a particular case. So we were up to our full complement of seven. The two replacement judges were unknowns. Of the remaining five, we counted one likely vote for our side, and three for our opponents. The usual swing justice was Paul E. Pfeifer, a notoriously unpredictable moderate.

David Brennan again agreed to organize a rally to follow the September 28 argument. Once more, the argument would be divided among Jeff Sutton, David Young, and me. It appeared to us that given the favorable language of the religion clause of the state constitution, First Amendment issues would predominate, and we prepared accordingly.

We were wrong. Early into Jeff's argument, the court asked a seemingly innocuous question about the uniformity clause, Ohio's version of the private or local bill clause. Because of some legislative changes made to the program's design in response to my urgings, we believed that issue would not be in play. The precedents were solidly on our side.

But unlike the Wisconsin Supreme Court, the Ohio Supreme Court didn't seem much concerned about precedents. Indeed, when Jeff explained that a decision striking down this program on uniformity clause grounds could imperil all manner of legislative enactments— usually a sobering prospect for state judges—I swear that the eyes of several of the justices actually lit up. This was going all wrong. Jeff argued gamely but was caught in a totally unexpected morass. Fortunately, I knew a great deal about the issue, but was unable to make much headway either. Still, when we left the courtroom, it was unclear what the court's ultimate decision would look like.

The rally, across the street at the state capitol, was a wonderful success. Bert Holt, the former program administrator who was deeply committed to the program, was an inspiring master of ceremonies. David Brennan was there, resplendent in his white cowboy hat, which of course brought to mind Bob Chanin's metaphor about wearing the black hat.

This time our adversaries came armed with a plan to mount a counterdemonstration. A plan, but not the execution. Ten or so union officials milled around near the curb alongside Chanin, all of them looking miserable and uncomfortable. When it was my turn at the microphone, I called to them to come over to our rally for some warm coffee, but they didn't accept the invitation. At least the rally took the sting off a very disorienting court argument.

By the end of the year we were awaiting decisions from four state supreme courts: Ohio, Vermont, Arizona, and Maine. The decisions came one after the other, starting in January. The Arizona Supreme Court ruled three-to-two that the scholarship tax credit did not violate either the First Amendment or the state constitution. Usually I'm pretty accurate in predicting where justices will come out, but I actually got three out of the five wrong—a good thing, because I had predicted following oral argument that we'd lose three-to-two.

Any victory under those circumstances would have been pleasing, but the decision was sensational. On the state constitutional issue, the court ruled that the provision limiting the appropriation of government funds was not implicated, because a tax credit is not an

129

appropriation—it's simply money that the state elects to leave in the hands of the taxpayer. That ruling could have important conceptual ramifications for tax credits and deductions in other states.

But even more salient was the court's ruling on the Blaine amendment. Arizona's provision could not be a Blaine amendment, the court reasoned, because Arizona became a state in 1912, long after Blaine's handiwork was complete. But citing the pathbreaking work of New York University professor Joseph Viteritti who has documented the nefarious history of the Blaine amendment, the court went on to say that if the Arizona provision could be traced to the Blaine amendment, "we would be hard pressed to divorce the amendment's language from the insidious discriminatory intent that prompted it."[6]

That language was cause for joy: we finally had a judicial decision recognizing, as the Arizona Supreme Court put it, that far from exemplifying some utopian notion of separation of church and state, the "Blaine Amendment was a clear manifestation of religious bigotry, part of a crusade manufactured by the contemporary Protestant establishment to counter what was perceived as a growing 'Catholic menace.'"[7] That precedent could prove enormously helpful in combating Blaine amendments in other states.

Following the decision, I trekked to Phoenix to meet with Lisa Keegan, Trent Franks, Jack and Isabelle McVaugh, and other tax credit stalwarts to determine whether we should support review in the U.S. Supreme Court if the union sought it. Because the program involved tax credits and so a precedent would not necessarily resolve the voucher issue, and because the program did not expressly encompass government school options, I recommended putting the decision in the bank. But Trent Franks would have none of it: the scholarship tax credit was a model for the nation, he argued with characteristic passion and eloquence, and we ought to take it to the U.S. Supreme Court if we could. Marching orders in hand, I filed a brief agreeing with the union that the Court should take the case—which once again demonstrated our confidence that we were correct in

[6] *Kotterman v. Killian*, 972 P.2d 606, 624 (Ariz. 1999). In a priceless bit of irony, the court also cited the academic work on the Blaine amendment by our nemesis Steven Green of Americans United for Separation of Church and State, who, as an attorney, has struggled mightily to apply the Blaine amendment to squelch school choice.

[7] Ibid.

interpreting constitutional standards. (When we later appealed the Cleveland decision, the unions did not exhibit the same confidence.) The bravado may have reflected more optimism than confidence; but in any event, the Court declined review, just as it had in the Milwaukee case.

The Maine Supreme Court followed with its decision in April. Despite the fact that the program was absolutely neutral as between public and private options, the Court ruled five-to-one that the state's policy of excluding religious schools was *required* by the First Amendment's Establishment Clause.[8] In an identical case brought by the American Center for Law and Justice, a religious liberties group, the U.S. Court of Appeals for the First Circuit ruled the same way.

Having lost our first case in a state supreme court, we thought the odds were decent for review in the U.S. Supreme Court, because we now could point to a split in authority. On the other hand, the Maine and Vermont tuitioning programs were not urban school choice programs, so the sense of urgency might not seem as great. In the end, the Court declined review. We were left wondering about the Court's reasons for ducking the issue: was it waiting for the "right" case, or were both sides indeed uncertain about winning the necessary fifth vote? In that case, we might never secure the constitutional certainty we so badly wanted.

The Vermont case seemed likely to present yet another vehicle but the Vermont Supreme Court threw an unexpected curveball. Only five years earlier, it had ruled that it was permissible for school authorities to refund tuition paid to religious schools by eligible families. In that decision, the court had not even addressed state constitutional issues. Nor did we view it as a serious problem. Vermont does not have a Blaine amendment, but rather a prohibition against "compelled support" of religion. Such clauses, typically of older vintage than the Blaine amendments, usually are interpreted harmoniously with the First Amendment.

Not this time. Seizing the opportunity to interpret its constitution more broadly than the First Amendment, the Vermont Supreme Court ruled unanimously that even if religious school tuitioning were permissible under the First Amendment, it violated the

---

[8] *Bagley v. Raymond School Dep't*, 728 A.2d 127 (Me. 1999).

Vermont Constitution.[9] Because the case was decided on independent state grounds, we could not appeal it to the U.S. Supreme Court. Moreover, the majority on the Chittenden school board had shifted and no longer supported including religious schools in the tuitioning program. The Vermont case, which initially held such promise, fell victim to the tide of political correctness that now dominates that state's institutions. So the overall scorecard recorded a tie—two victories and two defeats—with no immediate prospect of having the U.S. Supreme Court break it.

While the court decisions were rolling in, we were occupied as well in the legislative arena. In November 1998, Jeb Bush was elected governor of Florida, and part of his mandate was a plan for "opportunity scholarships," which was part of a much broader education reform program known as the A+ program. Unlike his brother George, Jeb Bush is a true policy enthusiast, deeply enmeshed in the details. He had swept a heavily Republican legislature into office with him, so prospects appeared excellent for legislative victory.

Education reform was the top priority for the new governor, so Matthew Berry and I flew down to Florida (a wintertime respite again) to meet with Patrick Heffernan, the president of Floridians for School Choice, and other activists, including T. Willard Fair, president of the Urban League of Greater Miami. Fair had broken ranks with the national leadership of his organization over vouchers. Fair had started a charter school in Miami and is an eloquent and passionate proponent of empowerment of economically disadvantaged minorities. He immediately became an important ally, willing to do whatever it took to get the program going and to keep it alive.

Jeb put together an impressive education policy team, which included his lieutenant governor, Frank Brogan, who had served as commissioner of education; Brewser Brown, a get-things-done aide to Brogan; and Reg Brown in the governor's counsel's office. We began to huddle immediately over the details of the plan so that Jeb could hit the ground running as soon as he was inaugurated. The opportunity scholarship component was designed to make

[9] *Chittenden Town School Dist. v. Dep't of Education*, 738 A.2d 539 (Vt. 1999).

meaningful the state's existing policy of grading each of its public schools. Any school that earned an A would receive a financial bonus. Schools receiving an F in any two years out of four would trigger two actions: first, the state would intervene to create a remedial program for the school, and the students would be offered scholarships to attend private schools or better-performing public schools. The program marked a policy breakthrough in two significant ways: it was the first potentially statewide voucher program, and it was the first to explicitly link public school accountability with private school choice.

Most of the details were easy, because Jeb had sketched out the program so carefully during the campaign. And it was ideal from a constitutional standpoint, because it included both public and private school choices. Florida has a Blaine amendment, but the courts have interpreted it fairly flexibly—though there are no recent precedents. The big issue was that Jeb had promised to include a provision allowing choice students to opt out of religious activities. I assured Jeb that such a provision was not constitutionally necessary, but he insisted on fulfilling his campaign pledge (a trait as rare in a politician as it is admirable). His insistence required a great deal of negotiation with Catholic school officials. Here, our experience in Milwaukee proved useful. The Milwaukee program also includes an opt-out. It turns out that Catholic schools in Milwaukee typically had such opt-out policies anyway—and none of their students availed themselves of them. Even non-Catholic parents, who comprise a majority in inner-city Catholic schools, usually do not have a problem with having their children attend religious services. We were able to suggest language that satisfied the governor and the Catholics.

The next step was getting the program through the legislature intact. Here we had a number of capable allies, including Tom Feeney, a longtime friend and school choice stalwart who had run as Jeb's lieutenant governor candidate in the 1994 campaign (and is now a congressman), as well as a few black Democrats. We sent Matthew to Tallahassee to serve as an on-the-spot adviser to the legislative team, providing legal counsel on each of the dozens of amendments, many of which were designed to stymie the program. Matthew spent nearly a week in toe-to-toe combat in the legislative trenches and acquitted himself superbly, far beyond his years. In the end, the program was adopted intact[10]—and that's when the real fun began.

The first problem was implementation. From a legal perspective, we were anxious to get the program up and running—and get kids into new schools—to increase the odds of a successful defense. But the accountability "standards" that the Bush administration had inherited from Gov. Lawton Chiles were a joke, and it wasn't clear that *any* schools would qualify. Jeb ratcheted up the standards, but we weren't sure that any of the failing schools would be receiving the second F necessary to qualify. Meanwhile, we had no idea where to look for clients, because the qualifying schools could be anywhere in the state.

The second problem was the court system, especially the Florida Supreme Court. Chiles had appointed the vast majority of judges in the state, and the Supreme Court—as the entire nation subsequently would learn in the aftermath of the 2000 presidential campaign[11]—was notoriously liberal. Hence we faced a painful paradox: never had we had a program more legally defensible—yet never were our odds of success so low. If the Florida program ever reached the U.S. Supreme Court, it would almost surely be upheld under existing precedent. Yet even with favorable Florida precedents, we had little confidence that it would survive in the Florida courts. If the program were enjoined at the outset, I feared that it would never get off the ground.

When the public school grades were announced, it turned out that two elementary schools—Spencer Bibbs and Dixon Elementary,

[10]The same legislature also adopted the McKay Scholarship program, an innovative program that allows youngsters with disabilities to use their state funds in private schools. Thousands of children with disabilities have transferred to private schools in the program. It's an especially good idea because many children in government schools are labeled "disabled" not because they need extra help, but because they need individualized attention. In private schools, they can receive the help without the label and the massive bureaucracy that goes along with it. Far from limiting options for children with disabilities, school choice expands them.

[11]My wife, Shawnna, and I were honeymooning in Australia shortly after the 2000 presidential election, and news coverage was ubiquitous even half the world away. When I heard a news report that the Florida Supreme Court was going to decide the outcome, I moaned, "Oh no! It's over." I also predicted that the U.S. Supreme Court *never* would review a state court's decision certifying its election results. Fortunately, my prognostications about school choice litigation proved closer to the mark.

both in Pensacola—had qualified. Unfortunately, the parents had no information about what was going on. We sprang into action. Pat Heffernan immediately put together an effort to coordinate sign-ups with the Florida Department of Education. We sent our outreach coordinator, Maureen Blum, to Pensacola to try to find parents to represent. Maureen is amazing. Before she had even checked into her motel, she learned from the desk clerk that one of their staffers was dissatisfied with her daughter's school, and Maureen met with her immediately. She also stood outside Bibbs and Dixon—subjecting herself to all manner of abuse—handing out flyers to parents. In no time we had several committed clients, including Dermita (Dee) Merkman and Tracy Richardson, who would become stalwarts for the program. We lined up the capable Kenneth Sukhia, a former U.S. Attorney, as our pro bono local counsel in Tallahassee and we were ready to go.

Maureen Blum and Pat Heffernan also worked with private schools to help bring them into the program. Unfortunately, the popular local Christian schools refused to participate, citing the random admissions and opt-out policies. The Catholic schools signed up, as did a Montessori school, which added a nonsectarian option to the program. Meanwhile, the Jeb Bush administration hustled to get the program up and running before the litigation commenced. The efforts were successful: out of about 600 eligible students in Bibbs and Dixon, more than 70 enrolled in new public schools and nearly 60 in private schools—a very satisfying mix. The signing ceremony, which took place in a Tallahassee elementary school, was spirited and touching. Jessica Merkman, Dee's adorable little daughter, fell asleep in the governor's arms, and he held her throughout the ceremony so that she wouldn't awaken.

The lawsuit was filed by the usual suspects, the two teachers unions (which subsequently merged), the ACLU, and the NAACP. We countered by intervening not only on behalf of the Pensacola families but also on behalf of the Urban League of Greater Miami. To my knowledge, it's the only time that the NAACP and Urban League have been on opposite sides of a civil rights lawsuit. It reflects the very different concerns and constituencies of the two organizations. The NAACP's base is primarily middle class and heavily wedded to government programs; the Urban League focuses more on urban underclass concerns. At the national level, both organizations oppose school choice—but while the NAACP long ago made a devil's pact with People for the American Way, Urban League president Hugh Price has been far more critical of public schools and open to alternatives. Moreover, while the NAACP routinely excommunicates local chapters or activists who stray from organizational dogma, the Urban League fosters innovation and independence at the local level. T. Willard Fair personifies the independent and innovative spirit that can flourish in the less-authoritarian environment of the National Urban League.

The lawsuit challenged the program under the religious establishment provisions of the First Amendment and the Florida Constitution as well as under the constitution's provision that guarantees a uniform and quality education, which the plaintiffs contended was violated because the scholarship program diverted money from public schools. The latter was especially worrisome, for if a court accepted the proposition, it would preclude the use of government funds in private schools for *any* purpose. I was peeved that the ACLU was signing on to such an argument, once again playing the role of the tail to the union's dog. If there is any organization on earth that has "diverted" funding from the public schools, it's the ACLU and its often-inane lawsuits. Yet here it was casting itself as the guardian of public schools.

The prospect of an injunction was imminent. Around that time, one of IJ's board members,[12] Arthur Dantchik, asked how he might help with a strategic philanthropic investment. I suggested that we take out full-page advertisements in the four biggest newspapers in Florida, once when the program was signed into law, and again when the lawsuit was filed. Arthur agreed. We decided to go after the ACLU directly and try to shame it—a tall order—into not seeking an injunction. Given that the plaintiffs had sought an injunction at the outset in every previous lawsuit, the odds were poor that they'd back off here.

IJ's talented production director, Don Wilson, designed an eye-catching advertisement featuring a sweet photograph of Dee and

---

[12] When Chip and I were starting IJ, one of the best suggestions we received came from Burt Pines, then at the Heritage Foundation, who urged us not to follow the "show board" model embraced by many Washington organizations, but rather to have a small group of highly committed individuals, and the kind of people with whom we'd want to drink beer (or in my case, wine). We heeded that advice and are lucky to have a superb board.

Jessica. In big type, it proclaimed that "Florida is giving Jessica Merkman—and every Florida child—a money-back guarantee on their public education." In bold print below that: "The ACLU wants to take it away." Then we went on to describe the opportunity scholarship program and the ACLU's lawsuit.

The reaction was far greater than we reasonably could have hoped for. The ACLU howled in protest. In addition to the advertisements running in the largest dailies, four newspapers editorialized about the advertisements—two in favor, two against—giving us huge secondary coverage. The issue was humanized and dramatized.

And, astonishingly, the ACLU blinked: it didn't ask for an injunction. That didn't mean our legal troubles in Florida were over—far from it—but it meant, crucially, that the program would start in the fall.

It is remarkable that the unions and ACLU blinked in Florida but didn't blink later that summer in Cleveland. Instead they decided to pursue an injunction there—with disastrous results. Had they done the reverse—sought an injunction in Florida but not in Cleveland—the whole history might have been different: we probably wouldn't have a functioning (and now expanded) opportunity scholarship program in Florida, and the movement would not have been so galvanized as it became later that summer as a result of the donnybrook in Cleveland.

As events were unfolding in Florida, so were they in Cleveland as a result of the May 27 ruling by the Ohio Supreme Court. The ruling split the difference: the Court by a four-to-three vote struck down the scholarship program because it had been enacted as part of the state budget, but four justices went on to uphold the program under the First Amendment.[13] Given the realm of the possible, we were pretty pleased: it was our third favorable First Amendment decision. But the budget bill ruling made our work cut out for us: we had to get the program passed as a separate bill, with only a few weeks left in the legislative session.

Our opponents faced a dilemma as well. Their strategy of securing a ruling on state constitutional grounds had succeeded too well: it was unclear whether they could file a petition with the U.S. Supreme Court even if the program were reenacted or whether they would

---

[13] *Simmons-Harris v. Goff*, 711 N.E.2d 203 (Ohio 1999).

be precluded from doing so because they had "won" on state constitutional grounds. Our research showed that they had all the legal process to which they were entitled, given that they had elected to file in state court. But it was very much an open—and highly unusual—question.

Our allies in Ohio moved quickly, with David Brennan and David Zanotti of the Ohio Roundtable working with Gov. Bob Taft, Secretary of State Ken Blackwell, Rep. Jim Jordan, and others to approve the program as a separate bill. Fortunately, they succeeded. So by the end of June, we all assumed that we could breathe a little easier, chuckling to ourselves at the mess the unions had managed to create for themselves and now had to sort out.

That was probably the only time in 12 years that we were overconfident and underprepared. I was attending a retreat in California when I received a call that the unions had done something totally unexpected: instead of filing a petition for review in the U.S. Supreme Court, they had filed a new First Amendment lawsuit in the federal district court in Cleveland. Not only that, they were seeking an injunction against the continuation of the program.

I flew back to Washington immediately. I was shocked by the unions' strategy for two reasons. First, the unions were asking a federal district court to relitigate an issue that already had been decided by the Ohio Supreme Court, violating the rule of *res judicata*.[14] Second, they were asking for an injunction against an *ongoing* program, just weeks before the start of the fourth school year. Given that the purpose of an injunction is to preserve the status quo, I didn't think there was a federal judge in the country who would grant one.

We quickly put together our intervention papers. Coordinating with Fannie Lewis, who was with us again for the fight, we recruited some new parents in this round of litigation, among them Christine Suma and Roberta Kitchen, who would become national spokespersons for school choice. Christine is the mother of 12 children and worked tirelessly to organize school choice parents in Cleveland. Roberta, who already had raised her own children, had taken in

---

[14] This is one of the Latin terms that lawyers have to learn. Under the doctrine of *res judicata*, the same parties cannot relitigate issues that already have been litigated to conclusion in a prior proceeding.

five more from a friend who was in trouble with drugs and alcohol. She could speak eloquently and with firsthand knowledge of the need to obtain educational opportunities outside of the Cleveland public schools.

Much had changed in the short time since the state court litigation. Jeff Sutton had resigned as solicitor general and returned to private practice. His replacement was Edward "Ned" Foley, a former professor of constitutional law at Ohio State University. Our initial contacts were pleasant, and it was clear that Ned possessed a strong intellectual grasp of the legal issues. Still, it wouldn't be the same team with which we had prevailed, by and large, in the state courts.

More significant, the state had adopted a charter school program (called community schools). Private nonsectarian schools were eligible to become charter schools, and would receive nearly twice as much per-pupil funding as they would in the scholarship program. David Brennan had converted his Hope Academies—previously the two largest nonsectarian schools in the scholarship program—into community schools. As a consequence, the percentage of scholarship students attending religious schools suddenly increased from about 83 percent to 97 percent.

We knew that would present what lawyers call "bad facts." To try to ameliorate them, we worked with Professor Jay Greene, who already had conducted cutting-edge research on publicly and privately funded school choice programs, to study the broader social, economic, and religious context of school choice in Cleveland. In a study published by the Buckeye Institute he found, not surprisingly, that the private schools were much more integrated in racial, economic, and religious terms than were the Cleveland Public Schools. Moreover, in analyzing *all* schools of choice in Cleveland—magnet schools, community schools, and scholarship schools—he found that only 16.5 percent of all Cleveland schoolchildren enrolled in schools of choice were attending religious schools.

We also brought in an affidavit from Howard Fuller, reporting on the evolution of school choice in Milwaukee. Since the end of the litigation, the number of nonsectarian private schools had increased—not surprisingly, new schools were started to accommodate the increased demand—and the percentage of students in the program who were attending nonsectarian private schools had increased as well. Under *Mueller* and *Agostini*, those facts should not be necessary, because the program was neutral on its face in that it invited all types of schools to participate. Still, 97 percent is a powerful statistic, and we were sure our opponents would wield it. Fuller's affidavit would help counter it.

We presented affidavits as well from scholarship families and school officials, warning of the dire real-world consequences of an injunction. The state also put together an admirable evidentiary submission, including an affidavit from Harvard professor Caroline Hoxby, an innovative researcher who has studied the positive effects of choice programs on public schools. We also reported that the Cleveland Public Schools were continuing to struggle, with the state reporting that the district had failed to satisfy a single one of its 18 performance criteria the previous year. Considering that we had only a few weeks to create a record, we managed to compile a remarkably solid one.

The judge assigned to the case was Solomon Oliver. Our research revealed that Judge Oliver had served as an official in the NAACP, which of course was dead-set against school choice, although the Cleveland chapter was not involved in the lawsuit. It was not clear whether Judge Oliver had ever considered the issue in that capacity, but it sounded alarm bells. Given the sensitivity of the legal issues— indeed, the unions only recently had succeeded in having two members of the Ohio Supreme Court recuse themselves, one because she was a social friend of David Brennan—we thought it appropriate to raise the issue with the judge and have him address it.

After I informed the state of our plans, Foley went ballistic. He demanded that we refrain from suggesting a recusal. Attorney General Betty Montgomery was furious that we were considering it, Foley reported, and now was having second thoughts about our participating in the lawsuit. If we didn't back off, Foley made clear, Montgomery would see to it that we would regret it.

I was flabbergasted. I'd never been threatened by a lawyer on the same side of a lawsuit before. And the venom with which it was delivered left me practically speechless. I explained that one of the major reasons we intervened in lawsuits was to take the heat for controversial strategies that the state's lawyers might be institutionally reluctant to endure. But Foley continued to insist that we change course.

The last thing we needed was a conflict. In the interest of harmony—and not feeling strongly about the recusal strategy in the first place—I agreed not to proceed. But I worried that the incident would be a harbinger of things to come, and indeed our relationship with the attorney general did prove to be a major problem throughout the litigation. We were accustomed to aboveboard, good-of-the-cause working relationships with both government and private-sector lawyers, but that was all but impossible in Ohio. A former colleague of Montgomery's explained that the attorney general is not ideological and in fact opposed school choice as a legislator, but nonetheless wanted the state (and her office in particular) to gain credit for defending the program. Not only did it make for an uneasy working relationship, but Montgomery's influence over politically connected Ohio activists complicated our ability to organize at the grass roots.

Once I agreed not to try to recuse Judge Oliver, Foley brought pressure to bear on another front, trying to convince me that he should provide the sole argument at the preliminary injunction hearing. Foley had produced a superb brief, but I had no idea whether he was a good oral advocate. And as I explained, it was vitally important to have the interests of the parents represented. Interveners are never in a particularly strong bargaining position with regard to oral argument, though they are entitled to some time except at the U.S. Supreme Court. But the parties are supposed to settle such issues among themselves, and the courts frown on disputes of that kind. This time I refused to back down, and Foley acquiesced. But he would have 40 minutes, with only 10 each for Dave Young and me.

The August 13 argument was a disaster. Foley and Judge Oliver did not click at all, with Foley misunderstanding the judge's questions and the judge growing visibly frustrated. Foley conceded that if the court found that *Nyquist* was controlling, it could issue an injunction, but should stay it. By the time it was my turn to argue, I had a lot of ground to cover. I started out by emphasizing that there was no occasion for an injunction, because the purpose of an injunction was to preserve the status quo, and the status quo was a school choice program about to enter its fourth year. Two numbers were dispositive on the equities, I argued: 12, which was the number of days before school was scheduled to begin, and 3,801, which was the number of children who would be forced to leave the only good schools they ever had known, and returned to a government school system that was in no condition to absorb them. An injunction would mean chaos for both the public and private schools, and more important, chaos for the children. On the law, I argued, *Nyquist* did not apply because the U.S. Supreme Court had reserved the very question presented by the Cleveland case: the constitutionality of a neutral parental choice program.

I was worried after the argument, but still could not believe that a court would order an injunction on the eve of the school year. Still, I discussed with Susan Mitchell the possibility of raising money to sustain the children in the program if the unthinkable occurred. We also had an emergency appeal drafted that we could file in the U.S. Court of Appeals for the Sixth Circuit if we needed it.

And we did: only hours before school was set to begin, Judge Oliver enjoined the entire program, sending it into bedlam.

The decision came down in midafternoon. We immediately moved into action, filing our emergency papers and contacting parents and schools to advise them to proceed as usual. We would do whatever we could to secure private funding so the program would continue. It turned out we didn't have to do anything: by five o'clock, philanthropists such as John Walton, Peter Flanagan, and the Bradley and Friedman Foundations had pledged $6 million if we were unable to get the injunction lifted. The response was head-spinning. At that point, we had to maintain a delicate balance, trying to communicate to the schools and parents that they shouldn't worry, while at the same time trying to keep the pledges quiet so as not to undercut our efforts to dissolve the injunction.

Meanwhile, we worked the phones contacting Ohio reporters and our friends on the editorial pages of the *Wall Street Journal, Cleveland Plain-Dealer, Columbus Post-Dispatch,* and *Cincinnati Enquirer.* As I spoke to reporters, I sensed a subtle shift had taken place: where before I usually had encountered detached objectivity at best or skepticism at worst, the sense was that the other side had gone too far.

The following day the newspapers were full of page-one stories and photographs chronicling the plight of children in the program. All three leading Ohio newspapers condemned the ruling in the editorial pages. And the cartoons followed. My favorite one depicted Judge Oliver driving a bus that had just run down two schoolchildren, who were labeled "School Choice."

The outcry was so intense that four days after issuing the injunction, Judge Oliver reversed most of it on his own accord, lifting it with respect to children who previously participated in the program, but leaving it intact for the four hundred or so who were entering the program for the first time in the 1999–2000 school year. That meant that a bailout would require far less philanthropy than we previously had feared.

Still, we pursued our appeal in the Sixth Circuit, a court known recently for its rancorous debates and ideological divisions. Remarkably, the court never ruled. In October, Ned Foley and we agreed that the state should seek to bypass the Sixth Circuit and appeal to the U.S. Supreme Court. Each circuit is supervised by a Supreme Court justice, in this case Justice John Paul Stevens, who was likely to be hostile to school choice. But Justice Stevens referred the matter to the entire Court. Though his action made us hopeful, the Court had recently denied review in both the Arizona and Maine cases, suggesting that it still did not have the stomach to take on a school choice case. And the Court rarely intervenes in such fashion in ongoing cases.

But the unexpected happened. In November, the Supreme Court voted five-to-four to lift the remainder of the injunction pending a decision by the U.S. Court of Appeals for the Sixth Circuit. The lineup was predictable, with Chief Justice William Rehnquist joined in the majority by Justices Sandra Day O'Connor, Anthony Kennedy, Antonin Scalia, and Clarence Thomas; with Justices Stevens, David Souter, Ruth Bader Ginsburg, and Stephen Breyer in dissent.

The decision was wonderful news on multiple fronts. Not only would the program continue for the pendency of the appeal, but the Court had sent its clearest signal yet on school choice. The Court will stay a lower court injunction only if it considers it likely that it will eventually review the case on the merits, and only if it believes the party seeking the stay will prevail. Neither was a foregone conclusion, but in November 1999, we were liking our chances—again, *if* we could get a case to the high court before a change in personnel.

There's an adage, be careful what you wish for because you might just get it. For the unions, the decision to seek an injunction against the Cleveland program was the gravest miscalculation in 12 years of litigation. By seeking to turn 4,000 children out of their schools on the eve of the school year, the unions abandoned any pretense that they cared about kids, and forever abdicated any moral claim. Not only that, they eventually lost the injunction, no doubt forming a lasting impression with the Supreme Court in the process. It was a strategic miscalculation of titanic significance.[15]

By contrast, the injunction galvanized the school choice movement like never before. The response to the injunction was the movement's proudest moment. Philanthropists from all over the country came forward to bail out the children, while school choice activists far and wide held vigils to express solidarity with Cleveland parents. Everyone in the movement now was focused on Cleveland, recognizing that the fate of school choice everywhere was bound up with the fate of the Cleveland program. Whatever obstacles might lie ahead, a flickering beacon of sunlight suddenly had appeared on the distant horizon. We marched toward it united, determined, and with a renewed sense of optimism.

---

[15] Following the U.S. Supreme Court decision in 2002, I debated American Federation of Teachers president Sandra Feldman on CNN. After I accused her of having tried to wrench 4,000 schoolchildren out of good schools in Cleveland in 1999, she angrily asserted that she had opposed the injunction motion. If so, it's too bad her lawyers didn't get the message.

8. Battles Within and Without

As the Cleveland battle raged in federal court, we also were fighting state court battles in Florida and Illinois.

In Florida, we were encountering serious problems with the trial court judge, L. Ralph "Bubba" Smith. The Florida affiliate of the American Federation of Teachers had hired a well-known Tallahassee lawyer, Dexter Douglas, to represent them. To put it mildly, Douglas was the anti-Chanin, making for an odd-couple litigation team. Whereas Chanin is an intellectual, silver-tongued, big-city labor lawyer, Dexter affects a back-country, good ol' boy demeanor. More important, he was well-connected in local Florida politics.

We gathered in November for a preliminary hearing in Tallahassee, bringing a van full of parents and children from Pensacola. Just as the hearing was to begin, the door from Judge Smith's chambers opened, and out bounded Dexter Douglas, parading across the courtroom to his place at plaintiffs' counsel table. Matthew Berry and I looked at each other in amazement: despite abundant experience with local customs and practice in courtrooms across America, that was a new one for us.

It did not take long for Judge Smith to evidence hostility toward our position. The judge bifurcated the issues, announcing that he would consider first the issue of whether public funds could be used under any circumstances in private schools. From a legal perspective, that was our easiest issue, because Florida (like every other state) sends government funds to private schools in a variety of circumstances, such as aid for college students and youngsters with disabilities. But it also posed enormous risks: were a court to rule that no public funds could be used in private schools, it would completely paralyze any efforts at school choice. The judge scheduled oral arguments for the following February.

In Illinois, the state enacted a tax credit for educational expenses, including tuition. It could be used by either public or private school students. This time, the NEA and AFT filed competing cases in different jurisdictions, forcing us to help defend the law in two different courts. But the divergent strategy evidenced a continuing split between the rival unions, which could work only to our advantage. Betraying something less than complete confidence in their federal constitutional theories, both groups challenged the tax credits solely on state constitutional grounds.

The Illinois cases were Matthew Berry's first as lead counsel. Dick Komer and I served as second-chair. Matthew took to the task with his usual gusto and enthusiasm. Working with well-organized Catholic activists, we identified a broad range of clients to represent as interveners in both cases, including Catholic, Protestant, Muslim, Jewish, and public school families. We also developed a close working relationship with the attorney general's office, dividing arguments evenly.

Matthew prepared assiduously for his first oral argument in tiny Benton, Illinois. We usually prepare advocates using practice sessions called moot courts, in which lawyers act as judges and pepper the advocate with questions. Matthew's only flaw was that he talked at about twice the speed of a normal human being. And as he rose to speak in court, he did exactly that. The judge smiled benignly but eventually stopped Matthew when the court reporter complained that she couldn't keep up. "If you don't want anyone to remember your eloquent words, you should keep on speaking like a runaway train. If, however, you'd like to preserve your remarks for posterity, you need to slow down," he advised. Matthew took a deep breath and started speaking more slowly. He's been a masterful oral advocate ever since.

In fact, Matthew put all his colleagues to shame: he won both cases in trial court, then in the courts of appeals,[1] without a single dissenting judge. He then joined with the state in persuading the Illinois Supreme Court not to disturb the rulings. Indeed, in three tax credit cases to date, we have yet (knock on wood) to lose a single round in court.

Unfortunately, events were not unfolding so well in Cleveland or Florida. Displaying his remarkable penchant for ironic timing, Judge Solomon Oliver delivered a lump of coal to the schoolchildren of

---

[1] *Toney v. Bower*, 744 N.E.2d 351 (Ill. App. 2001); *Griffith v. Bower*, 747 N.E.2d 423 (Ill. App. 2001).

Cleveland in the form of a final decision striking down the scholarship program five days before Christmas 1999.[2] It was not an unexpected decision. The judge based his ruling on the conclusion that too many students were enrolled in religious schools. How many is too many, constitutionally speaking, and the fact that the numbers varied from year to year, were issues that the court did not even address. Judge Oliver acknowledged that his decision conflicted with the ruling of the Wisconsin Supreme Court, which would improve our prospects for Supreme Court review. Best of all, his ruling had absolutely no effect because of the stay. In a memorandum to school choice allies on the day of the decision, I wrote, "Please don't allow this decision to dampen the holiday spirit. We fully intend that Judge Oliver's order will be short-lived."

In Florida, the oral argument also was disappointing. Despite the most one-sided argument we had ever presented, it was clear that Judge Smith intended to rule against us. The judge asked both sides to prepare orders, but we knew which one he would sign.

As we awaited the decision, we learned some news that seemed to help explain the judge's antipathy: his son reportedly was engaged to the daughter of a high-ranking official in the teachers union. That relationship, were it to be consummated, would be grounds for recusal. Seeking the judge's removal would be a high-stakes gambit. If he disliked us already, he would dislike us even more if we raised the specter of conflict and he denied our motion. But it was so clear the judge was biased against us that we decided to move forward.

After verifying the reports, we filed a recusal motion, only to have the judge's son and the union official's daughter sign affidavits attesting that they were not, and never had been, engaged. Despite the fact it was clear they had made public statements to acquaintances to the contrary, we concluded we had no choice but to take their word for it. With embarrassment, we withdrew the motion. Whereupon, Judge Smith promptly struck down the program, issuing verbatim the lengthy opinion drafted by the teachers union. Once again, though, we surmised that the union had overplayed its hand: its decision was extremely sweeping, which would make it easier to attack on appeal.

Because a court had struck down a state law, under Florida procedures the decision was immediately stayed pending appeal. Along with the state, we filed an appeal in the state court of appeals. The

[2] *Simmons-Harris v. Zelman*, 72 F.Supp. 2d 834 (N.D. Ohio 1999).

unions quickly countered with a motion to bypass the court of appeals and move directly to the Florida Supreme Court, which fortunately was denied. The plaintiffs mounted a feeble effort to convince Judge Smith to lift the stay, which we countered with extensive affidavits. The judge denied the motion and the program continued.

Meanwhile, the program was working its magic. Around 75 schools had received one F under the state's grading standards, meaning that their students would be eligible for scholarships if the schools flunked a second time. The schools responded with a flurry of activity, adopting such measures as tutors for failing students, Saturday classes, year-round schooling, and allocating a higher percentage of funds to classroom instruction—exactly the sort of things they should have been doing all along. Government school officials insisted, of course, that those reforms had nothing to do with the threat of school vouchers. We set out to prove otherwise. Through public records requests, we obtained internal documents from all of the school districts that had failing schools, and we hired retired *Washington Times* education writer Carol Innerst to review the documents. It turned out (surprise!) that public school officials adopting the reform measures repeatedly expressed concern about vouchers that would result if they did not lift their schools off the failing list. Imagine that: the laws of competition are not suspended at the schoolhouse doors, after all.

At the same time, Jay Greene was compiling impressive statistics regarding the impact of the opportunity scholarship program on public schools. He found substantial improvement in the test scores of the lowest-scoring students across the state—typically a group whose scores get worse, not better. Greene's findings were echoed in the school report cards in 2000. Everyone connected with the program assumed that some of the 75 or so schools that had received one F would receive a second. But when the grades came out, the results were shocking—every single failing school had lifted itself off the F list![3]

---

[3] Two years later, in 2002, after the Jeb Bush administration tightened accountability standards, several additional public schools received a second F, making their students eligible for scholarships for private schools or transfers to better-performing public schools. That year, 800 students from 10 public schools received opportunity scholarships to attend private schools.

The Florida results provided powerful new evidence that school choice is not just a life preserver for some children, but an essential catalyst for public school reform and improvement. In debates, I lauded the Florida program's innovation in that regard: if the teachers didn't want vouchers, they didn't have to file a lawsuit to stop them—they just had to do their jobs. And that's exactly what they did. Coupled with similar strong evidence to the same effect from Milwaukee, it was growing increasingly difficult for choice opponents to argue plausibly that school choice would harm public schools (though, predictably, they continued to make those arguments anyway).

As the litigation in the lower courts continued in earnest, the U.S. Supreme Court weighed in one more time. In a follow-up to *Agostini*, the Court considered whether the government could provide computers and other equipment directly to private and religious schools for remedial education purposes. Again, we drafted a neutral brief, this time with Matthew Berry taking the lead oar. Whatever the outcome in a case involving direct aid, we urged the Court to clearly reiterate the standards applicable to indirect aid, specifically neutrality and individual choice.

This time the Court created some confusion, upholding the program six-to-three, but without a single majority opinion.[4] Justice Clarence Thomas, writing for himself and for Chief Justice William Rehnquist and Justices Anthony Kennedy and Antonin Scalia, broke new jurisprudential ground. He concluded that an aid program was permissible so long as it is neutral, without regard to whether it was effectuated through individual choice.

But Justice Sandra Day O'Connor, joined by Justice Stephen Breyer, concurred only in the result. They reiterated the dual requirements of neutrality and "true private-choice" for indirect aid programs. For direct aid to religious schools, however, they found it relevant that the aid took the form of computers and other equipment, and hence that no government funds would reach the coffers of religious schools.

Nothing in the decision registered alarm. The swing justices had reiterated the standards we had emphasized all along. Moreover,

---

[4] *Mitchell v. Helms*, 530 U.S. 793 (2000).

Justice Breyer had signed onto that framework for the first time, giving us a potential sixth vote.

Still, the decision was unsettling. School choice opponents seized upon the language about government funds flowing to religious school coffers. And Justice O'Connor now was occupying middle ground with Justice Breyer, which was unusual, puzzling, and worrisome. When the school choice case came, would he try to nudge her in the wrong direction?[5]

If the Court meant what it said, we were in good shape. But after five solid precedents in a row, the fractured decision in *Mitchell* introduced new uncertainty at the worst possible time.

In June, the battlefront shifted back to Ohio. Again, the litigators were wracked with internal divisions. The IJ team was surprised to learn that on appeal the state planned to abandon its argument on *res judicata*—the doctrine that the same parties cannot relitigate an issue that had been fully litigated previously. Matthew Berry had thoroughly researched the issue and concluded that it could be a winning argument. The state, with an interest in protecting the decisional integrity of its own supreme court, was in the best position to make the argument. We decided that if they wouldn't, we would.

That decision prompted a series of angry phone calls from Ned Foley, demanding that we not pursue the *res judicata* argument. The disagreement reflected a divergence in goals. The state's lawyers wanted to address the core constitutional issues. We wanted that too, of course, but our overarching goal was to preserve the choice program. If we had a chance to hedge our bets with a procedural issue that might appeal to a wavering judge or justice, we wanted to provide that option. This time I was in no mood to appease Ned Foley, and the argument remained in our brief.

Recognizing that the Sixth Circuit argument might be a dress rehearsal for the Supreme Court, we also took the opportunity to revamp our briefing approach. By now we had written dozens of school choice briefs, and I was concerned after a while that the briefs would become rote and predictable, even though we always wrote

[5] In hindsight it appears exactly so. It appears that in joining Justice O'Connor in emphasizing "true private-choice," Justice Breyer meant to suggest that only a program that created an abundance of choices might be permissible. In the end, fortunately, Justice O'Connor remained true to the principles she set forth in her *Mitchell* concurrence; sadly, Justice Breyer did not.

each one from scratch. Also, I knew that Foley would write a good brief on the merits. So this time we decided to shake things up. Instead of arguing about the legal standard or presenting exhaustive case discussions that the other parties would exhaustively provide, we started off with the constitutional standard on which both sides agreed: primary effect. Our brief turned the legal standard into a factual analysis, examining the crisis in the Cleveland public schools, the broad emergency response of which the school choice program was only one component, and the resulting educational effects. As a factual matter, we argued, it required a tortured interpretation to conclude that the primary effect of the program was to establish religion. It was a novel approach that would carry forward into our U.S. Supreme Court brief, and reflected the strategy we had devised at the Shadow of the Beast conference.

As the June 20 argument date approached, Ned Foley called to once again ask for all of the argument time in the appellate court. I was amazed that he would do so in light of his performance in the trial court. He assured me he would be much better this time. I was not convinced, and I threatened to seek separate argument time if he refused to consent. Dave Young took the same position. But I knew that the court of appeals might deny time for the interveners. In the end, Dave Young and I reluctantly agreed to 5 minutes apiece, with Foley having 20 minutes.

Maureen Blum set out to organize a rally outside the Sixth Circuit courthouse in Cincinnati. Because the official activist network in Cleveland still was not organized, we had to cobble together a rally from disparate elements, with Fannie Lewis recruiting parents from Cleveland, aided by the Harmony Community School in Cincinnati as well as the Friedman Foundation, Children First America, the Greater Educational Opportunities Foundation, and the American Education Reform Foundation bringing parents from around the nation.

Dave Young and I discussed the oral argument with Ned Foley and agreed that our first line of defense should be the program's facial neutrality—that is, the inclusion of public as well as private school options. *Mueller* and *Agostini* had emphasized that neutrality should be determined within the four corners of the program, not with regard to the independent choices that third parties (here, private schools, public suburban schools, and parents) might choose to make. As a back-up argument, we would demonstrate that Cleveland parents had available a broad range of educational options, such as public magnet and nonsectarian community schools. Coming to this common understanding, I felt less apprehensive about Ned Foley having most of the argument.

As usual, the courtroom was packed to capacity. The Sixth Circuit is intensely ideologically polarized, and we expected a rough-and-tumble argument. The court panel comprised two Republicans and one Democrat, making the odds favorable to us. Ned Foley rose to make his argument—and proceeded immediately to discuss the broader context of school choices, jettisoning altogether our main argument about facial neutrality. I looked over at Dave Young and our jaws dropped. Judge Eric Clay, a liberal Democrat, challenged Foley on whether it was permissible to consider that context. Judge James L. Ryan, a conservative Republican, tried to jump to Foley's defense, but Foley fought off his efforts, giving contentious responses even to simple questions, such as whether Cleveland's schools were bad and whether most of its students were minority. Even Judge Ryan clearly was growing frustrated. I looked back at Chip Mellor and Susan Mitchell, who were sitting in the front of the gallery. They looked as glum and incredulous as I.

By the time it was my turn, the argument seemed all but hopeless. I had to make a split-second decision whether to use my five minutes on the merits, or on the *res judicata* argument. Concluding that the former was hopeless, I opted for the latter, to give the swing judge an out if he wanted it. But the court seemed unconvinced.

On the other side, Chanin divided his time with retired judge Marvin Frankel, who made another confused argument. At least Chanin has his cross to bear, too, I consoled myself. Judge Ryan grilled Chanin mercilessly, but Chanin sensed he was prevailing and he was as condescending as ever. At one point Judge Ryan asked whether it was a reality that Cleveland students enjoyed a range of school choices. To which Chanin gave a truly remarkable response: "Yes, but it is a constitutionally inappropriate reality."

When the argument ended, I couldn't wait to escape the courtroom. I was seething with anger. Court decisions rarely are won or lost in oral argument, but I was quite sure I had just witnessed the glaring exception to the rule.

It was incredibly difficult to go to the rally at which more than 150 people were gathered and anxiously awaiting word from the courtroom. Ohio Secretary of State Kenneth Blackwell, the most stalwart supporter of school choice among the state's elected officials, had given a rousing speech to the crowd, as had Fannie Lewis and Bert Holt. I whispered to Fannie and Bert that the argument had been a disaster. But we all put on a brave face to the assembled activists, emphasizing that the Sixth Circuit was merely the last stop before the U.S. Supreme Court. Or at least we hoped.

While we were busy litigating in Ohio, Florida, and Illinois, important school choice developments were occurring elsewhere. Two school choice initiatives were being prepared for the 2000 ballots in California and Michigan. Few in the school choice movement were very excited about initiatives—we had never come close in previous initiative battles, including a disastrous California initiative several years before that had turned much of the state against school choice. Initiatives by nature are uphill battles—most voters will vote "no" if it's a close call. The unions can spend copious amounts of money. More significant, they can raise scare tactics that push people toward an adverse vote, and the charges are tough to rebut in 30-second commercials. It takes five seconds to say that vouchers will destroy public schools; it takes a lot longer to demonstrate that they don't and, in the case of a draw, the electoral nod usually goes to the opponents.

In Michigan, proponents had no choice. The Michigan constitution contains the most stringent anti–school choice language in the nation, crafted precisely by the teachers unions in the 1960s to achieve that distinction. The proponents were led by Dick and Betsy DeVos, the Mackinac Center, and others. They put together a broad school choice coalition, including black pastors and inner-city parents, and invested sufficient money to get their message across. The effort drew broad support from the movement as a whole.

In California, the initiative was drafted by Silicon Valley entrepreneur Tim Draper, who promised a $20 million investment. As far as I know, everyone in the school choice movement—even former California governor Pete Wilson—urged Draper not to go forward. When I reviewed the proposal, I concluded that it would not survive constitutional challenge. It contained a provision—meritorious as a policy matter but vulnerable from a constitutional standpoint—that would allow students to bank any amount of the voucher in excess of a private school's tuition for future educational expenses. Because such benefits were unavailable to public school families, it could defeat the neutrality required of such programs. The broader advice given to Draper by school choice activists, including me, was that a big defeat in California would deal the movement a serious setback, at the very time we might be heading to the U.S. Supreme Court. Draper's retort was that his initiative wasn't going to fail.

Proponents fought with spirit in both states, but they were doomed to failure in light of the unions' fierce campaigns of demagoguery. In the end, neither initiative received even one-third of the vote. The results gave ammunition to school choice opponents who claimed that no one wanted vouchers, as they had been defeated wherever they were on the ballot.[6]

Fortunately, as the voters were rejecting school choice, parents were voting with their feet. Tens of thousands of low-income families in inner cities across the nation were applying for highly publicized private scholarships made available by Children First America and the Children's Scholarship Fund. The private scholarship programs demonstrated not only the widespread and urgent demand for school choice among families of modest economic means but also provided opportunities for additional studies on the efficacy of school choice that invariably yielded positive results.

The November initiative defeats in California and Michigan were harbingers of an adverse Sixth Circuit decision on December 11, 2000. The majority and dissenting opinions were about as vitriolic as I had ever seen in a judicial decision. Writing for a two-to-one panel, Judge Clay concluded that the scholarship program must be viewed in isolation rather than in the broader context of educational choices. The pro–school choice advocates' "argument concerning other options available to Cleveland parents such as the Community Schools," he asserted, "is at best irrelevant."[7] *Nyquist* controlled, the majority concluded, and it dictated the outcome. Because the amount of the scholarship was so small, Judge Clay remarked, the program was designed to discourage nonsectarian school participation, leading to 96 percent of the children being enrolled in religious schools.

[6]Notably, the Arizona Education Association backed off plans for a referendum over scholarship tax credits after they were passed in Arizona. That suggests that the unions understand that it is easier to challenge school choice in the abstract rather than once it is in practice and there are real beneficiaries identified with it.

[7]*Simmons-Harris v. Zelman*, 234 F.3d 945, 958 (6th Cir. 2000).

The choice was "illusory," for "there are no spaces available for children who wish to attend a suburban public school in place of a private school under the program. Therefore, the program clearly has the impermissible effect of promoting sectarian schools."[8]

In a passionate and thorough dissent, Judge Ryan castigated his colleagues for failing to apply relevant Supreme Court precedents. The program was not enriching religious schools—it was enlisting them to rescue children and paying them only a fraction of the cost. Judge Ryan minced no words in condemning the majority for concluding that the program was unconstitutional on the grounds that, in essence,

> the voucher program has too many voucher schools and that the schools are too religious. This argument should fail, first, because it is rooted in nativist hostility toward religious schools and, second, because it has been explicitly rejected by the Supreme Court as a legitimate determinant of whether the government is engaging in religious indoctrination. . . .
>
> This case and its result—sentencing nearly 4,000 poverty-level, mostly minority children in Cleveland to return to the indisputably failed Cleveland public schools from which, in many cases, they escaped as long as three years ago—is an exercise in raw judicial power having no basis in the First Amendment or in the Supreme Court's Establishment Clause jurisprudence.[9]

Judge Ryan urged the entire Sixth Circuit to review the panel's decision.

The result of the decision was stinging. At that point, I felt somewhat like a little kid who just had been flattened by the playground bully; and yet, I had him exactly where I wanted him. The Sixth Circuit's decision conflicted not only with the Wisconsin Supreme Court but also with the Ohio Supreme Court as well. We had precisely the type of conflict in authority that the U.S. Supreme Court likes to resolve. Moreover, this would be the first time that a case would go to the Supreme Court and, if the Court failed to review the decision, children actually would be forced to leave their schools.

---

[8] Ibid., p. 959.
[9] Ibid., pp. 973–74 (Ryan, J., concurring in part and dissenting in part).

That, presumably, was why the Court had dissolved Judge Oliver's injunction. So our prospects for Supreme Court review looked good.

Still, we could not afford to take anything for granted. Having lost in the Sixth Circuit, we absolutely had to secure review by the U.S. Supreme Court, and we absolutely had to win. It was as simple—and as nerve-wracking—as that.

Though we were anxious to get to the Supreme Court, we agreed with the state that we should exhaust all possibilities and seek review by the full (*en banc*) Sixth Circuit. Such review is discretionary, and the court had a slight majority of Democrats, but it seemed worth a shot. For the first time, we felt that we had the luxury of time: with the 2000 presidential election finally resolved, we were confident that a change in the composition of the Supreme Court no longer would jeopardize our chances.

Two days after the decision, I participated in a full-day conference on school choice in New York hosted by Mayor Rudolph Giuliani and the Manhattan Institute. The timing was propitious, with everyone speculating that the long-awaited resolution by the Supreme Court finally was drawing near.

On a panel with Robert Chanin, I predicted that the outcome would be favorable for the school choice movement either with a win or a loss. A win obviously would remove the federal constitutional cloud. But even a loss would provide a roadmap for the movement. I was quite confident, in light of recent decisions, that the Court would not categorically repudiate school choice. So regardless of the outcome, certainty would replace uncertainty; and if we lost, we could craft future programs to the Court's specifications.

Chanin in turn made a startling admission. The unions, he noted, had no particular interest in the Establishment Clause. If they lost on that issue, he promised, they would turn to the Blaine amendment. And if they lost on those, they would find other grounds in their "toolbox" on which to challenge school choice. I thought to myself: if only they could channel their ingenuity into improving government schools. But Chanin's remarks were sobering: he made it very clear that even if we won in the Supreme Court, we would have to fight a war of attrition for years to come.

Following the conference, Mayor Giuliani hosted a reception at Gracie Mansion that was a veritable pep rally for school choice supporters. He reiterated an earlier promise to coauthor a brief with

Milwaukee Mayor John Norquist. The reality finally was dawning on me: this was the moment for which we had been waiting and working for a solid decade.

Chip and I convened an IJ team meeting. This was a big moment for our organization, which was to celebrate its 10th anniversary the following year: our first case in the U.S. Supreme Court, and one of the most important constitutional cases ever. Our task inside the courtroom would be complicated by the fact that we were not the only—or even the lead—entity defending the program. And many other groups and individuals would want to contribute to the overall effort. As a result, we would have to do our best with respect to the matters under our control, and choreograph the overall effort to optimal effect. But because we had planned for this moment for several years, we were prepared to hit the ground running.

We knew that what happened outside the courtroom would be as important as what happened inside it. That made media and outreach paramount. Working closely with George Mitchell and Howard Fuller, John Kramer launched a painstaking effort to accumulate every bit of data on school choice that reporters could possibly want, from details about the various programs to scholarly studies to public opinion polls to court decisions to law review articles and on and on. The goal was to make IJ's Web site "Information Central" for school choice. The information had to be entirely credible, and that meant it had to be entirely accurate. Kramer and George Mitchell spent countless hours sweating the details so that the database would be beyond reproach—and it was.

At the same time, the Black Alliance for Educational Options launched an extensive advertising campaign designed to educate and influence opinion leaders. The goal was twofold: to humanize and personalize school choice and to debunk the mythology popularized by People for the American Way and the teachers unions. The advertisements appeared in key media outlets such as the *New York Times* and the *New Republic*, typically bearing the headline "School Choice Is Widespread—Unless You're Poor"—and as commercials on network public affairs shows. Opinion leaders were introduced to real parents like Tony Higgins of Milwaukee, a loving dad who poignantly related the story of what school choice meant to his family. The ads were unmatchable by the other side—they could spend the money (and they did), but they simply couldn't overcome

157

the message. A column by the AFT's Sandra Feldman or the NEA's Robert Chase just wouldn't cut it.

Meanwhile, we had to prepare the Cleveland program for the onslaught of attention it inevitably would receive if the Court granted review. That meant creating the infrastructure that had been sorely lacking throughout the litigation. Working closely with Sherry Schmeling at AERF, Maureen Blum made several trips to Cleveland to meet with school officials and to organize parents. We hired Rosalinda Demore-Brown, a close confidant of Fannie Lewis, as a part-time consultant, and Bert Holt continued to provide valuable guidance. Christine Suma and Roberta Kitchen led the parent organizing effort. It took nearly a year, but by the time the case was accepted for review, the Cleveland program was ready for prime time.

Dick Komer was in charge of recruiting and coordinating amicus briefs. Two would be key, in our opinion: the mayors' brief, arguing that the Court should preserve school choice as an urgently needed tool in the policy arsenal of big-city mayors and school boards; and an ecumenical brief signed by law professors reflecting a broad range of ideological diversity. Beyond those, we would need to match key legal talent with appropriate opportunities. Once again, Jeanne Allen's Center for Educational Freedom agreed to provide a brief for the large number of groups wanting to participate in the Supreme Court; this one to be authored by the talented Catholic University School of Law professor Robert Destro.

We were disappointed that the Sixth Circuit denied *en banc* review. But in March, Sixth Circuit Judge Clay ordered an extension of the stay of the injunction pending Supreme Court review. That gave rise to scheduling considerations: if we brought the case to the Supreme Court too early and it rejected review, the program would terminate before the new school year. We calculated that if we waited until the last permissible moment to file our petition for certiorari, in all likelihood the Court would not decide the petition until the following term in October. That meant that no matter what happened, the scholarship program would begin another year.

By this time, Ned Foley's term as Ohio solicitor general had expired and he was not re-appointed. Taking his place on the case was an assistant solicitor general, Judith French, who had no experience with the case or with education or religious establishment issues. Rumor had it that Attorney General Montgomery had designated French to argue before the Supreme Court. To put it mildly, in such a high-profile case it is very unusual—and perilous—to assign the argument to an advocate who is inexperienced in the case, the applicable law, and Supreme Court advocacy. Moreover, we thought it unfair that in designating a sole advocate, Montgomery would purport to make a unilateral decision, without so much as consulting the other parties. A number of experienced advocates were available to make the argument, including University of Utah Professor Michael McConnell (who could not be considered once President Bush nominated him for a federal appeals court judgeship), Pepperdine Law School professor (now Catholic Law School Dean) Douglas Kmiec, Harvard Law School Professor and former U.S. solicitor general Charles Fried, former Berkeley Law School dean Jesse Choper, and former U.S. solicitor general Walter Dellinger. We communicated to Montgomery our view that an experienced advocate should argue the case, and a number of intermediaries made a similar case to her. But unlike Florida and Wisconsin, which recognized the need for outside counsel, Montgomery considered it an institutional insult to consider anyone outside of the attorney general's office to argue the case—notwithstanding the office's unimpressive track record in the federal court litigation thus far. Montgomery made it clear she was sticking with Judith French, and played the gender card, publicly accusing me of sexism in urging a more experienced advocate.

She did, however, acknowledge the need for outside assistance, and retained Ken Starr as special counsel, which proved to be a splendid decision—in fact, probably more significant in the end than the decision of who would provide oral argument. Ken and I had worked closely together in the second Wisconsin Supreme Court argument and had developed an excellent relationship. Not only is Ken an outstanding lawyer who works tenaciously to master his subject, he is also a consummate diplomat. I've seen him work a crowd of 80 people and remember everyone's name the next day. Both his lawyering and diplomacy skills would play a vitally important part in the U.S. Supreme Court battle. I just wished that Montgomery had tapped him to argue the case, rather than to coach from the sidelines.

Despite the high stakes of our dispute with the state, we recognized that we had to develop a good working relationship with the state's team for the good of the case. Dick Komer and I flew to Columbus and spent a day with Judi French, who was busy getting up to speed, and with her colleagues. We discussed all manner of strategy and seemed to share a common perspective on how to approach the issues. Judi seemed bright, earnest, and conscientious, but she knew little about the case or about establishment clause jurisprudence. I urged her to spend time in the schools in Cleveland, absorbing the real-world texture of the case, and she took my advice. Dick and I offered to help in any way we could, even to try to secure funding for moot courts or other resources the state might lack.

We also agreed that we should file our petitions for certiorari on the last possible day, and that we would exchange drafts in advance. We thought both agreements crucial—the first to ensure the continuation of the program in the next school year, and the second to help compensate for the new state team's lack of familiarity with the case and the record.

A "cert" petition is a highly distinctive form of legal advocacy. Unlike the vast majority of written submissions, the attorneys are not arguing why they're right; they're arguing why the Court should take the case. The Court takes only a tiny fraction of cases presented to it—roughly three percent. Simply rearguing the case does not aid the Court at all in its determination of whether to review a case: the Court assumes that the parties that lost in the courts below think they're right. Rather, the Court wants to know, out of all the hundreds of cases that are brought to it, why it should take this one. Why is it important enough to merit the Court's attention?

Of course, with widespread media attention, the Court knew the case was coming. But we decided to strengthen our hand by encouraging the new administration to weigh in. The United States almost never asks the Court to grant certiorari in cases in which the federal government is not a party. That makes its advice to the Court all the more salient when it does so.

Prospects were dubious. Though George W. Bush nominally was pro–school choice as governor, he had expended almost no political capital on behalf of otherwise promising school choice legislative efforts in Texas. As president, he had proposed a school choice component in his "No Child Left Behind" federal education reform bill, but quickly jettisoned it. Still, a brief in support of cert would provide a symbolic yet tangible and low-capital way for the president to demonstrate his commitment to school choice.

Making the decision would be Theodore Olson, who just had been confirmed as solicitor general. I had long known Ted and his wife, Barbara, in Washington conservative circles. Ted is an outstanding appellate lawyer who successfully had navigated the Supreme Court thicket as the 2000 presidential election ended in the courts.

Both Ken Starr and IJ were engaged in parallel lobbying efforts to help persuade Ted to overcome institutional resistance and file a brief. We had several friends making our case for us inside the administration, including Nina Rees in the vice president's office. The solicitor general's office prepared a draft brief, but made no commitment to file it. At the very last minute, Brian Jones, the new general counsel at the U.S. Department of Education and a friend dating back to his days at the Center for New Black Leadership, prevailed upon Education Secretary Rod Paige to make a personal call to Ted Olson. Paige, an innovative reformer while public schools superintendent in Houston, is a strong school choice supporter. The combination of influence worked, and Olson filed a predictably fantastic brief. We were on our way.

For our part, the goal was to make our cert petition compelling. Our ace in the hole was the split in authority—not only between the Sixth Circuit on the one hand and the Wisconsin and Arizona Supreme Courts on the other but also between the Sixth Circuit and the Ohio Supreme Court with respect to the very same program. The case presented a highly unusual circumstance: the same program had been adjudicated by two different courts, each entitled to equal dignity under our federal system of government, reaching opposite results. The only forum in which a conflict of that type could be resolved was the U.S. Supreme Court.

Second, of course, were the equities. If the Court failed to review the case, it would sentence 4,000 economically disadvantaged school-children to educational deprivation. We presented extensive data about the abysmal conditions in the Cleveland public schools, the excellent educational opportunities that the schoolchildren were receiving in private schools, and the positive effects of school choice on public education reform. We observed that policymakers considering educational reform proposals repeatedly agonized about the constitutionality of school choice. The Cleveland program, we argued, presented an ideal vehicle by which to determine broadly the legality of school choice.

As we had promised, we sent an advance draft of the brief to the state, and Dave Young did likewise. We eagerly awaited the state's brief. Judi French told me they were still working on it. And then—even before the due date—the state filed its petition, accompanied by a news release trumpeting Attorney General Betty Montgomery's role in defending the program. Judi French sent an e-mail explaining that they had decided not to share a draft of the brief, because if they shared it with us, they'd have to share it with everyone. That was nonsense, of course, because we occupied a special role as co-counsel. Judi offered no explanation about why they filed in advance of our mutually agreed-on date, but the reason was all too obvious.

I was livid. I understood that Judi was in a tough position because of her boss. But for Montgomery to jeopardize the program by filing early, just for the sake of publicity, was too much. Moreover, the state's cert petition inexplicably omitted almost any discussion of the Ohio Supreme Court decision, whose conflict with the Sixth Circuit seemed to us the single most powerful argument in favor of review. Had we had a chance to discuss it, we would have raised that concern. Montgomery's refusal to share a draft was potentially damaging to our cause.

Fortunately, the Court's term expired before it took action on the petition, so the program would resume again in the fall. But any scintilla of trust we had in the state's team had been eroded. Still, overall I thought the submissions were strong, and I was fairly confident that the Court would agree to consider the case.

Meanwhile, we were about to lose one of the most important members of our own team. Matthew Berry had received a prestigious clerkship on the U.S. Supreme Court, commencing that August. Though he (and we) were ecstatic, it was bittersweet because he would have to recuse himself from a case and an issue in which he had invested his heart and soul. In a short time, Matthew had developed into a superb attorney and a stalwart and respected adviser to the school choice community.

But we would have one last hurrah together before he departed for the Court: specifically, argument in the Florida Court of Appeals over Judge Smith's decision that government funds could not be used in private schools. The state's team in Florida had changed also, decidedly for the better. Former member of Congress Charles Canady (R-Fla.), who had honored his term-limits commitment, had become legal counsel to Gov. Jeb Bush. Charles was a personal friend with whom I had worked frequently in his capacity as chairman of the Subcommittee on the Constitution of the House Judiciary Committee. Charles is a quick study and I looked forward to working with him.

Matthew and I flew down to Tallahassee for oral argument, which Charles and I presented for our side. We argued that aside from Judge Smith, no court anywhere in the nation ever had issued a categorical prohibition against the use of government funds in private schools. Such a ruling inevitably would jeopardize numerous programs, including aid for children with disabilities.

The three-judge panel was sharp and well-prepared. For the unions, Dexter Douglas rose first. It was clear that his special status with Judge Smith did not carry over to the appellate court and that he had not mastered the intricacies of his argument. I thought Bob Chanin was going to keel over in his chair. By the time it was his turn to argue, it was too late—a feeling with which I was all too painfully familiar. The judges swarmed upon Chanin, who is not at his best when under attack. I watched as he melted down for the second time in my presence. He exhibited obvious disdain for the panel, which reciprocated it. At one point, one of the judges asked Chanin a question, and he demurred. Please humor us with an answer, the judge retorted sarcastically, because after all, "courts are peculiar institutions." To which Chanin replied, "Increasingly so, your honor." The judges glared at Chanin in abject disbelief. I had a feeling I knew which way the panel would decide.

And indeed it did as I hoped, issuing a strong ruling in favor of the program, finding that the use of government funds used in private schools is consistent with the goals of public education.[10] We urged the Florida Supreme Court to decline to review the decision, because only one issue had been decided, and it would be better for the state supreme court ultimately to review the case after a complete and final judgment was issued. So the case was remanded to the trial court for determination of the remaining issues, including religious establishment.

And then we received a nice break. While the case was pending in the appellate court, guess who got married? Sure enough, the

[10] *Bush v. Holmes,* 767 So.2d 668 (Fla. Ct. App. 1st Dist. 2000).

judge's son and the union official's daughter. I guess we had stirred up a romance after all. So upon remand to the trial court, we promptly filed a motion to recuse Judge Smith. The judge angrily refused, and we appealed his denial. Matthew prepared the appeal with Clark Neily, an experienced trial litigator who had just joined IJ and the school choice team. Surprisingly, Judge Smith weighed in with a brief of his own, impugning IJ's motives in seeking recusal. That made the appellate court's decision an easy one: without even reaching the merits, the court ruled that Judge Smith had become an advocate in the proceedings before him, and thus had established a bias against one of the parties. Once again the other side had overplayed its hand. The court removed Judge Smith from the proceedings. And Matthew had his final victory before leaving IJ.

Florida also brought good tidings in other ways. Largely as a result of the tenacious efforts of philanthropist John Kirtley, Florida enacted a corporate scholarship tax credit (as did Pennsylvania). Florida also expanded the McKay Scholarship program, allowing all children with disabilities to choose private schools if their parents deemed them more appropriate than public schools. As the Cleveland case moved toward the Supreme Court, school choice continued to expand.

In the midst of all this, I was experiencing significant change in my personal and professional life. In November 2000, I married my sweetheart, Shawnna Matthews.[11] After 16 years inside the Beltway, I was hankering to leave, but didn't want to leave the work I love. Fortunately, IJ was preparing to launch an ambitious new program: state chapters. Over our first 10 years, we came to appreciate the largely untapped potential of state constitutions in the cause of expanding freedom. We decided to begin opening state chapters to supplement our national litigation by focusing exclusively on state constitutional issues. I volunteered to head up the effort. Arizona seemed an especially congenial place for our first chapter, with its strong tradition of individualism, its record of educational freedom,

---

[11] In addition to the many debts I owe the Heritage Foundation for its consistent and multifaceted support for school choice, I am indebted to it for introducing me to Shawnna Matthews, who at the time was working for Heritage as a talented research assistant in educational policy.

and its vibrant pro–free market community exemplified by the Gold-water Institute. In August 2001, Shawnna and I—with a baby on the way—set out to Phoenix to sink our roots in the desert soil.

As we were moving west, the focus of the school choice movement turned eastward. For better or worse, Washington, D.C., would be the center of our universe for much of the next year. That's where our destiny would be decided by nine individuals entrusted with the sober task of interpreting our nation's Constitution. Judgment day was coming at last.

9. The Road to the Supremes

IJ's main office is at 1717 Pennsylvania Avenue, N.W., a stone's throw from the White House—a distance I like to say I personally measured during the Clinton years. Our offices place us at the center of the Washington maelstrom. Though the vast majority of our work is outside the Beltway, our location positions us well when we're involved in controversies inside the capital.

We are constantly mindful that sometimes we're a bit too close. Whenever a presidential motorcade whizzes past, it snarls traffic. The World Bank, only a block away, draws frequent demonstrations and police blockades. Chip and I often wondered aloud what would happen if there ever was a terrorist attack at the White House, to which we were in precariously close proximity. The conversation always would turn to what we could do about it, to which the answer was always the same: nothing.

Watching from afar as the horrendous events of September 11 unfolded, trying to figure out if my colleagues were all right, and frantically trying to track down friends in New York such as John Fund of the *Wall Street Journal*, I felt very far away and very helpless. Then seeing Barbara Olson's face among the victims brought it painfully home. Like everyone who knew Barbara, I remember her fondly as a smiling, optimistic, tenacious stalwart for the principles of freedom. Every summer, I attended a picnic that Ted and Barbara Olson generously hosted for Federalist Society chapter presidents from around the country, and they were a very happy, well-matched couple. I mourned deeply Ted's loss.

The events of September 11 cast a pall over everything, not the least over our school choice efforts, which we pursued now with an even greater sense of sobriety and purpose. The Court, which later would move its operations briefly in the midst of the anthrax scare, would consider our petition only 14 days later.

On September 25, the Court announced its decision that it would review the Cleveland decision. The long journey that had begun 11 years earlier in a hot, crowded courtroom in Madison, Wisconsin, had finally reached its destination. For Cleveland parents, it would culminate six years of exhilaration, disappointment, turmoil, and uncertainty.

All of our efforts could be reduced to a single objective: it was our job to demonstrate to the Court, in every way possible, that this case was about education, not religion. If we succeeded, we would win. If we failed, our opponents would. Everything we did over the next five months, whether in our legal arguments, our media campaign, or our outreach efforts, was dedicated single-mindedly to that goal.

Immediately we convened our teams both inside and outside of IJ to deploy the strategy that had been several years in the making. John Kramer and his capable new assistant, Lisa Andaloro, would begin the drumbeat to stoke positive media coverage. That effort embodied two discrete components. First, the Supreme Court media would extensively cover the case. That coverage was very important because most of Supreme Court community follows it. The Supreme Court press corps consists of highly talented professionals such as Linda Greenhouse of the *New York Times*, Nina Totenberg of National Public Radio, Lyle Denniston of the *Baltimore Sun*, David Savage of the *Los Angeles Times*, Charles Lane of the *Washington Post*, and Jeffrey Rosen of the *New Republic*. We had cultivated good relationships with each of them over the years, carefully building our credibility by providing only accurate information and informed commentary on cases and issues on which we commented.

Likewise, we knew that every major newspaper, magazine, and television network in the nation would cover the case extensively. Our goals in the broader media were three: to convince as many journalists as possible to actually visit Cleveland or one of the other programs, to connect them with parents and children to personalize and humanize the story, and to provide all of the background research they needed. Fortunately, the background information was ready to go, thanks to the painstaking efforts of George Mitchell and Kramer. Now it was a matter of working with as many journalists as we could.

The campaign in the court of public opinion depended on a solid grassroots infrastructure. Toward that end, Maureen Blum of IJ and Sherry Shmeling of AERF made repeated trips to Cleveland to help organize the parents and the schools. It was prime time, and everyone involved in the program was a potential spokesperson. We also began preparations for a massive rally, an effort complicated by the fact that we would not know the argument date for quite some time. Compounding that uncertainty, the argument almost certainly would take place smack in the middle of the winter, and travel was now a very vexing complication. But the goal was a vitally important one: we wanted every bit of news coverage to feature not only the argument but also the parents and children. It would be our last opportunity to illustrate the equities.

An effort of that magnitude required far more resources than IJ had at its disposal. Fortunately, the coalition to pull it off was already in place, consisting at the national level primarily of AERF, the Friedman Foundation, and Children First America. Having gone over the logistics for so long, each of us was ready to do what needed to be done, and it was a wonderfully efficient overall operation.

On the legal front, we had to prepare our own brief and choreograph as best we could a strong amicus effort. Over the summer, I had assigned two law clerks to research exhaustively the historical context of *Nyquist*, so that we could help distinguish it, and to identify every shred of social science research on school choice. We wanted to leave no stone unturned. And I was intent that this brief would be our best ever.

On the amicus front, our goal was to demonstrate the depth and diversity of support for school choice. In particular, we thought that the two briefs we had conceived at the Shadow of the Beast conference—the mayors' brief and the law professors' brief—could help accomplish that. To that task we assigned the newest IJ attorney, Robert Freedman, who had joined us from the State Department. We figured that Bob's diplomatic skills would come in handy in bringing together a disparate group of individuals.

They did. For a while it looked as if the Rudolph Giuliani-John Norquist brief wouldn't come together. The mayors' designated representatives, Anthony Coles and David Riemer, respectively, were pulling in different policy directions. But in the end they cohered behind a unified brief urging the Court to preserve a vitally important policy option for urban schools. Meanwhile, on the basis of advice from Jack Coons, we recruited Professor Jesse Choper to draft a brief for the law professors. Choper was the retired dean of the Berkeley law school, and a politically moderate, enormously well-respected constitutional scholar. Having Choper author the brief allowed us to attract more than three dozen other law professors, spanning the ideological spectrum.

To further bolster our own brief, we invited Harvard Law School Professor Charles Fried to sign on. Fried was solicitor general during the Reagan Administration and had served on the Massachusetts Supreme Judicial Council. His name and insights helped bolster the credentials of IJ's legal team.

Because Ohio Attorney General Betty Montgomery had presented the matter of oral argument as a fait accompli, we submitted a motion for divided oral argument as soon as the Court granted review. Because the Court does not like to narrowly address the facts of specific cases but rather prefers to speak broadly to the issues at hand, we argued that the Court would benefit from hearing an advocate with a broad range of experience with school choice programs. The Court rarely grants divided argument, but we thought it might do so in this case, and that by filing the motion we could goad the state into a more cooperative posture. Dave Young also filed a motion after we filed ours.

Ken Starr called to discuss the situation. Though he was working now for Betty Montgomery, I thought he might be more reasonable, and he was. He told me there was a decent chance that Ted Olson would ask to argue for the United States. Notwithstanding his recent grievous loss, Ted was throwing himself into his work, and cared deeply about the case. I told Ken that having Ted share the argument would alleviate our concerns about inexperienced counsel presenting the argument. But I emphasized that we needed to have a more cooperative relationship with the state's team. Specifically, we wanted to see an advance draft of the state's brief on the merits, we wanted to participate extensively in moot courts, and we wanted to sit at counsel table so we could make suggestions during oral argument. Ken thought all of the requests were reasonable and he set out to fulfill them. The only one that proved difficult was counsel table, which ordinarily seats only three attorneys per side. Having served as solicitor general aided Ken in that endeavor: he was able to arrange eight seats per side. Not only would I be able to sit there, but Dick Komer would as well. Having reached an acceptable accommodation, we withdrew our motion for divided argument. Ken Starr's shuttle diplomacy had worked well.

Meanwhile, Kramer was working the media. We brought parents from school choice programs around the country to Washington for several media events. In particular, Tony Higgins of Milwaukee, Tracy Richardson from Florida, and Christine Suma and Roberta Kitchen from Cleveland made regular forays, presenting firsthand testimony on the urgent need for school choice.

Back in Phoenix, it was nose to the grindstone on our brief. I wanted to make it passionate yet moderate at the same time—in a word, to make a revolutionary brief seem decidedly un-revolutionary. The tone was set in our summary of argument:

> This program is part of a rescue plan for children in one of the worst urban school systems in the country. It enlists an array of schools—suburban public schools, private non-sectarian schools, and religious private schools—to educate several thousand economically disadvantaged schoolchildren. That the schools answering the rescue call were mainly religious provides the basis for much of the courts' finding below that the program establishes religion—a truly anomalous decision staking a program's constitutionality on the independent choices made by private third parties.

In reality, I argued, the state had constructed the program carefully in accord with the Court's precedents. "Petitioners do not ask this Court to endorse parental choice as a matter of public policy, nor would it be proper for the Court to do so. Rather, we ask this Court to find that the program fits well within the boundaries of neutrality and true private-choice set forth in this Court's establishment clause jurisprudence," we urged. "In doing so, the Court will affirm good-faith efforts directed toward the constitutional imperative of extending educational opportunities to children who need them desperately."

In an attempt to assert control over the terms of the debate, we began our substantive argument not by plunging into the Establishment Clause, but by discussing "four background principles that should help inform this Court's deliberations." The first was parental liberty, drawing on the *Pierce v. Society of Sisters* line of cases. Second was equality of educational opportunity, as proclaimed by *Brown v. Board of Education*. Third was federalism. Under our federal system, the states serve as laboratories for public policy experimentation, which the national government is supposed to respect. Justice

O'Connor in particular is a strong adherent of federalism, and we hoped that argument would appeal to her. Finally, we discussed the free exercise of religion, pointing out that the Court's neutrality framework was the only way to accommodate both guarantees of the First Amendment regarding religion.

We began our Establishment Clause argument by discussing the history of education in America, which for more than a century was tied to religion. The common schooling movement initially embraced Protestantism and then secularism, but the latter was a modern trend. *Nyquist* grew out of an effort to bail out failing religious schools. But school choice developed out of a urgent need to address the crisis of urban public education. Hence the benefits in *Nyquist* were aimed exclusively at private schools and their patrons, whereas here private schools were only one of the many options embraced to expand opportunities for children in a failing government school system. To support the real-world argument, we cited not only Jay Greene's Cleveland study, but an array of social science that comprised a full five pages in our table of contents.

Finally we turned our attention to the absurdities of the Sixth Circuit's decision. Basing a program's constitutionality on year-to-year statistics would create a hopelessly subjective standard, we argued. As had been the experience in Milwaukee, the numbers could (and probably would) change so that the percentage of children attending nonsectarian schools likely would increase. Moreover, the program was not just neutral, it was "neutral-plus": every tip of the scale (such as the amount of tuition, the availability of tutorial assistance grants, etc.) operated to favor public or nonsectarian schools to the detriment of religious schools. Finally, it made no sense to view the program in isolation. We provided a multicolor, pullout chart illustrating the range of choices available to Cleveland schoolchildren—magnet schools, community schools, and scholarship schools—and the relative amount of money available to them from the state. Amid the hundreds of pages the justices and their clerks would have to read in this case, we figured that the pullout chart would be memorable and provide some welcome relief for tired eyes.

We finished our brief with the following passages:

> Many of the themes in this case reflect those raised 47 years ago in *Brown v. Board of Education*. There, children were

forced to travel past good neighborhood schools to attend inferior schools because the children happened to be black; today, many poor children are forced to travel past good schools to attend inferior schools because the schools happen to be private. In the quest to fulfill the promise of equal educational opportunity, we must enlist every resource at our disposal.

The Cleveland Pilot Scholarship Program was not designed to test the boundaries of constitutional law, but to fit safely within them. We respectfully ask this honorable Court to affirm that it does.

One of IJ's key strategy devices is the SOCO, an acronym for strategic overriding communications objective. The idea is that in preparing for any public forum—whether a court or the court of public opinion—the advocate should distill the message into two or three crisp statements that convey it powerfully. The method is to ask yourself what message you want to be absolutely sure to leave with the audience. Once devised, no matter what question is asked, the advocate incorporates the SOCOs. That way the advocate can be sure that the audience is hearing the most important message.

At the Supreme Court, our preeminent SOCO, reflected in our brief, was "This is the most important education case since *Brown v. Board of Education*."[1] The purpose was twofold: to seize the moral high ground and to convey that the case was about education, not religion. It precipitated some disagreement, particularly from Howard Fuller and *New York Times* columnist Brent Staples, a school choice supporter. Both believed that the school choice movement was distinct from the civil rights movement. I intensely respect both Fuller and Staples, but I disagree with them on this question. The battle to achieve equal educational opportunities is not over, and historically it has been one continuous struggle. For the many families we have represented over the course of the past dozen years, the promise of *Brown v. Board of Education* was illusory—until school choice. My colleagues and I repeated the line as mantra, and it stuck.

---

[1] The use of that language, which President Bush also embraced after the decision, was discussed in a thoughtful analysis by Supreme Court correspondent Linda Greenhouse, "Win the Debate, Not Just the Case," *New York Times*, July 14, 2002, sec. 4, p. 4.

When the briefs were filed on November 9, our side had put together an amazing showing. The state's brief was solid. Among amici, in addition to the mayors' and the law professors' briefs, we presented several distinctive voices. BAEO was represented in a brief by New York University law professor Samuel Estreicher, a former clerk to Justice O'Connor. An IJ alumnus, Mark Chenoweth, enlisted two senior partners in his firm, former White House counsel Boyden Gray and former Baltimore mayor Kurt Schmoke, to draft a brief for AERF. Excellent briefs were filed on behalf of Wisconsin Gov. Scott McCallum, Florida Gov. Jeb Bush, New Mexico Gov. Gary Johnson, and Florida's Democratic Attorney General Robert Butterworth as well as for the Friedman Foundation, the Center for Education Reform (on behalf of a broad coalition of pro–school choice groups), Children First America, and the Cato Institute. In all, more than two dozen briefs, reflecting a very broad and ecumenical range of interests and philosophical perspectives, weighed in for school choice.

I expected a barrage of briefs from the other side, but they failed to materialize in anything approaching the number or quality filed on our side. Initially I was surprised, then realized that the unions had made a huge tactical error early on in the litigation. When they filed their lawsuits, they wanted to disguise the fact that the unions were orchestrating the litigation by surrounding themselves with a multitude of fellow travelers such as the American Civil Liberties Union, People for the American Way, and Americans United for Separation of Church and State. The gambit fooled nobody; but when it came time for amicus briefs in the Supreme Court, the cupboard was all but bare: the very groups that ordinarily would have weighed in were precluded from doing so because they were already part of the case, representing the plaintiffs. So the advantage in numbers that left-wing groups usually can bring to bear was neutralized by the groups themselves.

The unions' briefs broke little new ground, though they revealed an emerging strategic divergence. The NEA, realizing that it was dangerous to pin all its hopes on *Nyquist*, now sought to invoke *Witters*, while the AFT continued to argue that *Witters* was irrelevant. Dick Komer, who authored our reply brief, took delight in pointing out that curious inconsistency. The opposition's overall amicus effort was feeble. The only noteworthy brief was from the NAACP Legal

Defense Fund, which devoted its entire argument to excoriating IJ for daring to invoke *Brown v. Board of Education*—with the fortuitous consequence of bestowing on our brief additional attention.

Now it was time to begin preparing for oral argument, which the Court scheduled for February 20. Facing the prospect of dividing his argument with Marvin Frankel, Robert Chanin filed a motion to extend each side's time from 30 to 40 minutes. The Court surprisingly approved the motion, allowing divided oral argument time for Chanin and Frankel on the other side and for Judi French, Ted Olson, and David Young on ours. It was obvious that if we had maintained our motion for divided argument time, the Court probably would have granted it. But by that point, we had established a good working relationship with the state's team, thanks to Ken Starr; and I was apprehensive enough about having our side's time divided three ways, much less four.

In preparing for argument, we researched every oral argument in the previous Supreme Court cases raising related issues, and compiled lists of questions that each justice might ask. We provided those to Ken Starr to help Judi French prepare. The state put together a number of moot courts, and both Judi French and David Young planned to come to Washington for more in the days preceding the argument.

Almost everyone was concentrating on Justice O'Connor, but I didn't think we could afford such a narrow focus. In fact, I didn't think we should write off a single justice, or take any for granted, so we researched all of their distinctive Establishment Clause jurisprudence. It appeared in particular that Justice Stephen Breyer might be in play. Breyer, after all, had joined Justice O'Connor's concurring opinion in *Mitchell v. Helms*. Was he trying to influence her, was she trying to influence him, or did they both mean what they said? If the latter, we had a shot at both.

While we were preparing for oral argument, Jeff Rosen wrote an interesting analysis of Breyer's jurisprudence in the *New Republic*, suggesting that Breyer is a true conservative who defers to the collective will expressed through decisionmaking processes. I was skeptical: Breyer's record is consistently statist, supporting whichever outcome expands government power. But if Jeff was right, Breyer should be a vote in favor of school choice because it is the reflection of community will. It seemed worth a shot. I was especially delighted that Jeff's article was the cover story—and on the back cover was a BAEO advertisement for school choice. I thought, that's one school choice ad a Supreme Court justice surely will read.

As the lawyers prepared for argument inside the Court, IJ and its principal allies were busy preparing the events that would occur outside. Maureen Blum and AERF's Jodi Goldberg were in charge of organizing large numbers of buses, overnight accommodations, food, speakers, and the Supreme Court venue for the rally. We could not reserve a space in front of the Supreme Court, which was first-come, first-served, so we would have to outflank the unions, which we knew were organizing a rally as well. Maureen and Jodi also were in charge of the weather. February 20 in Washington, D.C.? A tall order. We truly would find out which side God was on.

As the argument date approached, the media campaign was in full swing. The first major article, however, was a huge setback. A couple of weeks before the argument, the *New York Times* published a front-page story with a photo of white students at a Catholic school in Cleveland. The story suggested that a large percentage of the scholarship students were white and from middle-class families— exactly the opposite of the official statistical picture. We had no idea where the reporter had obtained his information, but the depiction was at odds with the reality in Cleveland. Inaccurate or not, the story was devastating.

But over the duration, it proved to be the only discordant note. Among the positive media were superb analyses by Stuart Taylor in *Legal Times* and Jeffrey Rosen in the *New Republic,* supportive editorials by the *Washington Post* and *Wall Street Journal,* and articles in nearly all of the nation's major magazines and newspapers. My personal favorite was the article in the ever-insightful *Economist,* whose cover pictured the raised arm of the Statue of Liberty responding to the instruction, "Hands up all those who think vouchers would improve America's schools."[2]

Christine Suma, Roberta Kitchen, Tracy Richardson, and Tony Higgins came to town for a media barnstorming tour the week before the argument. Along with John Kramer, we had lunch with columnist George Will, one of the quickest studies in Washington, D.C. The parents recounted their stories and Will eloquently

[2]*The Economist,* February 23/March 1, 2002.

reported them. There was one line of argumentation that I thought our advocates in the Supreme Court would not make, and I tried it out on Will. The Supreme Court, in the First Amendment freedom-of-speech context, had coined the concept of the "heckler's veto": the notion that a bystander should not be able to prevent speech because he objects to it and threatens to make a fuss. Wasn't that the role that the suburban public schools were playing by trying to veto the constitutionality of the choice program by refusing to participate? Will loved the idea and the point was made, in a column read by nearly everyone inside the Beltway.

Meanwhile, we helped prepare the advocates for oral argument in a series of moot courts. One was sponsored by the Heritage Foundation and hosted by former attorney general Edwin Meese, the ecumenical elder statesman of the conservative public interest law movement. Judi French, Ted Olson, and Dave Young all rehearsed their arguments and took criticisms gamely. Ted was intensely focused, making me respect him all the more. Watching Judi, it became clear that she would provide an excellent foil for Robert Chanin. Judi is diminutive, forceful yet soft-spoken, and unfailingly proper, in stark contrast to Chanin's demeanor. I also figured that if anyone could induce a Chanin meltdown, it would be Justice Scalia, probably the most intense questioner in the history of the U.S. Supreme Court. Ken Starr continued to play an extremely active role, corralling people's suggestions and digesting them to improve Judi's performance. Everyone agreed that the tone should be moderate, in an effort to encourage Justice O'Connor not just to vote with the majority to uphold the program, but to join the opinion in full. The team finally was operating in harmony, and I was beginning to feel fairly optimistic.

But in the blizzard of media appearances during that week— during which I spent way too much time with our nemeses Elliott Mincberg and Barry Lynn—I took a very cautious approach. The Court either would rule in our favor, or it would give us a "constitutional roadmap" by which to chart future school choice programs, I argued. Either way, we would achieve the constitutional certainty that had been our goal since the beginning. In other words, regardless of the outcome, school choice would win.

The forecast for February 20 was for cold rain. (Fortunately, weather forecasts in Washington, D.C., are notoriously inaccurate.)

If it was raining badly, we would have a big problem: we would have to move the rally several blocks away to Union Station. A key to successful media, as John Kramer has taught me, is to make the reporters' lives as easy as possible. If the rally was a distance away, we simply would not receive the coverage we wanted.

The night before the argument was a catharsis. First we went to the hotel in which hundreds of out-of-town parents and children were gathered, enjoying a buffet dinner. Seeing Fannie Lewis was uplifting. She had remained stoic and confident throughout five years of ups and downs, and true to form she was predicting victory. It's impossible for me to see Fannie without smiling—our relationship has been wonderful from the first instant, total kindred spirits. And now she had brought hundreds of people from Cleveland with her to the culmination of the journey.

From there we went to Boyden Gray's lovely Georgetown home, where he hosted a reception. All the stalwarts were there, from Ken Starr to Susan Mitchell to Pilar Gomez to District of Columbia activist Virginia Walden-Ford to Robert Enlow to Fritz Steiger to David Brennan to Chip Mellor and the entire IJ litigation, media, and outreach teams. Milton Friedman called in to share his well-wishes by speaker-phone. It was an evening of camaraderie, celebration, and intense anticipation.

The next morning I awoke to gorgeous sunshine and balmy 60 degree temperatures, amazingly rare in February in the nation's capital, which put an instant smile on my face. Seating in the Supreme Court is limited, so a dozen IJers spent the night outside the Court, fortified with portable heaters and hot chocolate, saving places for school choice parents and supporters. As I walked into the Court I exchanged hugs and handshakes with people I had grown to know so well.

The Supreme Court courtroom is a truly august place, and an argument is the best show in Washington. I positioned myself at counsel table right behind Ken Starr and Judi French, to facilitate the delivery of notes. The advocates and their associates filtered in as the galleries filled. I shook hands with Robert Chanin's team and with Marvin Frankel's. The elderly former judge was ill and wheelchair-bound; sadly, he would pass away a few weeks after oral argument.

The galleries had their share of celebrities such as Secretary of Health and Human Services Tommy Thompson and Sen. Ted Kennedy. My colleague Clark Neily came up to counsel table and told me, "I think Bo Derek is here." He pointed her out, and sure enough. I decided to lighten the nervous mood of the advocates on our side by sharing the news, and evoked several over-the-shoulder glances and nervous smiles.

Then all nine justices entered the courtroom with a crack of the gavel and a loud voice announcing, "Oyez! Oyez! Oyez!" And they start asking questions almost as soon as arguments begin. The justices sit with the chief in the middle emanating outward in order of seniority. My eyes would be focused primarily on Justice O'Connor, sitting next to Chief Justice Rehnquist, and Justice Breyer, on the far right.

Judi French was first up and started with precisely the right tone. "In 1995, the Ohio General Assembly responded to an unprecedented educational crisis by enacting the Ohio Scholarship and Tutorial Program. Under this Court's decisions, especially *Mueller*, *Witters*, and *Zobrest*, and most recently in *Agostini* and *Mitchell*, the Ohio program is constitutional because it offers a neutral program that offers true private choice to parents." French crisply fielded a barrage of questions, evidencing a mastery of the record that is essential to a successful Supreme Court argument. The point of demarcation among the justices grew quickly apparent, with some questioning whether any real choices existed in the Cleveland program, and others asking whether community schools should be taken into account. It appeared that Justice O'Connor, who always is a careful and active questioner, was positioned into the latter category, which made for a hospitable argument.

Dave Young went next, just as the justices were getting warmed up. Justice Breyer asked a convoluted question that indicated he was not looking favorably on the program:

> [I]magine you came from Europe or Africa, or a different place, and said, what do they do in the United States by way of educating their children, and you're told, well, $60 billion a year, $40 billion, or some very large amount of money is being spent by the Government to give children K through 12 what is basically a religious oriented education taught by a parochial school. Wouldn't you then say, in the United

States of America, like France or England, the Government
of the United States endorses a religious education by putting
up massive amounts?

Young responded by arguing that there is no endorsement of religion
because the scholarship amount is far below the average public
school subsidy and the program clearly was a response to a serious
public school crisis. He could also have pointed out that the government already provides billions of dollars every year—through such
programs as the G.I. Bill and Pell Grants—to students who spend
such money in religious schools. No one perceives it as an endorsement of religion because students choose where to spend the money
and the government also provides its own comprehensive system
of schools—precisely the criteria of true private choice and neutrality
that the Court has set forth.

But Breyer was back at him. "[T]he irony," he said, "is that the
better the parochial school, in a sense, the less the freedom of choice.
I mean, I—if it were my children and I saw these comparisons, I'd
say, send them to a parochial school." For most people, that would
be a reason to uphold the program; but for Justice Breyer, it appeared
to constitute a government endorsement of religion. My skepticism
had, unfortunately, been well-founded. Clearly we were not going
to get his vote.

Following Dave Young, Ted Olson focused on the endorsement
question as well. Pointing to the nifty fold-out chart in our brief, he
observed that the program operates amidst a wide range of secular
options. His argument seemed to play well for the program's supporters on the Court and to respond effectively to the naysayers. It
was all about context, Olson stressed, and the context was education,
not religion.

Then it was Robert Chanin's turn. Momentarily, the experience
turned bittersweet for me: it would be the first time among many
court arguments that I would not rise to rebut the union lawyer's
rhetoric. The instinct to stand was almost Pavlovian, but I managed
to restrain myself.

Chanin began with a familiar and powerful argument:

> Under the Cleveland voucher program, millions of dollars
> of unrestricted public funds are transferred each year from
> the State Treasury into the general coffers of sectarian private
> schools and the money is used by those schools to provide

an educational program in which the sectarian and the secular are interwoven. It is a given that, if those funds are properly attributable to the State, the program violates the Establishment Clause.

We submit that the answer to that attribution question is yes, and it is yes because, regardless of the decision that individual parents make, it is inevitable, it is a mathematical certainty that almost all of the students will end up going to religious schools that provide a religious education.

But that was as far as he got. Justice O'Connor interrupted with a question that began inauspiciously and got worse. "Well, Mr. Chanin, wait just a minute," she said. "Do we not have to look at all of the choices open to the students, the community schools, the magnet schools, et cetera? How is it that we can look only at the ones looking to the religious schools?"

At that point, everyone on our side must have heaved a collective sigh of relief. The message we had struggled so mightily to communicate had been heard.

Chanin responded that the narrow focus was dictated by both precedent and logic. To which Justice O'Connor responded, "I don't understand either point, to tell you the truth. I mean, if you want to look at what the parents' choices are, do you not have to look in reality at the whole program?"

Two minutes into the argument, Chanin was growing testy; and it wasn't Justice Scalia who was getting under his skin, it was Justice O'Connor (though Scalia, as always, would have his turn). Chanin began arguing with O'Connor and interrupting her. She accused him of asking "us to put on blinders, . . . to make a decision based on a fictional premise." As they bantered back and forth, Justice O'Connor made what seemed to be a dispositive observation: "If anything, it's skewed against the religious schools."

Justice Kennedy then jumped in, telling Chanin to the laughter of the spectators, "So far, you're doing a very good job of not answering Justice O'Connor's question." The spectacle was somehow both vicariously painful and exquisitely enjoyable to watch at the same time. Surely feeling himself in quicksand, Chanin fought to get out, but the effort brought out his worst qualities as an advocate. He started speaking over the justices. At one point, Chief Justice Rehnquist stopped in mid-sentence and leaned back in his chair. Chanin

181

finally realized what he was doing and apologized. "I didn't mean to interrupt you, Your Honor," he said. To which the chief justice quipped, "You'd better not!"

Finally, Justice Scalia asked how the state could deliver high-quality educational opportunities without including religious options. Chanin responded that the state needed to "provide resources" to public schools. To which Scalia delivered the most memorable line of the argument: "They've spent already $7,000 per child, which is above the average in the rest of the country. It isn't a money problem. It's a monopoly problem."

Chanin argued the point, but sat down even before his argument time expired, finishing with the tepid and decidedly unlawyerly assertion that vouchers are a "lousy option."

Following a brief and unfocused argument by Marvin Frankel, Judi French rose for rebuttal. Picking up on the weaknesses in Chanin's argument, she used a line I suggested, characterizing the scholarship program as the "poor relative" among educational choices in Cleveland in terms of the resources devoted to it. By now there were few questions, and French repeated the themes that seemed to have resonated with a majority of the Court.

When the argument was over, everyone on our side wore huge smiles. It appeared that the vote would be 5–4, but the direction of the Court was much clearer than we had expected.

I bounded toward the exit and the rally. I was anxious to see whether our side secured the prime position in front of the Court.

We did. Maureen Blum and our other organizers had scored the key terrain in front of the Court, while the teachers were relegated to the sidelines and earned themselves a "tardy." Our rally dwarfed theirs. Hundreds of parents and children, waving signs and wearing the red, white, and blue school choice buttons that had become the movement's trademark, waited expectantly for word from inside the Court. Bert Holt, Kaleem Caire, and other speakers had stoked the crowd to a fever pitch. I plunged into the crowd, shaking dozens of hands and exchanging high fives along the way. At the microphone, I talked about the long journey we had traveled together, but noted that the real journey had begun many years before when Thurgood Marshall made his argument in *Brown v. Board of Education*. Victory seemed likely, I told spectators with a lawyer's usual caution but my never-play-poker face telling them everything they wanted to know.

But characteristically, Fannie Lewis exhibited no such equivocation. If there was any doubt in anyone's mind about how it had gone inside the courtroom, it was dispelled when the grande dame of the Cleveland school choice movement emerged onto the steps of the Supreme Court. In a moment captured the next morning on the front pages of newspapers around the country, she held up her arms and proclaimed, "We won!"

And I smiled and said to myself: I think we did.

10. D-Day

We've had our share of victories and defeats since opening the Institute for Justice in 1990 in the areas of school choice, economic liberty, private property rights, equal protection of the laws, and freedom of speech. But perhaps above all we have learned that we don't like to lose. That is one reason why our efforts outside of the courtroom in outreach and communications are so intense. Given that the odds inside of the courtroom usually are against us, we do whatever we can to improve them. That is because our interests are bound together with the interests of the people we represent, and we can't bear to let them down.

I remember back in the early 1990s, when we were representing Leroy Jones and his colleagues in Denver in their struggle to bust the government-imposed taxicab monopoly and to start their own company, aptly named Freedom Cabs. The legal battle wasn't going well. Not surprisingly, Leroy had lost his job driving for Yellow Cabs, and now was hawking sodas at Mile-High Stadium. One night his van burned down and he lost all of his inventory. Leroy's lawyer, my partner Chip Mellor, made some phone calls and secured loans to keep Leroy's interim business afloat. Eventually, though we lost the lawsuit, the state capitulated under the glare of adverse publicity, and Freedom Cabs was born. It thrives today. Chip's example of going above and beyond to help keep Leroy's business afloat was an inspiration to me.

We would need to draw on that inspiration if the worst should happen and the Cleveland school choice program were declared unconstitutional. Though the argument had gone extremely well, we needed to be prepared if we lost. That possibility was not altogether remote given it was clear that, as usual, we had no votes on the Court to spare.

We expected that the Court would render its decision on one of the last days of the term, as it usually does with its most controversial cases. No one seems to know why—perhaps the justices like to leave town before all hell breaks loose. In this term, the school choice case was the most controversial. So we anticipated a decision in late June—four months after oral argument. Over the years, I've learned to not think (too much) about cases after they're argued. It hearkens back to grade school days when teachers always seemed to take forever to grade exams. At least the U.S. Supreme Court, unlike most courts, nearly always gets its work done on schedule. Still, it was impossible not to think about the impending decision and indeed it seemed that everyone I knew was speculating about it as well.

My anxiety was not lessened when we heard a rumor in May, supposedly emanating from the Department of Justice, that Justice O'Connor had gone south (figuratively, not literally). After her fierce questioning in oral argument, that seemed improbable, but certainly not outside the realm of possibility.

If the Court rendered an adverse decision, it seemed likely that it would focus on some quirk of the Cleveland program, such as the amount of the scholarship or the nonparticipation of suburban government schools. Bob Freedman in our office drafted curative legislation, addressed to the program's possible vulnerabilities, so that our allies in Ohio could move swiftly to keep the program afloat. I spoke with Susan Mitchell about a philanthropic response as well. My colleagues and I brainstormed about how to inoculate other programs, especially Florida's and Milwaukee's, from an adverse decision. The state trial court in Florida already had abated proceedings in the opportunity scholarship case to await the decision in *Zelman*. We suspected that the unions also were waiting for a Supreme Court decision to decide whether to challenge scholarship tax credits in Florida and Pennsylvania, the McKay scholarship program for disabled children with disabilities in Florida, and a new preschool choice program in Louisiana. A lot was riding on this decision.

Much more fun was planning to shift from defense to offense in the event of a favorable decision, and my colleagues and I spent many hours over the spring preparing for that possibility (knocking wood all the while). Our first and most urgent endeavor would be to file federal challenges to Blaine amendments that were construed by state courts to discriminate against religious options. We could continue to fight them state by state—as we would have to, for instance, in Florida—or seek a national precedent that would establish that such provisions violate the federal requirement of neutrality toward religion. Dick Komer, in particular, was anxious to return to Maine and Vermont to make precisely that argument.

As June rolled around, we dispatched a law clerk to the Supreme Court on each decision day, predictably to no avail. John Kramer had me draft three news releases—one for a victory, one for a defeat, and one for an ambiguous outcome—so we could be ready the moment a decision came down.

Once it came down to the final week of the Court's term, I flew back to Washington to be on hand. By that point I was studying for the obligatory Arizona bar examination. So I packed up my books and tapes and set up shop in my former venue. Happily I was joined by my wife, Shawnna, and by the newest school choice supporter, our son Ryne Austin, who had joined our family on April 11.

The Court announced it would render its last decisions on Monday, June 24, and Thursday, June 27. I expected our decision would come down on the last day, but went over to the Court on Monday to hear the case announcements. Ken Starr and Ted Olson were there, along with several lawyers from the other side, but our decision was not announced. Thursday would be D-day.

It was good to have a dress rehearsal that Monday: everything that logistically could go wrong did. A frustrated Kramer convened the whole school choice team that morning and gave us our marching orders once again so that Thursday would proceed seamlessly.

By that time, the rumor mill was on overdrive. Our case was the only one to have been argued in February that had not yet been decided. Ordinarily, each justice is assigned at least one decision to write each month. For cases argued in February, there were only two justices who had not yet authored an opinion: Justices Anthony Kennedy and Antonin Scalia. It was a very good harbinger.

Before leaving Phoenix, I had written a letter to Robert Chanin, telling him how much I had enjoyed our litigation experiences, and that I had learned a great deal from him over the years. Though Bob and I see the world in fundamentally different ways, I grew to respect him as a tenacious yet highly ethical lawyer, which is just about the highest compliment one can render in highly charged, policy-oriented litigation. Chanin tracked me down in Washington and thanked me for the letter. But then he surprised me. For an advocate who had projected dogged confidence every step of the way, he virtually conceded defeat. "We can do the math as well as you can," he told me. "I would be happy to trade places with you."

As decision day approached, my assignment changed. Kramer wanted me not inside the courtroom, but outside the press office. The Supreme Court press corps receives decisions as the Court issues them, whereas the public at large receive them only when the Court concludes. Spectators inside the courtroom must wait for all of the decisions before leaving. CNN wanted Barry Lynn of Americans United for Separation of Church and State and me to provide instant commentary on the decision, so we would know as soon as the media did.

On the morning of June 27, I awoke with a nervous stomach. As I showered, I rehearsed my SOCOs for an adverse decision. The decision was not the end for school choice, but a new beginning. The court had given us a constitutional roadmap for school choice programs. School choice was the most promising education reform in America, and it would continue to open educational opportunities to schoolchildren who desperately needed them. It all sounded so brave and optimistic, and yet it depressed the heck out of me even to say it. I hoped those words would be confined to the shower.

If argument day had been splendid, June 27 was a classic summer day in the nation's capital, with oppressive heat and humidity. For all of the desert heat in Phoenix, humidity is something for which a person quickly loses acclimation, and Shawnna, Ryne, and I were already wilting as we piled into a cab to travel the mile or two to IJ. There we hooked up with Chip, Kramer, and several other colleagues for the trek to the Supreme Court.

From there we stood in line in the basement outside the press office. A very stern marshal kept us quiet and in order. Also in line were Barry Lynn, somehow appearing even more dour than usual, and Ralph Neas of People for the American Way. Ralph and I had sparred repeatedly in the early 1990s over racial preferences, but since becoming president of People for the American Way, he had ducked debates over school choice. I hoped that his appearance at the Court would mean that he was coming out on the issue. As Neas's roots were in the civil rights establishment, I was eager to challenge him on his opposition to school choice.

The Court had four decisions remaining in its term. After the 10 A.M. start of the court session, reporters left the press office first with one decision (not ours), then another (not ours), and finally a third (maddeningly, still not ours). The school choice decision would be the last case decided by the U.S. Supreme Court in its 2001–2002 term.

And then. . .nothing. Five minutes. Ten minutes. Fifteen. I walked over to Chip and murmured, "Someone is reading a dissent from the bench." He said, "That's exactly what I was thinking."

Typically, the justice who writes the Court's decision summarizes it briefly, and announces which justices have joined, concurred, or dissented. In an extraordinary case, a justice will read part or all of a dissent from the bench to underscore how strongly he or she feels. Someone was doing that now. And Chip and I both knew that one justice above all makes a practice of reading dissents from the bench: Justice Scalia. Our spirits plunged.

Then, finally, the CNN reporter walked by with the decision, Barry Lynn in tow. She wouldn't let us see it until we left the building, however, lest she unleash a feeding frenzy. I followed her practically in a run, Kramer and Chip closely behind.

As we left the building, she handed Barry and me the decision as we moved quickly toward the front steps where the CNN camera awaited. The scene recalled images of the *Bush v. Gore* decision, when reporters were thumbing through the decision trying to determine who had won the presidential election. There were only two things I needed to know to start pontificating: who authored the decision, and whether Justice O'Connor had joined the decision or separately concurred. I could find both answers a few pages into the decision.

I flipped the pages and saw: Decision by Rehnquist, C.J. And: Joined by O'Connor, J., Kennedy, J., Scalia, J., and Thomas, J.

We had won.

And not only that, we had won an outright majority decision. No equivocation.

As the CNN team placed microphones on Barry Lynn and me, I flashed a huge grin and a thumbs up to Chip, Kramer, and Shawnna. An enormous media corps awaited on the steps to the Court, but CNN had first dibs.

Barry Lynn announced that the Supreme Court had taken a "wrecking ball" to the First Amendment. He spoke for a few moments and then it was my turn to speak the words I had been waiting 12 years to say.

"This is the most important education decision since *Brown v. Board of Education*. This was the Super Bowl for school choice, and the kids won."

From there the day was a total blur. I climbed the steps of the Court and spoke to the cameras, then to a sea of individual reporters. Ryne was dressed in red, white, and blue and adorned with a school choice sticker. He slept through most of the proceedings, but Shawnna thoughtfully borrowed his hat and some diaper wipes to help me stem the flow of sweat from the humidity.

We had won! Back at IJ, the entire office was jubilant. We were making calls, receiving calls, sending e-mails, doing media interviews, everything to get the word out about the victory for school choice. Best of all were the phone calls to the Cleveland parents, who had gathered for the news and were ecstatic. Our director, Arthur Dantchik, sent us a case of Dom Perignon. I had never smelled Dom Perignon, much less tasted it, and it was exquisite. At 5 P.M., we had a staff toast, and the champagne was every bit as sweet as the victory. The credit, I told the staff, belonged to everyone who had played a part in the programs and the litigation—a team that spanned from coast to coast. I singled out Chip and our development team for special praise. In a decade of expensive litigation encompassing more than a dozen cases against very well-heeled opponents, the litigation team had never once been asked to cut corners. Every resource we needed we secured, thanks to dedicated supporters who were determined that school choice ultimately would be vindicated in the U.S. Supreme Court.

That night we celebrated with school choice supporters at our offices. I wished that some of the Milwaukee and Cleveland parents could have been there. But Virginia Walden-Ford, who has worked indefatigably for school choice in the District of Columbia, was there, and I hugged her for all school choice parents I had worked with over the years. It was the happiest, most gratifying day of my professional life.

Eventually I had time to actually review the Supreme Court decision. Apart from the vote, the Court's decision vindicated the most optimistic hopes of school choice supporters. Though it was a five-to-four decision, the Court majority spoke with a single, decisive voice, providing precisely the clarity necessary for the school choice movement to progress.

Within the Supreme Court, opinions are assigned to a particular justice to write by the chief justice if he is in the majority or, if not, by the next senior justice among the majority. School choice supporters owe a debt to Chief Justice Rehnquist for assigning the opinion to himself.[1] Though Rehnquist is staunchly conservative, he is politically savvy. Instead of writing a sweeping opinion breaking new jurisprudential ground that could have compelled Justice O'Connor to concur separately, he understood that it was important to keep her in the fold in order to produce a majority opinion. The chief justice adroitly moderated his previous position from *Mitchell*, accommodating Justice O'Connor by retaining the "true private choice" criterion that the *Mitchell* plurality had sought to jettison.

In addition to Rehnquist, four justices fully joined the majority opinion: O'Connor, Anthony Kennedy, Scalia, and Thomas. The chief justice began by recounting the grievous educational conditions giving rise to the Cleveland scholarship program. It was against that backdrop, the Court observed, that the scholarship program was adopted as "part of a broader undertaking by the State to enhance the educational options of Cleveland's schoolchildren" in response to the education crisis.[2] The Court examined other educational options, including magnet and community schools as well as the higher dollar amount they commanded relative to the scholarships.

Applying the law, Rehnquist observed that "our decisions have drawn a consistent distinction between government programs that provide aid directly to religious schools, . . . and programs of true private choice, in which government aid reaches religious schools only as a result of the genuine and independent choices of private individuals. . . ."[3] Whereas the Court's recent cases had expanded the permissible realm of direct aid, "our jurisprudence with respect to true private choice programs has remained consistent and unbroken."[4] Recounting that jurisprudence, Chief Justice Rehnquist declared that "where a government aid program is neutral with respect to religion, and provides assistance to a broad class of citizens who, in turn, direct government aid to religious schools wholly as

---

[1] It was fitting that the chief justice wrote the majority opinion, for he also authored the *Mueller* decision in 1983, which inaugurated the modern era of Establishment Clause jurisprudence.

[2] *Zelman v. Simmons-Harris*, 122 S.Ct. 2460, 2464 (2002).

[3] Ibid., p. 2465.

[4] Ibid., p. 2466.

a result of their own genuine and independent private choice, is not readily subject to challenge under the Establishment Clause."[5]

The Court was convinced that the program was both neutral and "a program of true private choice," as part of "a general and multi-faceted undertaking by the State of Ohio to provide educational opportunities to the children of a failed school district."[6] "It confers educational assistance directly to a broad class of individuals defined without reference to religion. . . ."[7] Moreover, "[t]he program permits the participation of *all* schools within the district, religious or nonreligious. Adjacent public schools also may participate and have a financial incentive to do so."[8] By contrast, the program did not provide a financial incentive for parents to choose religious schools; to the contrary, it creates "financial *dis*incentives for religious schools."[9] Parents receiving scholarships have to copay a part of their tuition ($250), whereas parents choosing traditional, magnet, or community schools pay nothing. Emphasizing that while "such features of the program are not necessary to its constitutionality," they "clearly dispel" any notion that the program is skewed toward religion.[10] By making that observation, the Court went out of its way to broadly sanction school choice programs, even if they did not arise from the dire circumstances that led to the Cleveland program.

Citing the Jay Greene study, the Court viewed the program in the broader context of the wide range of school choices in Cleveland, and rejected the statistical snapshot as a touchstone of constitutionality. "The Establishment Clause question is whether Ohio is coercing parents into sending their children to religious schools, and that question must be answered by evaluating *all* options Ohio provides Cleveland schoolchildren, only one of which is to obtain a private scholarship and then choose a religious school."[11] Beyond that, the Court emphasized, "The constitutionality of a neutral educational

[5] Ibid., p. 2467.
[6] Ibid., pp. 2467–68.
[7] Ibid., p. 2468 (citations omitted).
[8] Ibid. (emphasis in original).
[9] Ibid. (emphasis in original).
[10] Ibid.
[11] Ibid., p. 2469 (emphasis in original).

aid program simply does not turn on whether and why, in a particular area, at a particular time, most private schools are run by religious organizations, or most recipients choose to use the aid at a religious school."[12]

Finally, the Court confronted *Nyquist*, finding no reason to overrule it because it did not compel the Court to strike down the program. After all, *Nyquist* involved programs that were designed unmistakably to aid religious schools, and the Court expressly had left open the question—answered subsequently in *Mueller* and other cases—of the constitutionality of a genuinely neutral aid program. Hence, the Court's ruling changed jurisprudence not at all.

In closing, the Court underscored the moderation of its decision:

> In sum, the Ohio program is entirely neutral with respect to religion. It provides benefits directly to a wide spectrum of individuals, defined only by financial need and residence in a particular school district. It permits such individuals to exercise genuine choice among options public and private, secular and religious. The program is therefore a program of true private choice. In keeping with an unbroken line of decisions rejecting challenges to similar programs, we hold that the program does not offend the Establishment Clause.[13]

Justice O'Connor, staying true to her concurring opinion in *Mitchell*, wrote separately to emphasize two points: that the decision does not mark "a dramatic break from the past," and that the inquiry regarding "true private choice" should "consider all reasonable educational alternatives to religious schools that are available to parents."[14] In the overall context of school choices in Cleveland, Justice O'Connor emphasized, religious schools played a small role. Moreover, government policies in general, including tax exemptions for religious institutions, already bestow a substantial financial benefit. That context, she explained, "places in broader perspective the alarmist claims about implications of the Cleveland program" sounded by the dissenters.[15]

---

[12] Ibid., p. 2470.
[13] Ibid., p. 2473.
[14] Ibid. (O'Connor, J., concurring).
[15] Ibid., p. 2475.

Justice Thomas's concurring opinion was especially poignant, remarking that "[t]oday many of our inner-city public schools deny emancipation to urban minority students," who "have been forced into a system that continually fails them."[16] He observed, "While the romanticized ideal of universal public education resonates with the cognoscenti who oppose vouchers, poor urban families just want the best education for their children, who will certainly need it to function in our high-tech and advanced society."[17] The Cleveland scholarship program, he concluded, "does not force any individual to submit to religious indoctrination or education. It simply gives parents a greater choice as to where and in what manner to educate their children. This is a choice that those with greater means have routinely exercised."[18]

Displaying a penchant for original intent jurisprudence that makes him one of the Court's greatest modern justices, Justice Thomas also raised the question about whether the Establishment Clause should be construed to limit state action. By its terms, the First Amendment is addressed to Congress. Most of the provisions of the Bill of Rights have been "incorporated" to apply to the states through the Fourteenth Amendment. But as Justice Thomas observed, "When rights are incorporated against the States through the Fourteenth Amendment they should advance, not constrain, individual liberty."[19] He concluded that "[t]here would be a tragic irony in converting the Fourteenth Amendment from a guarantee of opportunity to an obstacle against education reform," leaving intact a status quo that "distorts our constitutional values and disserves those in the greatest need."[20]

Justices John Paul Stevens, Souter, and Breyer penned strident dissents. All of them rejected the Establishment Clause framework that the Court has applied for the past two decades. Justice Stevens raised concerns about "religious strife," raising the specter of "the Balkans, Northern Ireland, and the Middle East"[21]—concerns echoed

[16] Ibid., p. 2480 (Thomas, J., concurring).
[17] Ibid., p. 2483.
[18] Ibid., p. 2482.
[19] Ibid., p. 2481.
[20] Ibid., p. 2482.
[21] Ibid., p. 2485 (Stevens, J., dissenting).

194

by Justice Souter's claims of "divisiveness"[22] and Justice Breyer's warnings of "religiously based conflict"[23]—all notwithstanding that, as the majority pointed out, "the program has ignited no 'divisiveness' or 'strife' other than this litigation."[24] Nor, as the majority observed, did the dissenters propose any rule of law by which the Court could discern when a program is too religiously divisive to sustain.

The fact is that the government already dispenses billions of dollars through the G.I. Bill, Pell Grants, student loans, and other programs that can be used for religious education. Yet Americans are not at each other's throats in religious conflict. The reason why we do not see strife is that allowing benefits to be used in a nondiscriminatory fashion and directed by individual choice actually promotes a value that liberals are supposed to support: diversity. No one views a Pell Grant used at Georgetown University or Yeshiva University as primarily advancing religion, because of the plethora of available options. Nor have the Cleveland, Milwaukee, or Florida school choice programs created religious strife because they correctly are perceived as educational programs. By engaging in totally unfounded hyperbole, the dissenters undercut their own credibility.

The main dissenting opinion, written by Justice Souter and signed by Justices Stevens, Ruth Bader Ginsburg, and Breyer, castigated the Court's jurisprudence beginning with *Mueller*. It also concluded that no true private choice exists in Cleveland, but that instead parents are presented with a "Hobson's choice."[25] The dissenters on this point maintained that the public schools are so bad—and the religious schools by comparison so good—that Cleveland parents have no realistic choice. It seems odd that the proposed solution would be to eliminate the only positive choice. Justice Souter conceded that in his view there is nothing the state permissibly can do to make religious options available. "The majority notes that I argue both that the Ohio program is unconstitutional because the voucher amount is too low to create real private choice and that any greater expenditure would be unconstitutional as well," he observed. "The

[22] Ibid., p. 2502 (Souter, J., dissenting).
[23] Ibid., p. 2508 (Breyer, J., dissenting).
[24] Ibid., p. 2472, n.7.
[25] Ibid., p. 2497 (Souter, J., dissenting).

majority is dead right about this. . . ."[26] For the dissenters, the only constitutionally permissible option is for the state to consign students to government schools, no matter how defective.

Moving to the verge of panic, the dissenters warned that "the amount of federal aid that may go to religious education after today's decision is startling: according to one estimate,[27] the cost of a national voucher program would be $73 billion, 25% more than the current national public-education budget."[28] It is comforting that the four liberal justices have suddenly assumed the role of guardians of the public fisc; but as a matter of factual analysis and establishment clause jurisprudence, it is off base. Not only does the government already spend a great deal on private education—not only at the post-secondary level but also at the elementary and secondary levels through the Individuals with Disabilities Education Act—but private school education in the lower grades can actually save the government money (as witness the $2,250 expended for full payment of private school tuition in the Cleveland program). Moreover, establishment clause jurisprudence never has turned on the amount of money spent—in the view of rigid separationists, one dollar is too much—but rather on whether government coercion is present. The dissenters would return us to an era in which the U.S. Supreme Court grafted on the Constitution a requirement of discrimination against religion—perhaps one in which, imagining the unfathomable, a court might even rule it impermissible for a public school to sponsor a salute to the American flag because it contains the words "under God"!

Finally, the four dissenters took up the role of lobbyists, beseeching the "political branches [to] save us from the consequences of the majority's decision," and expressing the "hope that a future Court will reconsider today's dramatic departure from basic Establishment Clause principle."[29]

---

[26] Ibid., p. 2496 n.16.

[27] You guessed it: the "projection" is from the militantly anti–school choice People for the American Way, whose studies are copiously cited by the dissenters, although they are not part of the case record.

[28] *Zelman*, p. 2498 n.20 (Souter, J., dissenting).

[29] Ibid., p. 2502. Justice Souter took the additional dramatic step of reading his dissent from the bench.

Not content with Justice Souter's 34-page opus, Justice Breyer presented a separate dissent, joined by Justices Stevens and Souter (but curiously, not by Justice Ginsburg). He wrote separately "because I believe that the Establishment Clause concern for protecting the Nation's social fabric from religious conflict poses an overriding obstacle to the implementation of this well-intentioned school voucher program."[30] For Justice Breyer, it is not enough to vindicate the express intent of the First Amendment—to prohibit laws "respecting an establishment of religion"—it must also avoid "religiously based social conflict."[31] In this regard, it doesn't seem to matter that the program, in its sixth year of existence, has not created religious conflict, nor that its aim is educational. Instead, Breyer viewed the program against the backdrop of religious strife both in the United States and abroad. Helpfully, he informed us that in the United States, "Major religions include, among others, Protestants, Catholics, Jews, Muslims, Buddhists, Hindus, and Sikhs. . . . And several of these major religions contain different subsidiary sects with different religious beliefs."[32] Apparently, the only way we can all get along is if individuals are denied the opportunity to use government benefits as they see fit—or, even worse, to direct them across religious lines, as with the large percentage of non-Catholic families sending their children to inner-city Catholic schools.

Justice Breyer conceded that the "consequence" of existing aid programs that include religious options "has not been great turmoil."[33] Nor is there evidence that the Cleveland program—or any other school choice program—has caused religious strife. But a voucher program, in Justice Breyer's view, "risks creating a form of religiously based conflict potentially harmful to the Nation's social fabric."[34] Note the hypothetical language: it does not *do* it, it only *risks* it; and what it risks is not invariable harm but *potential* harm. On this double hypothetical, the dissenters would substitute their abstract concerns for the State of Ohio's urgent effort to deliver educational opportunities in the all-too-real bedlam of Cleveland.

[30] Ibid. (Breyer, J., dissenting).
[31] Ibid., p. 2505.
[32] Ibid.
[33] Ibid., p. 2506.
[34] Ibid., p. 2508.

One wonders if in five years, or 10, when the dire prognostications of religious strife pass unfulfilled, the dissenters will reconsider their opinions. Likewise, it is curious that the dissenters focused on an argument that the plaintiffs made only in passing. Instead, the plaintiffs focused mainly on efforts to shoehorn the Cleveland program into the *Nyquist* construct. The dissenters implicitly acknowledged that the past 20 years of jurisprudence firmly sanction school choice programs. Instead, they embraced an ends-justifies-the-means rationale that substitutes the subjective fears of individual justices for the clear command of governmental neutrality embodied in the First Amendment's religion clauses. Fortunately, that view did not prevail, but it is genuinely alarming that it attracted four votes.

But the majority decision is the law of the land, and it has dissipated the largest single legal obstacle standing in the way of school choice. In the news show debates that followed the ruling, the defenders of the status quo acknowledged that. I finally had the chance to debate Ralph Neas on the Diane Rehm Show on National Public Radio, and he seemed truly deflated. The shrill warnings of religious conflict simply don't carry much currency. On one show, Barry Lynn confessed he did not see a single "silver lining" in the Court's opinion and, for once, I take him at his word. It is an uncommonly strong and unequivocal opinion.

It seems remarkable that it took 12 years of intense litigation to establish the baseline principle that parents may be entrusted with the decision of how to direct the spending devoted to their children's education. It will take much more work to establish even more ambitious principles of educational freedom but, in a free society, the task is an essential one. To paraphrase Winston Churchill, this triumph marks only the end of the beginning.

But for now, advocates of educational freedom have much to celebrate. In common cause with economically disadvantaged families, we have prevailed in our first big test in the U.S. Supreme Court. The special interest groups dedicated to the status quo are momentarily vanquished. The empire will strike back for sure; but this decision shows that they can be beaten, that David can indeed slay Goliath.

In the end, the unions failed to understand that this legal battle required more than courtroom advocacy. Only belatedly have they made even a halfhearted attempt to address themselves to the catastrophic problems confronting urban government schools. And even then, the proposals are always self-serving, focusing on more money that will strengthen the unions with more jobs and greater power. Their expensive advertising campaigns are aimed at improving the image of public schools even as the reality gets worse. It takes a lot for an organization representing schoolteachers, perhaps the most noble of professions, to squander its moral capital. But that is exactly what the unions did. And their lawyers never recognized how devastating that abdication would prove to be for them inside the courtroom.

As my colleagues and our allies and I savored the victory in the hours following the decision, I thought back to how the unions had characterized the parents as "inconsequential conduits" when they first challenged the Cleveland scholarship program in 1997. The unions, as usual, got it exactly backward: the parents *used to be* inconsequential, but thanks to school choice, they no longer are. In fact, in Cleveland and Milwaukee and other pockets in America, the parents are finally, and forever, in charge.

Let's hope it's a phenomenon that proves contagious.

11. Road Ahead

Given the wheel-spinning that has characterized public school reform efforts over the past few decades—resulting in additional generations of economically disadvantaged inner-city children being consigned to educational cesspools—it is clear that systemic public school reform *will not* occur without the competitive impetus of school choice. More recently it has become clearer than ever that such reform *cannot* occur without school choice.

Shortly after the inauguration of President George W. Bush, Congress enacted bipartisan legislation dubbed "No Child Left Behind" that ostensibly imposed new accountability requirements on government schools. Early in the legislative deliberations, the Bush administration agreed to strip school choice provisions from the bill to appease pro-education establishment politicians such as Sen. Edward Kennedy (D-Mass.). Still, one salient provision of the bill remained intact: the requirement that where a particular government school has failed according to the state's performance criteria, the district must allow students in that school to transfer to better-performing public schools if space is available.

Even taking into account the restriction of choice options to government schools, the law's guarantee is tepid. First, states have to apply meaningful performance standards to identify any failing schools. Some states do and some don't. Then the school districts have to publicize the available options. Again, some districts do and some don't. Finally, parents have to be willing to abandon their neighborhood schools and send their children a considerable distance to a better-performing government school. By contrast to the tens of thousands of inner-city parents who have applied for private school scholarships, relatively few parents sought the ephemeral benefits of government school choice even when it was made available to them for the first time under the new federal law in 2002.

Even with all of that, the 2002 results underscore graphically the utter inadequacy of government school options in meeting the needs of inner-city youngsters. In Baltimore, 30,000 children were identified as attending failing schools—but there were only 194 slots in better-performing government schools. In Chicago, 145,000 children were theoretically eligible to leave failing government schools—but only 1,170 seats were available in better-performing public schools. In Los Angeles, there were 223,000 students enrolled in 120 failing schools—and *zero* seats were available in better-performing public schools.[1] School choice is not even on the horizon in Baltimore, Chicago, or Los Angeles because of the vise-grip control the unions exercise over the school districts and state legislatures. It is nothing less than criminal to fail to consider private options in a rescue mission for those children's futures.

Despite the victory for school choice in the U.S. Supreme Court, not only political but legal barriers continue to stand in the way of school choice. But we now start from a much stronger legal vantage point than when the legal battle began 12 years ago. *Zelman* removed the federal constitutional cloud in the broadest possible terms. All recent voucher programs and proposals satisfy the applicable criteria of neutrality and true private choice. Likewise, so do scholarship and tuition tax credit programs.[2] Indeed, it now seems entirely permissible for the government to adopt a program in which *all* education funding is channeled through students, to government and private schools alike.

From a tactical standpoint, what is momentous about the *Zelman* decision is that it allows advocates of school choice to shift, for the first time in 12 years, from defense to offense. And we need to do so with gusto.

Every good team (here I go again with the sports metaphors) plots offense even as it is playing defense, and my colleagues and I have been eager to deploy a legal offensive for quite some time. Its initial parameters are predictable: challenging the notorious Blaine amendment, the state constitutional provisions that in some states are construed to require discrimination against religious educational options.

---

[1] Diana Jean Schemo, "Few Exercise New Right to Leave Failing Schools," *New York Times*, August 28, 2002, p. A1.

[2] Indeed, because *Mueller* is so closely on point, tax credit programs have fared better in litigation so far. In our three cases defending tax credits, we have not lost a single round in any court.

The new battles began to play themselves out within weeks of the *Zelman* ruling. The ink was barely dry on the opinion when the plaintiffs in the challenge to the Florida opportunity scholarship program withdrew their First Amendment claims, acknowledging that their federal constitutional claim against well-crafted school choice programs had evaporated. Instead, they will rely solely on their state constitutional claims, especially the Blaine amendment. That parallels the unions' new national strategy, which amounts to a war of attrition fought out state by state.

Florida swiftly emerged as a key battleground. The Florida Constitution prohibits both direct and indirect aid to religious institutions, but the state courts traditionally have taken a commonsense approach that looks to whether the purpose and effect of the program is for the general welfare or for the benefit of religious institutions. In 2002, the stakes increased significantly when the state strengthened the performance criteria applicable to public schools. As a consequence, several public schools in different parts of the state recorded a second failing grade, allowing a total of 800 children to leave for private schools. The lawsuit against the growing opportunity scholarship program also is a stalking horse for future challenges to the state's scholarship tax credit program and the McKay scholarships for children with disablilities, which between them allow tens of thousands of students to attend private schools at government expense. To strengthen our legal defense of the opportunity scholarship program, we moved swiftly to add new parents from Miami to bolster the Pensacola families that had been defending the program since 1999.

As my colleague Clark Neily was preparing to argue the Florida case in trial court, a panel of the U.S. Court of Appeals for the Ninth Circuit issued the opening salvo in the post-*Zelman* fight over school choice, in a case filed by the American Center for Law and Justice concerning a Washington State post-secondary scholarship program that singles out for exclusion students pursuing a degree in theology. The program is similar to the program in *Witters* that was struck down by the Washington Supreme Court under the state's Blaine amendment. Judge Pamela Ann Rymer applied the neutrality framework of *Zelman* to hold that the exclusion of theology students violates the First Amendment.[3]

---

[3] *Davey v. Locke*, No. 00-35962, 2002 U.S. App. LEXIS 14461 (9th Cir. July 18, 2002).

The Ninth Circuit ruling reflects precisely the counterattack against the Blaine amendment that forms the nucleus of the school choice movement's post-*Zelman* offensive. The neutrality requirement works in both directions, forbidding discrimination in favor of religion, but against religion as well. Instead of fighting the battle in every single state, we will seek a national precedent from the U.S. Supreme Court holding that state constitutions that are construed to require discrimination against religious options themselves violate the First Amendment. The Institute for Justice began filing test cases to produce such a definitive ruling within three months of the *Zelman* decision.

Meanwhile, the Florida litigation underscored the importance of the effort. In August, the state trial court, without even reaching the First Amendment issues, struck down the opportunity scholarship program under the state's Blaine amendment.[4] Faced with evidence of the harm that would result from an injunction, the judge declined to halt either the initial program or its expansion. Still, it was clear that the Florida battle could be the one that will resolve the question in the U.S. Supreme Court.

Though the Blaine amendments present a serious obstacle,[5] they should not deter school choice advocates. Several state supreme courts, such as the Wisconsin and Arizona Supreme Courts, have construed them in a narrow fashion; and others may find occasion to overturn hostile past precedents in light of the recent teachings of the U.S. Supreme Court. The unions have contrived a new strategy in Blaine amendment states by contending that school choice would require an amendment to the state constitution, when in nearly all of the states that is not true. One would think that the credibility of the unions and their allies on constitutional prognostication might have diminished in light of *Zelman*; but if nothing else, the unions have shown themselves remarkably adept at polishing new pearls of conventional wisdom whenever the need arises. School choice advocates should press forward with policy initiatives and address

[4]*Holmes v. Bush*, No. CV 99-3370, slip op. (Fla. Cir. Ct. August 5, 2002).

[5]Forty-seven states have either a Blaine amendment, or a provision forbidding "compelled support" for religion, or both. Only Maine, North Carolina, and Louisiana have neither.

the legal issues in due course. With luck, a national precedent will settle the issue once and for all.

Likewise, the school choice movement now can open a second litigation front on issues of educational equity. Many state constitutions guarantee public education that is "uniform," "thorough and efficient," "high quality," or consistent with some other standard. In at least a dozen states, state courts have found that certain tax schemes (such as property taxation) violate those provisions because poorer school districts receive less state funds. In New Jersey, where since 1969 the state Supreme Court has twice ruled that the state's school funding system is unconstitutional, higher taxes have fueled government school spending that now exceeds $10,000 per student; and in urban centers like Newark, it now exceeds $16,000.[6]

For years, I was dubious about educational equity theories. After all, years of equity litigation by liberal groups had opened the spigots of tax dollars for failing government schools without any demonstrable improvement in educational quality. But my friend Lisa Graham Keegan, the former Arizona secretary of public instruction and now chief executive officer of the Education Leaders Council, persuaded me that the liberal groups had hijacked a principle that conservatives and libertarians should use to promote market-oriented education reforms. Liberal groups want equalized funding, but without allowing children to opt out of the government system. As Lisa argues, equal funding, whether on a district or statewide basis, is not enough: every child in a district should receive an equal amount of funding that is "strapped to the child's back" and follows that child to the school of the parent's choice, public or private.

In an educational equity context, we should argue forcefully that instead of remedies calling for more money, cases of educational deprivations under state constitutional guarantees can be remedied through vouchers. The idea can best be illustrated by analogy to another consumer product. If you were to buy a car and it turned out to be a lemon, the courts would not order consumers to pay the car manufacturer billions of dollars to develop a better car. Rather

---

[6] The U.S. Supreme Court rejected a similar claim, finding that no right to education exists under the federal Constitution. *San Antonio School Dist. v. Rodriguez*, 411 U.S. 1 (1973).

they would order a refund to the consumer. That is the difference between the liberals' view of equity remedies and a voucher remedy.

The problem with the funding-equalization remedies pushed by liberals is that they do not accrue to the intended beneficiaries of the constitutional guarantees: children. Moreover, giving more money to failing school districts rewards those who are failing. Much of the money is siphoned off by the bureaucracy before it ever reaches the classroom. And there is no assurance that greater funding will produce improved outcomes. Only a monetary damages remedy— that is, vouchers—will allow students to acquire high-quality education without delay. That is precisely the remedy children with disabilities have when public schools default on their obligations under the federal Individuals with Disabilities Education Act. It's time that economically disadvantaged children in failing urban schools have the same remedy.[7]

As I recounted in chapter 3, we previously pursued such an approach in Chicago and Los Angeles in the early 1990s, with less than spectacular results. But sometimes the situation has to get worse before it can get better. California now ranks roughly in the bottom one-third of K–12 academic performance despite decades of funding equalization. New Jersey is spending record-setting amounts on its government schools, the state has taken over several urban school districts, and the educational equity litigation still is in court 33 years after it started—yet with nothing to show for it in terms of improved educational performance. Taxpayers in the suburbs, who typically resist school choice, are tired of footing the bill for failing school districts like Newark and Camden. Are they ready to support a voucher-type remedy that will allow children to opt out of failing schools? Considering the alternatives, probably so. Other states such as New York, Connecticut, North Carolina, and Arizona are mired in educational equity litigation. To prevent those states from following the same disastrous path taken by New Jersey and California, which started this mess, school choice supporters need to come forward and propose an alternative. And if you want to see *real* public school reform, just imagine the fire that a voucher remedy

[7]Under the IDEA, school districts are required to pay the entire cost of private school tuition when they fail to provide a "free appropriate public education." In the general education context, it should be more than sufficient for a child to receive his or her pro rata share of public school expenditures.

would light under recalcitrant, special-interest dominated govern-ment school systems. So after the Blaine amendment offensive, edu-cational equity should be a major litigation focus.

A third litigation priority should be to unleash the public educa-tional system. One argument that school choice opponents have made is that government schools are not on a level playing field, because private schools have greater autonomy. Their response, of course, is not to deal with the problem of excess government school regulation, but to resist school choice or to impose regulations on private schools participating in such programs.

By contrast, I have promoted the three Ds of public school reform: deregulation, decentralization, and depoliticization. Wherever we see opportunities to litigate to achieve those goals, we should do so. For instance, federal mandates cripple government schools. The strings attached to federal money vastly outweigh the benefits. We should look for ways to challenge them, and back state officials who do so.

We should defend bona fide deregulated charter schools, which are just as tenaciously attacked by pro–status quo special interest groups as are school choice programs. Here too the empire is striking back, trying to limit charter schools, unionize them, or otherwise take them down the failed pathways of other government schools. The school choice movement and the charter school movement have not aligned closely, but in light of common adversaries, they need to. And after all, they are two sides of the same coin of parental choice, aiming in the same general direction.

We should challenge teacher certification requirements that keep highly qualified potential teachers out of public school classrooms. I can attest that most of what a prospective teacher learns in courses required for teacher certification is of marginal usefulness, and of course every moment spent in such courses is time spent away from the teacher's supposed area of substantive expertise. Albert Einstein would not be allowed to teach physics under teacher certification requirements in most states.

And we should look for ways to help government schools establish and enforce disciplinary standards. The biggest single difference I have witnessed between urban public and private schools is that in private schools, behavioral standards are clear and consistently enforced. Because public schools are government institutions, they are required to adhere to stringent due process requirements imposed by the federal courts in the 1960s and 1970s. That is appropriate under our federal constitution. But it leads to chaos in many schools. It seems to me that where a school community supports more stringent disciplinary standards, it should be able to freely and voluntarily contract for them, so long as alternatives are made available for those who disagree with the standards. Should such a contract be challenged, I would wager that the U.S. Supreme Court would uphold it.

Ultimately, however, problems of educational policy should be settled not in the courtroom but in the policy arena. If we've learned anything from 12 years of school choice litigation, it is that whenever systemic reform is achieved, litigation follows as inevitably as death and taxes. My colleagues and I have only one request in that regard: please give us more school choice programs to defend. The *Zelman* decision is an invitation for policymakers to be as bold and innovative as our nation's education crisis demands.

My own thinking has evolved greatly over the years of litigation. I was drawn to school choice first as a philosophical idea, then as a life preserver for children in failing government schools, and finally as a vital facet of broader public education reform. My colleague Scott Bullock used to (and probably still does) make fun of me for saying to one audience that school choice is the first step toward achieving the libertarian goal of separation of school and state, and to the next audience that school choice is essential to saving public schools.

Yet as irreconcilable as the two statements seem to be, I believe they are both true. By making the parent sovereign over matters of school selection, the mechanism of choice reduces the control that government can exert over education. The *Zelman* decision could help usher in an era of child-centered public education reform whereby the state becomes primarily a *funder* rather than a *provider* of education. And yet, school choice can strengthen public schools. As we have seen in Milwaukee and Florida, competition forces public schools to improve. The rules of economics are not suspended at the schoolhouse doors.[8]

[8] Caroline Hoxby at Harvard University has conducted extensive cutting-edge research demonstrating the positive effects of various types of educational competition on public school performance. See, for example, Caroline M. Hoxby, "School Choice and School Productivity (or Could School Choice Be the Tide That Lifts All Boats)," NBER Working Paper W8873, April 2002. Available at http://post.economics.harvard.edu/faculty/hoxby/papers.html.

Likewise, Howard Fuller has helped me understand that public education and public schools are different things. Public schools are a means of achieving public education, but the defenders of the status quo have confused the means and the ends and struggle to support the public school system as an end in itself, and even at the expense of the public education. We should care less about *where* children are educated and more about *whether* children are educated. A child receiving a poor education in a public school does not advance the true goal of public education, whereas a child receiving a good education in a private school does.

Zelman has renewed the debate among libertarians about whether school choice is a good idea. The concern is that we will sacrifice private schools to government regulation. Anti–school choice libertarians point to the worst-case scenario of post-secondary education, where student funding has been accompanied by government strings. Unquestionably, regulation presents an omnipresent concern. But our post-secondary education system, even with its flaws, is vastly superior to our K–12 educational system. In post-secondary education, we have a vibrant private and public sector. Students may use student aid at public or private institutions, indeed, even at sectarian institutions, which are free to be as sectarian as they like. The resulting competition has made our post-secondary system of education by far the greatest in the world. Students from every nation flock to our colleges and universities. By contrast, 89 percent of our nation's K–12 students are in government schools, and the system as a whole is appallingly bad. The status quo is not likely to change if the massive resources we invest in K–12 education are not made transportable between the public and private sectors, with control placed in the hands of consumers.

Moreover, we cannot be certain that the increased regulations we have witnessed in the post-secondary setting will be replicated in the K–12 arena. A number of safeguards do exist to help resist regulation. Drawing from the post-secondary experience, school choice programs can create "firewalls" against regulation; indeed, they can give private schools greater protections against excessive regulation than now exist. Further, the federal Establishment Clause itself protects against "excessive entanglement" between the government and religious schools.

And as a matter of economics, whereas few college students can afford to attend school without financial assistance, a substantial (yet all-too-small) number demonstrably can do so at the K–12 level. There always will be a significant number of private schools that will not participate in voucher programs. After all, school choice means choice for schools, too. In Florida, for instance, many evangelical Christian schools have chosen not to participate in the opportunity scholarship program, while many Catholic schools have chosen to do so. It all comes down to the school's mission. If a school wants to serve as many children as possible or children of modest economic means, it makes sense to accept vouchers. If it wants to maintain a distinctive focus or student population, it may make sense not to accept vouchers. Part of the problem with the anti-voucher position is that it deprives schools of making the choice about what is in their best interest, and tends to prop up the status quo.

Finally, experience demonstrates that school choice has fomented as much of a demand to *deregulate* government schools as to regulate private schools, and so far that phenomenon has prevailed. Ultimately, the consequence of school choice unquestionably is to expand freedom. In Milwaukee, for instance, we see a substantially larger private educational sector *and* a substantially deregulated public school sector, with a proliferation of charter schools as well as more autonomous regular public schools. The marketplace now is dynamic and focused on consumer satisfaction, rather than on the dictates of politicians and the demands of special-interest groups.

As school choice grows, we will see the stark dichotomy between public and private schools (weighted heavily in favor of public schools) diminished in favor of a continuum that includes ordinary public schools, deregulated charter schools (many of which are private nonprofit or for-profit enterprises), lightly regulated voucher-redeeming schools, and unregulated nonvoucher-redeeming private schools (some of whose students may be aided by tax credits). The percentage of students in ordinary public schools will decrease and, with luck, the regulation of those schools will decrease as well. In sum, we will have a true educational marketplace, oriented toward the specific needs and talents of individual students rather than one-size-fits-all. And it will be an environment that is markedly freer and more competitive than the one we have now.

And if that is not enough, just look at who supports school choice and who opposes it. If I see Milton Friedman on one side of an issue and Sandra Feldman on the other, it's pretty obvious which side I belong on. The unions are not kidding when they invest what passes for their heart and soul into resisting school choice. If school choice is really a plot to subvert private schools, it is a curious one. Yes, strings on private schools are a real threat, but we can nonetheless demonstrate with proven experience that school choice is a catalyst for freedom.

So in which direction should we go, school vouchers or tax credits? I still believe it is too early in the movement's history to choose either one to the exclusion of the other. Until school choice is so accepted that we can win at the ballot box, I believe we cannot afford the luxury of opposing anything that can move the effort forward.

It is true vouchers are more susceptible to regulation and legal challenge. But scholarship tax credits have vulnerabilities as well. Unlike vouchers, they are not targeted to specific student populations or school districts. As a result, their effect as an educational life preserver may not be as direct or immediate as vouchers. Existing tax credit programs are not limited exclusively, or even mainly, to low-income children. Whereas some tax credit organizations, such as the Arizona School Choice Trust, direct their efforts toward low-income children, others are focused on specific schools. As a result, wealthier parents sometimes benefit, which is fine if that is the program's purpose, but not if the goal is to assist low-income families to choose private schools. If the programs are truly intended to benefit economically disadvantaged children, they should provide tax credits for contributions to organizations that offer scholarships to low-income children. But even generalized tuition tax credit programs benefit most those at the economic margins for whom the credits may make the difference between government or private schools. Tax credits of any variety plainly expand choice, and they can be universal in scope or targeted to specific populations.

Indeed, with any kind of school choice that encompasses private options, the benefits outweigh the burdens. My colleagues and I have defended with equal tenacity school vouchers, tuition tax credits, and scholarship tax credits—and we hope to have many more opportunities to do so. We cannot afford to be anything other than supportive of efforts to expand parental choice.

Having said that, I think it is imperative to concentrate our energies on school choice for economically disadvantaged families. I support universal vouchers, and I believe that the benefits of such a

211

program would mostly accrue to the disadvantaged because poorer families have fewer options. But we should place our priorities where the need is greatest, and we have a moral imperative to do so. That is especially true given that public policy presently skews the system to the detriment of the poor who reside disproportionately in large urban centers where school systems are especially impervious to reform. Wealthier families, by contrast, receive income tax deductions for mortgage interest and property taxes, which provide an economic boost for people who move into affluent communities to avail themselves of good public schools.

Moreover, as we build beachheads for school choice, school choice in troubled inner-city school districts is politically most feasible. As Terry M. Moe points out in his sophisticated recent analysis of polling data, *Schools, Vouchers, and the American Public*[9]—a book so probative and insightful that it should provide a strategic roadmap for the school choice movement—the popular consensus is strongest for school choice targeted to economically disadvantaged families. As we have seen in Milwaukee, choice in urban centers can help build support for universal choice.

Though I counsel a small-step approach, ultimately I think the movement's successes have been limited not because they are ambitious but because they are not ambitious enough. Instead of presenting school choice as a distinct educational reform, we should encompass it within a broader discussion of educational funding and universal school choice. After all, it is only by extending school choice to a larger constituency that we can feel truly confident about preserving our gains and improving through market competition the overall quality of education.

Consider how clever the teachers unions are in the way they devise questions in polling surveys. In typical surveys asking opinions about school choice, a plurality or majority usually back the concept. But when the unions frame the question, they ask: Do you support increased support for public schools *or* a voucher program? Put that way, a large majority of respondents choose the former. And that is the same tactic that the unions use successfully to crush school choice initiatives.

[9] Brookings Institution, Washington, D.C., 2001.

It is a false dichotomy, of course, even if commitment to public schools is measured in terms of government subsidies. Florida has poured more than a billion new dollars into government schools at the same time as it has created a school choice program. And Wisconsin has substantially increased support for the Milwaukee Public Schools even as the school choice program has grown. But by supporting school vouchers or tax credits as programs separate and distinct from public education, we play into that rhetoric.

Again taking a page from Lisa Graham Keegan's playbook, we should pursue a broader agenda of student-based education funding. The idea begins with the premise that an equal amount of funding should follow every child (perhaps with funding supplements for children with special needs). The funding would follow every child to the school of the parents' choice. To take it a step further, the funding need not go to a school at all: it could be used for distance learning, or home schooling, or tutoring, or some combination of formal and informal schooling geared toward the individual student's needs.

Obviously, such a program would be, in a sense, a universal voucher program. But government schools, too, would receive their funding through parental choice. That would engender both a burden and benefit for government schools. A burden, because it would dry up the entitlement—and, of course, foment competition. A benefit, because the money would come through the student rather than through the central bureaucracy. The school then would decide how to spend it—and I suspect its priorities might not be the same as the central bureaucracy's. Indeed, it would mean a much larger share of public school funding spent in the classroom, probably with less of it spent on bureaucrat salaries and more on teacher salaries. School districts would become providers of specialized services rather than dictators of educational policy.

When I was in the Mariana Islands several years ago proselytizing (Did I say proselytizing? I mean providing counsel) for school choice, our group visited a small public school. We spent time with a beleaguered but dedicated teacher who was eager to share her opinions. I asked her if she supported vouchers, and she replied that she opposed them. Then I asked her if she would support a system in which students could choose public or private schools; but if they chose public schools, the schools would decide how the funds would be spent. Her eyes lit up and she pointed outside to some forlorn rusting playground equipment. "We could finally get some new supplies and equipment!" she exclaimed.

That conversation made me realize that perhaps we're fighting the right battle in the wrong venue. Student-based funding is not about private schools; it's about public education. It places an equal amount of funding behind every child. It frees public schools to compete on a level playing field. And it leaves no child behind— all while it expands educational freedom, especially for parents who lack it.

If we were starting a system of public education from scratch, surely it would not look like the bricks-and-mortar, top-down, homogeneous, bureaucratic system that we have today. Technology makes individualized instruction possible like never before. Instead of the nation's best teachers instructing 30 children, they can teach 3,000. At the same time, tried and true methods of teaching like phonics are making a comeback in public schools. We live in a society characterized by consumer choices—just about everywhere except in the most important service of all, elementary and secondary education. We should create institutions that adapt to technological advances and individual needs.

Thankfully, *Zelman* allows us to think in such exciting, expansive ways. The decision conjoins the two most important principles of educational jurisprudence: parental liberty and equal educational opportunities. In vindicating those principles, the realm of the possible now is constrained only by our imagination and our energy.

Let's hope they turn out to be boundless.

12. Lessons

When I started writing this book some months ago, I did not know how the Supreme Court case was going to turn out. Similarly, before the decision, I started accepting speaking engagements scheduled for after the decision. Some of them, happily, were contingent on a successful outcome. I remember one awkward invitation that went something like this: "Um, we're sort of assuming that you're going to win and were wondering, um, if you don't win, if you would mind, you know, not coming." I guess it's a good thing for my dance card that we won.

But painful as those speaking engagements—and writing this book—would have been if we had not prevailed, either way I felt it was important to get the message out. Everyone involved in the school choice movement over the past decade has learned a great deal. The movement has matured and blossomed immeasurably. Not only did we achieve a truly landmark Supreme Court victory, but we have also influenced the debate over, and the reality of, public education. There is no going back. Along the way, we all have learned valuable lessons not only for the school choice movement but also for the freedom movement generally. In these final few pages, I'll share some of them.

With regard to school choice, a threshold issue is that good things come in small packages. From the seed of a tiny program encompassing nine schools and fewer than a thousand students in one midwestern city, we now have a substantial number of privately and publicly funded school choice programs, with tens of thousands of students receiving a high-quality education in schools chosen by their parents.

Though I would love to see nationwide, or statewide, choice programs, in any particular venue it is more important to get *something* going than to await the ideal. The unions understood that when they threw all of the resources at their disposal to defeating the Milwaukee school choice program in its infancy. They understood that if unchecked, the program would succeed and that it would grow. And it has. When one considers the baseline of inner-city public schooling, it is all but impossible for a choice program not to succeed by comparison.

Ultimately we want programs that are large and concentrated enough to influence behavior in the government schools. But initially, even a small program—publicly or privately funded—begins to introduce inner-city parents to a previously unknown concept, and thereby to create a constituency for a larger program. Moreover, any functioning program, no matter how small, will begin the process of replacing a debate about hypotheticals with a debate about realities. The more the debate shifts from the former to the latter, the better off we are. When we can show that competition *helps* public schools, and that the families are choosing good schools rather than witchcraft schools, we can begin to debunk conventional mythology purveyed by our adversaries and win over skeptics. In Milwaukee, for instance, public opinion polls show that support for the program is strongest the closer one is to the program. Now, not only do inner-city parents support school choice but suburban parents do as well.

Program design should reflect the realm of the possible in the local community. In some places, vouchers are viable; in others, tax credits are. Indeed, in some states, it is still even difficult to get charter schools up and running. We constantly have to push the envelope, recognizing however that there is no proper top-down, one-size-fits-all approach. We all need to render assistance to our allies, even if progress is measured in inches.

Still, design is important. We must design programs that will *succeed*—and target resources to make sure that they do. That means not relying on the government to provide information to parents about their choices. That means making sure that the schools and parents are organized and that problems such as transportation are factored into the equation. And that means helping to ensure that the supply of private-sector schools will keep pace with demand. A substantial portion of school choice philanthropy now is being devoted to the infrastructure requirements of successful school choice programs, again reflecting the movement's growing sophistication.

We should take care not to promise more than we can deliver. We now know that school choice programs do not skim the cream, as our detractors like to say. Instead, not surprisingly, school choice programs usually attract children who are experiencing academic or disciplinary problems in government schools. Many such children are on a downward trajectory. Even arresting that trajectory reflects tangible progress, but it won't show up right away in improved test scores. Academic research by Harvard's Paul Peterson and others fairly consistently shows that academic gains are slight in the first year or two of a school choice program, and begin to accelerate afterward. I am very excited about the prospect of longitudinal studies, showing where choice students end up (even if they return to government schools for part of their schooling). I am certain that the foundation of basic skills, coupled with higher expectations, that they obtain in private schools will manifest in much higher high school graduation and college enrollment rates. If that happens, regardless of relative test scores, the debate over the efficacy of school choice will be over. To the extent that we also can demonstrate the beneficial effects of competition on public school performance— and the early research by Caroline Hoxby and Jay Greene is extremely hopeful—we will have pointed the way to systemic public education reform.

Another lesson we have learned is that the cause takes perspicacity and stamina. When I consider how many times we lost court decisions over the past 12 years, I realize we were able to endure only because we recognized that the ultimate decision was still yet to come. As difficult an ordeal as that was, it's important to keep it in perspective. When I think of others like Milton Friedman and Martin and Mae Duggan who have been at this longer than I've been alive, it makes those 12 years seem like a momentary blip. And when we consider how far we have yet to go and that the education establishment is going to fight us every inch of the way, it is truly daunting. We need to pace ourselves for the long haul, and buck each other up. But the prize is worth it.

Finally, we have achieved much with our ecumenical spirit. School choice is coalition politics at its best. The movement elicits support from both ends of the ideological spectrum and every place in between. It needs to. We're up against some very powerful folks. A lot of work remains to be done on multiple fronts, and we need to welcome and encourage all people of good will to our ranks.

The freedom movement generally has much to learn from the school choice movement. For those of us who consider ourselves

217

libertarians, the school choice movement is a textbook example of effectively reducing the scope and power of government.

It begins with setting priorities. If our goal is to expand freedom, it seems to me that our principal priority should be making common cause with those in our society who are least free. Typically, that encompasses disproportionately the poor and members of minority groups. Low-income people in the inner cities, in particular, are isolated by misguided government policies from basic opportunities most of us take for granted: the chance to walk down safe streets, to send our children to good schools, to start a business or pursue a chosen livelihood, to own and enjoy property. As Americans, none of us are truly free so long as any among us is not free. We should focus our energies on helping secure for all Americans the liberties that are their birthright.

This is not only a moral imperative but also a practical one. As the school choice movement demonstrates, there is enormous potential to change the world through nontraditional alliances. We need to bypass self-anointed leadership elites and work directly with the people and communities that are our natural allies. As I recounted in my last book, *Transformation*, "empowerment" policies are mutually reinforcing. Once we make common cause on an issue like school choice, other pieces of the puzzle, such as economic liberty and private property rights, seem to follow logically. We can expand the constituency for freedom by helping give more people a tangible stake in freedom. That is one of the things that most excites me about the potential for school choice.

That point dovetails with the need to humanize the freedom philosophy. Too often we ignore the human dimension of our philosophical arguments, making the freedom philosophy antiseptic. We need to remember that behind every principle is a human consequence. For those of us who are fighting to expand freedom, we should embrace the ennobling human dimension of our cause. The school choice movement has been effective precisely because we are not just fighting for a principle—we are fighting for kids.

Likewise, we must deploy not only words but also actions and concentrate not on abstract utopias but on expanding freedom as far as we can through principled pragmatism. Too often we spend our time arguing fine points of philosophical esoterica into the wee hours, and some of us tend to focus on philosophical differences

218

that divide us from others rather than on common denominators that might give rise to common cause. That too can make our philosophy unappealing. Given that our goal is to give people greater control over their destinies, we should never cede either the moral high ground or the opportunity to put a human, compassionate face on our philosophy.

And beyond all, we need to get on with it. It seems to me that the one obligation we all share as Americans is to leave a nation that is at least as free as the one we inherited. We've got to make up for lost time. And freeing up our nation's educational system is a great place to start. The kids don't have any time to waste. We've got to get going. Today. This minute.

Those of us who have managed to gain admittance to the legal cartel are often accused (usually rightly) of speaking Latin to justify exorbitant fees. To this lawyer, there are only two Latin words that matter: carpe diem. Seize the day.

The future is ours to chart. Let ours be the generation in which our nation finally, at long last, lives up to its sacred vow of equal educational opportunities for every child.

Appendix

Brief of the Institute for Justice in *Taylor v. Simmons-Harris,* one of three cases consolidated and reported as *Zelman v. Simmons-Harris,* June 27, 2002.

No. 00-1779

In The

Supreme Court of the United States
♦

SENEL TAYLOR, *et al.*,
Petitioners,

v.

DORIS SIMMONS-HARRIS, *et al.*,
Respondents.

♦

**On Writ Of Certiorari To The
United States Court Of Appeals
For The Sixth Circuit**

♦

BRIEF ON THE MERITS

♦

CHARLES FRIED
1545 Massachusetts Avenue
Cambridge, MA 02138
Of Counsel

INSTITUTE FOR JUSTICE
CLINT BOLICK*
WILLIAM H. MELLOR
RICHARD D. KOMER
ROBERT FREEDMAN
1717 Pennsylvania Ave.,
NW, Suite 200
Washington, DC 20006
(202) 955-1300

* Counsel of Record

PORTER, WRIGHT, MORRIS &
ARTHUR, L.L.P.
DAVID TRYON
1700 Huntington Building
925 Euclid Avenue
Cleveland, OH 44114
(216) 443-2560

Counsel for Petitioners

QUESTION PRESENTED

Does a program designed to rescue economically disadvantaged children from a failing public school system by providing scholarships that they may use in private, religious, or suburban public schools that choose to participate in the program—and which operates in the context of a broad array of public school choices—violate the First Amendment because in the early stages of the program most of the schools that have agreed to take on scholarship students are religiously affiliated?

PARTIES TO THE PROCEEDINGS

Petitioners are Senel Taylor, on his own behalf and as natural guardian of his daughter Saletta Taylor, Johnietta McGrady, on her own behalf and as natural guardian of her children Trinnietta and Atlas McGrady, Christine Suma, on her own behalf and as natural guardian of her children Dominic, Gloria, Emeric and Emily Suma, Arkela Winston, on her own behalf and as natural guardian of her children, Tanashia and Devonte Winston, and Amy Hudock, on her own behalf and as natural guardian of her daughter, Amber Lee Angelo.[1]

The State petitioners are Dr. Susan Tave Zelman, in her official capacity as Superintendent of Public Instruction for the State of Ohio, the State of Ohio, and Saundra Berry, in her official capacity as Director of the Cleveland Scholarship and Tutoring Program.

Additional petitioners are Hanna Perkins School, Ivy Chambers, Carol Lambert, Our Lady of Peace School, Westpark Lutheran Association, Inc., Lutheran Memorial Association of Cleveland, and Deloris Jones.

Respondents are Doris Simmons-Harris, Marla Franklin, Rev. Steven Behr, Sue Gatton, Mary Murphy, Rev. Michael DuBose, Cheryl DuBose, Glenn Altschuld, and Deidra Peterson.

---

[1]None of the petitioners are corporations, and have no parent companies or subsidiaries.

TABLE OF CONTENTS

OPINIONS BELOW

The opinion of the court of appeals is reported at 234 F.3d 945 (6th Cir. 2000) (Pet. App. at A.1). The decision of the district court is reported at 72 F. Supp. 834 (N.D. Ohio 1999) (Pet. App. at A.65).

———————— ◆ ————————

JURISDICTION

The court of appeals entered judgment on December 11, 2000 (Pet. App. at A.1). The court of appeals denied the petitions for rehearing and rehearing en banc on February 28, 2001 (Pet. App. at A.150). The jurisdiction of this Court is proper under 28 U.S.C. § 1254(1).

———————— ◆ ————————

CONSTITUTIONAL AND STATUTORY PROVISIONS

The First Amendment to the United States Constitution provides, "Congress shall make no law respecting an establishment of religion, or prohibiting the free exercise thereof. . . ."

The Cleveland Pilot Scholarship Program is codified at Ohio Rev. Code §§ 3313.974–3313.979 (reprinted in full in Pet. App. at A.152).

———————— ◆ ————————

STATEMENT OF THE CASE

A. Statement of Facts. Petitioners are five parents of children who are participating in the challenged Cleveland Pilot Project Scholarship Program, Ohio Rev. Code §§ 3313.974–3313.979 (J.A. 21a–40a). They intervened as defendants in this action, on their own behalf and on behalf of their minor children, to safeguard their children's precious educational opportunities.

The scholarship program was enacted in 1995 in response to an unprecedented crisis in the Cleveland City Public Schools (CCSD). A combination of paralyzing administrative mismanagement and abysmal educational quality led the U.S. District Court for the Northern District of Ohio, in the context of an ongoing desegregation lawsuit, to transfer control of CCSD to the State of Ohio. *Reed v. Rhodes*, slip op., No. 1:73 CV 1300 (N.D. Ohio, Mar. 3, 1995). The following year, the court commended the State for taking swift, aggressive, multifaceted action to "alleviate the emergency" in CCSD, *Reed v. Rhodes*, 934 F. Supp. 1533, 1539 (N.D. Ohio 1996), such as reorganization, a financial infusion, and providing "choices to each child which will include the opportunity to attend schools and programs of the family's selection." *Id.* at 1557.

One of the choice programs created by the State was the Cleveland Pilot Scholarship Program. Enacted in the 1995 State budget and made operational in the 1996–97 school year, the program embodies two components: (1) it expanded the pre-existing range of educational options for Cleveland schoolchildren to now include private and suburban public schools that opt to participate in the program; and (2) it created a tutorial assistance program for students remaining in CCSD.

Under the parental choice component, students may receive scholarships of either 75 or 90 percent of tuition (depending on family income) to attend the participating private schools of their parents' choice. The scholarships are capped at $2,500 (of which a maximum of $2,250 is provided by the State) or the price of tuition, whichever is less. Participating private schools may not charge more than $2,500 for tuition. Participating suburban public schools would receive the scholarship amount plus the "average daily membership" expenditure under State law (approximately $4,294 per student), for a total of about $6,544. Ohio Rev. Code §§ 3317.03(I)(1), 3327.06, 3317.08(A)(1). The program began with students in grades K–3, expanding one grade each year through eighth grade. If more children apply for the program each year than there are spaces, as routinely occurs, they are chosen by lottery with a preference for economically disadvantaged children and a ceiling on the percentage of children who were already enrolled in private schools. Participating schools also must choose students on a random selection basis. Checks are made payable to the parents and disbursed to them at the schools they designate. *Simmons-Harris v. Zelman*, 72 F. Supp.2d 834, 836 (N.D. Ohio 1999).

The program's second component provides an equal number of tutorial assistance grants for students remaining in CCSD. These grants are capped at $500 and may be used to obtain additional academic assistance outside regular school hours.

In the 1999–2000 school year, 3,761 students received scholarships under the program. No suburban public schools have elected to accept CCSD students under the program. However, in the same school year, 46 religious and ten nonsectarian private schools volunteered to enroll students using scholarships. Of the students in the program that year, 96 percent enrolled in religiously affiliated schools. *Id.* at 837. The program is only one of multiple school choice options available to CCSD students, including magnet schools and community (charter) schools. In 1999–2000, 16,184 Cleveland students were enrolled in magnet schools and 2,087 were enrolled in community (charter) schools. See Jay P. Greene, *The Racial, Economic, and Religious Context of Parental Choice in Cleveland* (1999) (J.A. 217a–18a).

B. Statement of the Case. This litigation was commenced in 1996 in state court, raising the First Amendment claim at issue here along with state claims. The Ohio Supreme Court struck down the program on the grounds of a subsequently corrected defect in the manner of its legislative enactment, but upheld it against the First Amendment challenge. *Simmons-Harris v. Goff*, 711 N.E.2d 203 (Ohio 1999). Subsequently, the plaintiffs filed the First Amendment challenge anew in federal court. In August 1999, just hours before the start of the program's fourth year, the U.S. District Court for the Northern District of Ohio enjoined the program. Four days later, the court stayed most of its own injunction. In November 1999, this Court stayed the remainder of the injunction pending disposition of the case. *Zelman v. Simmons-Harris*, 528 U.S. 983 (1999). The district court subsequently struck down the program on cross-motions for summary judgment. *Simmons-Harris v. Zelman, supra.* A panel of the U.S. Court of Appeals affirmed the ruling over a dissent by Judge James Ryan. *Simmons-Harris v. Zelman*, 234 F.3d 945 (6th Cir. 2000). After denying a motion for rehearing *en banc*, the Sixth Circuit granted motions to stay the mandate pending disposition in this Court.

Aside from a four-day period in the fall of 1999, the Cleveland Pilot Project Scholarship Program has been continuously operational since the 1996–97 school year, and now is in its sixth year of operation.

———— ♦ ————

SUMMARY OF ARGUMENT

Forty-seven years ago, in *Brown v. Board of Education*, 347 U.S. 483 (1954), this Court set forth a sacred promise of equal educational opportunities for all American schoolchildren. Since that ruling, we have traveled a long and often-painful distance. Along the way, the promise has become reality for many. But for others, especially minority schoolchildren mired in many of our nation's worst urban school systems, that promise has been an illusion.

The respondents have made known their theory of the case and their disdain for the scholarship program from the earliest days of the state court case, when they contended that the parents are "inconsequential conduits" in the transmission of funds to religious schools. Reply Br. of Plaintiffs' Sue Gatton, et al. in *Gatton v. Goff*, No. 96 CVH 01-01093 (Ohio Ct. of Common Pleas, Franklin County) at 17. Respondents have it exactly backward: as a result of this program, for the first time the parents are *not* inconsequential with respect to the education of their children. Like parents of greater affluence, they have the power to choose good schools for their children now.

This program is part of a rescue plan for children in one of the worst urban school systems in the country. It enlists an array of schools—suburban public schools, private nonsectarian schools, and religious private schools—to educate several thousand economically disadvantaged schoolchildren. That the schools answering the rescue call were mainly religious provides the basis for much of the courts' finding below that the program establishes religion—a truly anomalous decision staking a statute's constitutionality on the independent choices made by private third parties.

In reality, when it designed the Cleveland Pilot Project Scholarship Program, the State and its advisors had available to them this Court's carefully articulated establishment clause guidelines with respect to aid programs in which beneficiaries may choose religious providers.[2] Specifically, the Court has instructed that such aid is permissible so

---

[2] As Judge Ryan observed in his dissent, *Simmons-Harris v. Zelman*, 234 F.3d at 967 (Ryan, J.) (emphasis in original):

> We may safely assume that in fashioning the new law, the Ohio legislators and the governor knew that the challenge they faced was to design a law that would survive a federal constitutional challenge on Establishment Clause grounds. That is not to say that the statute the legislators wrote and the governor signed into law is insulated from federal judicial constitutional scrutiny. Rather, it is to say what the majority does not even acknowledge: this statute is *presumed* to be constitutional. [Citations omitted.] This presumption is not a mere literary figure for rote recitation in all appellate opinions addressing the constitutionality of legislative enactments; it is a bedrock rule of statutory construction, one we are bound assiduously to honor as we begin our assessment of the validity of the Ohio statute.

long as (1) the program includes religious entities among a broader range of choices and (2) the choice of where to expend funds is made independently by third parties. See *Mueller v. Allen*, 463 U.S. 388 (1983); *Witters v. Wash. Dep't of Services for the Blind*, 474 U.S. 481 (1986); *Zobrest v. Catalina Foothills School Dist.*, 509 U.S. 1 (1993); *Rosenberger v. Rector & Visitors of Univ. of Va.*, 515 U.S. 819 (1995). The State applied those teachings in good faith to develop a program whose primary effect is not to advance religion but to expand educational opportunities.

Petitioners do not ask this Court to endorse parental choice as a matter of public policy, nor would it be proper for the Court to do so. Rather, we ask this Court to find that the program fits well within the boundaries of neutrality and true private-choice set forth in this Court's establishment clause jurisprudence.[3] See, e.g., *Mitchell v. Helms*, 530 U.S. 793, 842 (2000) (O'Connor, J., concurring in the judgment). In doing so, the Court will affirm good-faith efforts directed toward the constitutional imperative of extending educational opportunities to children who need them desperately.

———— ♦ ————

ARGUMENT

I. THE COURT SHOULD ASSESS THIS PROGRAM NOT IN A VACUUM BUT IN LIGHT OF OUR RICH CONSTITUTIONAL TRADITION THAT ACCORDS GREAT WEIGHT TO PARENTAL AUTONOMY, EQUAL EDUCATIONAL OPPORTUNITIES, FEDERALISM, AND RELIGIOUS LIBERTY.

In any lawsuit, the plaintiffs enjoy a certain logistical advantage in initially framing the terms of the debate. For the respondents here, the establishment clause is the beginning and the end of the

---

[3]See, e.g., Michael W. McConnell, "Governments, Families, and Power: A Defense of Educational Choice," 31 *Conn. L. Rev.* 847 (1999); Catherine L. Crisham, "The Writing Is on the Wall of Separation: Why the Supreme Court Should and Will Uphold Full-Choice School Voucher Programs," 89 *Geo. L.J.* 225 (2000); Jason T. Vail, "School Vouchers and the Establishment Clause: Is the First Amendment a Barrier to Improving Education for Low-Income Children?" 35 *Gonz. L. Rev.* 187 (2000); Nicole Stelle Garnett and Richard W. Garnett, "School Choice, the First Amendment, and Social Justice," 4 *Tex. Rev. of L. & Politics* 301 (2000); Andrew A. Adams, "Cleveland, School Choice, and Laws Respecting an Establishment of Religion," 2 *Tex. Rev. of L. & Politics* 166 (1997).

analytical construct—and we are more than happy to engage in that debate. But it would be a mistake for this Court to decide this case bereft of other vital constitutional principles that this program implicates directly. We briefly discuss below four background principles that should help inform this Court's deliberations.

1. At its core, the Cleveland Pilot Project Scholarship Program effects a transfer of power over one of the most basic decisions in a child's education—the decision about which school a child will attend—from State officials to parents.[4]

Far from representing some radical departure, the program harmonizes with our rich constitutional tradition that recognizes the central role of parents in the educational upbringing of their children. See, e.g., *Meyer v. Nebraska*, 262 U.S. 390 (1923); *Farrington v. Tokushige*, 273 U.S. 284 (1927); *Wisconsin v. Yoder*, 406 U.S. 205 (1972); *Troxel v. Granville*, 530 U.S. 57 (2000). As the Court declared in *Pierce v. Society of Sisters*, 268 U.S. 510, 535 (1925),

> The fundamental theory of liberty upon which all governments in this Union repose excludes any general power of the State to standardize its children by forcing them to accept instruction from public teachers only. The child is not the mere creature of the State; those who nurture him and direct his destiny have the right, coupled with the high duty, to recognize and prepare him for additional obligations.

Quite apart from the thrust of the *Pierce* line of cases with regard to limiting state power, surely it is *permissible*, even laudatory, for the State to promote the "fundamental rights of the individual" by allowing parents "fair opportunity to procure for their children instruction which they think important. . . ." *Farrington*, 273 U.S. at 298–299.

---

[4]Parents with sufficient economic means already possess such power. If they are dissatisfied with their children's public schools, they either can send them to private schools or move into communities that have better public schools (with mortgages and property taxes that qualify for federal tax deductions). Indeed, over half of U.S. families with incomes above $60,000 report that they chose their neighborhood at least in part due to the quality of the public schools. Moe, *Schools, Vouchers, and the American Public* (2001) at 81. By contrast, it is beyond dispute that the vast majority of families in this program lack the essential attributes of school choice that many wealthier families enjoy. See, e.g., Greene (J.A. 215a) (average family income of scholarship recipients is $15,769); Affidavit of Senel Taylor, ¶ 8 (J.A. 174a) (parent could not afford to send his child to private school without scholarship).

2. Equality of educational opportunity is one of our most basic and essential civil rights. This Court declared in *Brown*, 347 U.S. at 493, that education, "where the state has undertaken to provide it, is a right which must be made available to all on equal terms." Indeed, "[t]he provision of education is one of the most important tasks performed by government: it ranks at the very apex of the function of a State." *Rendell-Baker v. Kohn*, 457 U.S. 830, 848 (1982). Private schools may be enlisted to fulfill the mandate of educational opportunity. This Court has recognized in the context of the federal Individuals with Disabilities Education Act that where the public schools have defaulted on the obligation to provide a free appropriate education, students are entitled to obtain such education in private schools at public expense. *School Comm. of Burlington v. Dep't of Educ. of Mass.*, 471 U.S. 359 (1985).[5] Likewise, parental choice programs can operate as "a life preserver to ... children caught in the cruel riptide of a school system floundering upon the shoals of poverty, status-quo thinking, and despair." *Davis v. Grover*, 480 N.W.2d 460, 477 (Wis. 1992) (Ceci, J., concurring) (describing the Milwaukee Parental Choice Program).

Despite federal court intervention and the expenditure of billions of dollars, the goal of equalizing educational opportunities and boosting student achievement has been an elusive one. See, e.g., *Missouri v. Jenkins*, 515 U.S. 70 (1995). Again, if equal educational opportunity is a constitutional imperative, a State's efforts to promote such goals ought to merit substantial judicial deference.

3. "Courts and commentators have recognized that the 50 States serve as laboratories for the development of new social, economic, and political ideas. This state innovation is no judicial myth." *FERC v. Mississippi*, 456 U.S. 742, 788 (1982) (O'Connor, J., concurring in the judgment in part and dissenting in part); accord, *New State Ice Co. v. Liebmann*, 285 U.S. 262, 311 (1932) (Brandeis, J., dissenting). As Justice Powell observed in *San Antonio Indep. Sch. Dist. v. Rodriguez*, 411 U.S. 1, 50 (1973), "No area of social concern stands to profit more from a multiplicity of viewpoints and from a diversity of

[5]Such a parentally directed private placement may be made in a religious school without violating the establishment clause. *Christen G. v. Lower Merion Sch. Dist.*, 919 F. Supp. 793 (E.D. Pa. 1996); *Matthew J. v. Mass. Dep't of Educ.*, 989 F. Supp. 380 (D. Mass. 1998).

approaches than does public education." In particular, "[e]ach locality is free to tailor local programs to local needs. Pluralism also affords some opportunity for experimentation, innovation, and a healthy competition for educational excellence." *Id.*

The proliferation of parental choice programs reflects federalism at its best.[6] Most states now provide parents with some choice of schools for their children, whether through open enrollment, magnet schools, charter schools,[7] private school scholarships, or a combination of those means.[8] Moffit, et al., *School Choice 2001: What's Happening in the States* (Heritage Foundation, 2001). Those policy experiments have yielded abundant data on the efficacy of choice. See, e.g., Peterson & Hassel, eds., *Learning from School Choice* (1998); Paul E. Peterson, "School Choice: A Report Card," 6 *Va. J. Soc. Pol'y & L.* 47 (1998).

Several states provide public assistance for parents choosing private schools, employing a wide variety of means. See *Mueller, supra* (upholding Minnesota's tuition tax deductions). Like Ohio, Wisconsin provides tuition vouchers for economically disadvantaged children in its largest city to choose private schools.[9] Wis. Stat. § 119.23. Florida provides opportunity scholarships for children in failing public schools to use in private or better-performing public schools. Fla. Stat. § 229.0537. For more than a century, Maine and Vermont

---

[6]Though school choice for people of modest economic means is a fairly recent phenomenon at the K–12 level of U.S. education, it is of course ubiquitous at the post-secondary level. Programs such as the G.I. Bill, Pell Grants, and student loans at the federal level, and similar student grant and loan programs operated by the states, typically allow students to apply public assistance at public, private, or religious institutions. Indeed, this Court unanimously approved the use of public funds for a blind student to study for the ministry at a school of divinity. *Witters, supra.*

[7]Charter schools are semi-autonomous publicly funded schools. In Ohio, they are called community schools. Community schools may be operated by private entities. They must be nonsectarian and tuition-free. Affidavit of Steven M. Puckett, ¶ 3 (J.A. 158a).

[8]With the increasing range of public school options, Catholic school enrollment has actually decreased, while the numbers of children attending schools of choice has increased substantially. Between 1965–90, enrollment in Catholic schools nationwide decreased by 50 percent. Affidavit of Joseph Viteritti, ¶ 11 (6th Cir. J.A. 01310). Today, 11 percent of all American schoolchildren attend private schools, while 13 percent attend public schools of choice. Affidavit of Paul Peterson at 251 (J.A. 87a).

[9]The Milwaukee Parental Choice Program was upheld against a First Amendment challenge in *Jackson v. Benson*, 578 N.W.2d 602 (Wis.), *cert. denied*, 525 U.S. 997 (1998).

have paid private or public school tuition for children in towns that do not have their own public schools.[10] 16 Vt. Stat. Ann. § 822; 20-A Me. Rev. St. Ann. § 5204(4). Illinois provides income tax credits for public and private school tuition. 35 Ill. St. Ch. 35 § 5/201(m). Arizona, Florida, and Pennsylvania all provide individual or corporate tax credits for contributions to private school tuition scholarship organizations.[11] Ariz. Rev. Stat. § 43-1089; 2001 Fla. Laws ch. 225; 2001 Pa. Laws 4. Florida provides scholarships for children with disabilities who opt out of their public school placements. 2001 Fla. Laws ch. 82.

This case obviously has serious ramifications for education reform all across America. In our federalist system, the State of Ohio's good-faith efforts to expand educational opportunities through parental choice merit this Court's deference.

4. This Court has defined the establishment clause standard for aid programs as encompassing the central requirement that "its principal or primary effect must be one that neither advances nor inhibits religion. . . ." *Lemon v. Kurtzman*, 403 U.S. 602, 612–13 (1971). The inclusion of the words "or inhibits" indicates that the Court intended to recognize a species of establishment clause violation occasioned by state action that inhibits religion. Surely this arises from the Court's sensitivity to the fact that the establishment clause is not the only clause in the First Amendment that speaks to religion; it is followed by a command that the State shall not impair the free exercise of religion.

Accordingly, this Court has charted a course of neutrality. As this Court stated in *Rosenberger*, 515 U.S. at 839, "A central lesson of our decisions is that a significant factor in upholding governmental programs in the face of Establishment Clause attack is their neutrality toward religion." Indeed, upon finding no establishment clause violation in the funding of a religious publication by student fees, the Court found that the exclusion of the publication violated the free-speech clause of the First Amendment. *Id.* at 834–36. The Court has invalidated state action that discriminates against religion. See, e.g.,

---

[10] The Vermont tuitioning program was upheld against a First Amendment challenge in *Campbell v. Manchester Bd. of Sch. Directors*, 641 A.2d 352 (Vt. 1994).

[11] The Arizona tax credit was sustained against a First Amendment challenge in *Kotterman v. Killian*, 972 P.2d 606 (Ariz.), *cert. denied*, 528 U.S. 921 (1999).

Good News Club v. Milford Central Sch., 121 S.Ct. 2093 (2001); *Lamb's Chapel v. Center Moriches Union Free Sch. Dist.*, 508 U.S. 384 (1993); *Bd. of Educ. of Westside Comm. Schools v. Mergens*, 496 U.S. 226 (1990); *Widmar v. Vincent*, 454 U.S. 263 (1981).

Were religious schools not allowed to participate here, we would be left with parental choice programs in Cleveland that include private schools but single religious schools out for exclusion.[12] The primary effect of such an outcome would discriminate against religion. Although the First Amendment does not create an affirmative obligation on the part of the State to create parental choice options that include public, private, and religious schools, surely it follows from the command of neutrality that it is constitutionally *permissible*—even prudent—to do exactly that. That is precisely the course of neutrality the State has charted in designing this program (see Parts II-4 and III, *infra*).

Given that the Pilot Project Scholarship Program accords with the fundamental constitutional principles of parental autonomy, equal educational opportunities, federalism, and religious liberty, respondents ought to face a mighty burden in seeking to invalidate it on establishment clause grounds.

II. THE PRIMARY EFFECT OF THE SCHOLARSHIP PROGRAM IS TO EXPAND EDUCATIONAL OPPORTUNITIES.

All parties agree that the main legal question is the scholarship program's "primary effect."[13] The courts below found the outcome dictated by *Committee for Public Education v. Nyquist*, 413 U.S. 756 (1973), and distinguished away nearly three decades of intervening

---

[12]Respondents have no remaining claim against a scholarship program encompassing nonsectarian private schools. Likewise, in Ohio, nonsectarian private schools may qualify for community school status, entitling them to direct public funding. Ohio Rev. Code 3314.01, *et seq.*

[13]Respondents do not seriously contend that the program lacks a secular purpose or creates an excessive entanglement between the State and religion. See *Lemon, supra*. As Judge Ryan stated, *Simmons-Harris v. Zelman*, 234 F.3d at 967–68 (Ryan, J.),

> The *sole* purpose of the voucher program is to save Cleveland's mostly poor, mostly minority, public school children from the devastating consequences of requiring them to remain in the failed Cleveland schools, if they wish to escape. There is also no serious claim that the statute is constitutionally invalid solely because it fosters an "excessive entanglement" between government and religion.

establishment clause precedents.[14] Yet, Justice Powell, the author of *Nyquist*, admonished that the proper analytical framework is "the nature and consequences of the program *viewed as a whole.*" *Witters*, 474 U.S. at 492 (Powell, J., concurring) (emphasis in original).[15]

In this section, we examine the markedly different contexts in which the programs in *Nyquist* and the current program were adopted. To put it simply, in *Nyquist*, religious schools were the *ends*, while here religious schools are part of the *means* toward the goal of broadening educational opportunities. As a consequence, a secular primary effect is manifest.[16]

1. Respondents' extreme position that no public funds may be used in religious schools is curious not only in light of this Court's precedents over the past two decades, but in light of history. Early American education took place mainly in private and religious schools, often with direct public support. See Viteritti, *Choosing Equality: School Choice, the Constitution, and Civil Society* (1999) at 147. Indeed, Ohio's Constitution, which derived from the Northwest Ordinance, provides an affirmative constitutional mandate in that

---

[14] That is true despite the fact that this Court has observed that "our Establishment Clause law has 'significantly changed'" over the past two decades, *Agostini v. Felton*, 521 U.S. 203, 237 (1997); specifically, "our understanding of the criteria used to assess whether aid to religion has an impermissible effect." *Id.* at 223. For the reasons set forth in Parts II and III, we believe that the program comports with the criteria set forth in *Nyquist*. However, to the extent that *Nyquist* conflicts with the more recent teachings of this Court, we urge the Court to reconsider and overrule *Nyquist*.

[15] Although *Witters* was unanimous, it is significant that a majority of justices either joined Justice Powell's concurring opinion (*id.* at 490) or attached themselves to its underlying reasoning. *Id.* at 490 (White, J., concurring); *id.* at 493 (O'Connor, J., concurring).

[16] That this program is about education, not religion, is nowhere more evident than in the identities of the prime movers behind this litigation, the National Education Association (*Simmons-Harris* respondents) and American Federation of Teachers (*Gatton* respondents). A perusal of their websites (www.nea.org and www.aft.org) contains plenty of anti-parental choice propaganda from an education policy perspective, but sparse mention of the issue from a First Amendment standpoint. After all, the purpose of unions is to advance their members' interests, not to vindicate First Amendment establishment clause concerns. As education researcher Terry M. Moe explains, "There is a lot at stake. The current education system spends more than $300 billion annually, provides millions of jobs, and is a motherlode of power for the public officials, administrators, and unions that are the established players in its operation. Vouchers threaten all this." Moe at 26. See also Lieberman, *The Teacher Unions* (1997).

regard: "Religion, morality and knowledge, however, being essential to good government, it shall be the duty of the general assembly ... to encourage schools and the means of instruction." Ohio Const. Art. I, sec. 7.

In the middle of the 19th Century, the idea of the common school took hold widely. Religious disputes arose because the public schools often expressly promoted Protestant teachings. Viteritti at 147–51. Resistance among Catholic immigrants, who developed their own private schools, prompted an anti-Catholic backlash among those who believed that all children should be subject to the dominant Protestant common school teachings. That backlash manifested itself in a proposed constitutional amendment sponsored by Sen. James G. Blaine to forbid public support for religious schools. The amendment was defeated in Congress, but subsequently was adopted in many state constitutions.[17] *Id.* at 151–56; see also *Mitchell*, 530 U.S. at 828 (plurality) ("a shameful pedigree that we do not hesitate to disavow"); Toby J. Heytens, "School Choice and State Constitutions," 86 *Va. L. Rev.* 117, 131–141 (2000); Joseph P. Viteritti, "Blaine's Wake: School Choice, the First Amendment, and State Constitutional Law," 21 *Harv. J. L. & Pub. Pol'y* 657 (1998). In other words, respondents' position, which would shift the constitutional standard from neutrality to exclusion, was proposed—and *rejected*—as an amendment to the Constitution.[18]

2. Over the next century, the American public's attitude toward nonpublic schools changed. Justice Powell reflected the contemporary view that "[p]arochial schools, quite apart from their sectarian purpose, have provided an educational alternative for millions of young Americans; they often afford wholesome competition with our public schools; and in some States they relieve substantially the tax burden incident to the operation of public schools." *Wolman v.*

---

[17] Interpreting its own constitution, the Arizona Supreme Court refused to apply Blaine-style language to strike down the State's income tax credit for private school scholarship contributions because it "would be hard pressed to divorce the amendment's language from the insidious discriminatory intent that prompted it." *Kotterman*, 972 P.2d at 624.

[18] Indeed, even if the Blaine Amendment had been adopted, the scholarship program would survive scrutiny because it provides "aid" and "support" to students, not to schools. See *Jackson*, 578 N.W.2d at 621–23 (sustaining the Milwaukee Parental Choice Program under the Wisconsin Constitution's Blaine Amendment).

Walter, 433 U.S. 229, 262–264 (1977) (Powell, J., concurring in part, concurring in the judgment in part, and dissenting in part).

The New York program struck down in *Nyquist* was part of a broader effort to rescue Catholic schools. In the 1970s, Catholic schools faced a fiscal crisis created by declining student enrollments. Nationally, the number of Catholic schools declined from 13,000 in 1967 to 10,000 in 1972. Evan Jenkins, "High Court Dims Parochial Hopes," *New York Times* (June 27, 1973) at 19. A New York State-sponsored report predicted that at least 70 percent of Catholic grade schools and 50 percent of Catholic high schools would close by 1980. See Fleishmann, *The Collapse of Nonpublic Education* (1971). The Catholic school crisis in turn would reverberate in public schools, which would be faced with rising enrollments and costs.

The result was "parochaid," exemplified by the New York statutes struck down in *Nyquist*. The Legislature found that "the fiscal crisis in nonpublic education . . . has caused a diminution of proper maintenance and repair programs, threatening the health, welfare and safety of nonpublic school children. . . ." N.Y. Educ. Law, Art. 12-A, § 549(2). Likewise, "any precipitous decline in the number of nonpublic school pupils would cause a massive increase in public school enrollment and costs," which "would seriously jeopardize quality education for all children. . . ." *Id.*, § 559(3). See *Nyquist*, 413 U.S. at 764–65.

Accordingly, the Legislature crafted an aid program comprised of (1) direct money grants to qualifying private schools for maintenance and repair, (2) a tuition reimbursement plan for parents of nonpublic school students, and (3) a tax deduction for nonpublic school tuition. All three programs conferred benefits, expressly and exclusively, to private schools and their patrons. Given the context of the aid programs as a whole—designed as they were to bail out religious schools—it is quite understandable that the Court could conclude that the New York statutes were among those "ingenious plans for channeling state aid to sectarian schools that periodically reach this Court," *id.* at 785, for the aim and design of the programs was to prop up religious schools.

3. By contrast, the aim and design of contemporary parental choice programs is exactly the opposite: to enlist private and religious schools to bail out failing public schools. The origins of the modern parental choice movement trace to religious-school advocates and the free-market economics of Milton Friedman; but more

recently, parental choice has evolved into a central component of the broader quest for education reform and educational equity. See Moe at 32–33; Bolick, *Transformation: The Promise and Politics of Empowerment* (1998) at 43–53; Floyd H. Flake, "School Choice: Why Poor Kids Need It Most of All," 2 *Amer. Experiment Q.* 35 (Spring 1999); Diane Ravitch, "The Right Thing," *The New Republic* 31 (Oct. 8, 2001).

The movement was precipitated by a 1983 report finding the quality of public schooling to be in serious decline. National Commission on Excellence in Education, *A Nation at Risk* (1983). Most dire were the educational circumstances of low-income minority youngsters in the inner cities.[19] The trends have persisted. The 1994 National Assessment of Education Progress reported that only 23 percent of fourth-graders in high-poverty urban schools satisfied basic reading requirements compared to 63 percent in non-urban schools nationally. Ravitch, "A New Era in Urban Education?" at 2. Likewise, last year NAEP revealed that 63 percent of black and 56 percent of Hispanic fourth-graders are below the most basic levels of proficiency in reading. The report found that the black/white achievement gap actually has widened since 1992. National Center for Education Statistics, *The Nation's Report Card: Fourth-Grade Reading 2000* at 31 and 33.[20]

Graduation rates are equally grim: only 70 percent of black students and 50 percent of Hispanic students graduate on time. Robert M. Huelskamp, "Perspectives on Education in America," *Phi Delta Kappan* (May 1993) at 719. These rates have huge spillover effects:

[19]Urban public schools enroll 24 percent of all public school students in the United States, 25 percent of poor students, and 43 percent of minority students. Diane Ravitch, "A New Era in Urban Education?" *Brookings Institution Policy Brief #35* (Aug. 1998) at 1. (This report can be found at http://www.brook.edu/comm/PolicyBriefs/pb035/pb35.htm.)

[20]Although black students were making academic gains relative to whites until the 1980s, the situation reversed and the academic gap began to widen between 1988 and 1994. Thernstrom and Thernstrom, *America in Black and White* (1997) at 355–59. The gap in reading between blacks and whites closed by 3.5 academic years between 1980 and 1988, but then widened again by nearly a year and a half from 1988 to 1994, so that "in 1994 blacks aged seventeen could read as well as the typical white child who was a month past his or her *thirteenth* birthday." *Id.* at 357 (emphasis in original). Likewise, in math the racial gap of 2.5 years in 1990 grew to 3.4 years by 1994. *Id.*

about 90 percent of prison inmates are high school dropouts. Jake Thompson, "Jackson Calls Nation's Attention to Its Educational 'Emergency'," *Kansas City Star* (Feb. 22, 1997), p. A1. At the same time, violence and disorder caused chaos in many inner-city schools.[21] Thernstrom and Thernstrom at 376–82; Bolick at 34–36.

In 1990, two Brookings Institution scholars explored the differences between failing inner-city public schools and more-successful inner-city private schools and suburban public schools, and found the former to include bloated administrative bureaucracies more responsive to political influences than parental concerns; a lack of autonomy and mission; and a lack of parental choice. Chubb and Moe, *Politics, Markets & America's Schools* (1990), cited with approval in *Davis v. Grover*, 480 N.W.2d at 471. Around the same time, social scientists including James Coleman began to report that private schools, particularly Catholic schools, promoted greater educational attainment for minority children, regardless of background, because they provided a common academic curriculum and high academic expectations. See, e.g., Coleman, Kilgore, and Hoffer, *High School Achievement: Public, Catholic, and Private Schools Compared* (1982); Greeley, *Catholic High Schools and Minority Students* (1982). See also Ravitch, *Left Back: A Century of Battles Over School Reform* (2001) at 417–18; Derek Neal, "The Effects of Catholic Secondary Schools on Educational Achievement," 15 *J. Labor Econ.* 98 (1997);[22] Stern, "The

[21]Student behavior problems, particularly in areas of student absenteeism, classroom discipline, weapons possession, and student pregnancy, are more prevalent in urban public schools than other schools. Likewise, teacher absenteeism, an indicator of morale, is more of a problem in urban poverty schools. Laura Lippman, Shelley Burns, and Edith McArthur, *Urban Schools: The Challenge of Location and Poverty* (National Center for Education Statistics, 1996) at 5. (This report can be found at http://nces.ed.gov/pubs/96184ex.html.)

[22]Neal found in his 1997 study that although Catholic schools produce negligible academic effects for suburban and white students, they strongly improve educational outcomes for urban minority children. Holding background factors constant, Neal found that the odds for high school graduation for urban black and Hispanic children increase from 62 to at least 88 percent in Catholic schools. In turn, he found that the likelihood of college attendance is tripled for urban minority students who attend Catholic schools. Not surprisingly, those gains translate into substantially higher wages in the labor market. Neal concludes bluntly, "Urban minorities receive significant benefits from Catholic schooling because their public school alternatives are substantially worse than those of whites and other minorities who live in rural or suburban areas." *Id.* at 98–100. See also Jeff Grogger and Derek Neal, "Further Evidence on the Effects of Catholic Secondary Schools," *Brookings Wharton Papers on Urban Affairs* (Nov. 1999).

Invisible Miracle of Catholic Schools," *City Journal* (Summer 1996) at 14–16; Paul Hill, Gail E. Foster, and Tamar Gendler, *High Schools with Character* (Rand Corporation, 1990).

Many states responded with various types of parental choice programs, including open enrollment, magnet schools, and charter schools. Moe at 39–40. But institutional inertia and an inadequate supply of high-quality public schools motivated reformers to look beyond the public system. In Milwaukee, the nation's first parental choice program for economically disadvantaged children was created in 1990. Initially, it was limited to nonsectarian private schools, but capacity limits led to its expansion to include religious schools in 1995.[23] See McGroarty, *Break These Chains* (1996); Mikel Holt, *Not Yet "Free at Last"* (2000).

Not surprisingly, "the appeal of private schools is especially strong among parents who are low in income, minority, and live in low-performing districts: precisely the parents who are most disadvantaged under the current system." Moe at 164; see also *id.* at 211 (minority and low-income parents most strongly support parental choice), *id.* at 147 (also the most strongly interested in moving their children from public to private schools), *id.* at 165 (the main motivation for wanting to make a shift is academic performance). Perhaps the most tangible evidence of this phenomenon occurred in 1998, when philanthropists made 40,000 privately funded scholarships available for economically disadvantaged children nationwide and *1.25 million* youngsters applied for them. *Id.* at 38.

Debate rages among social scientists regarding the effects of parental choice, but the main focus is not on *whether* parental choice improves educational opportunities but in *what ways and how much.* See, e.g., Paul E. Peterson, "School Choice: A Report Card," in Hassel,

---

[23] As Moe notes, presently 85 percent of all private school students are enrolled in religious schools. "This means that a voucher system that includes religious schools could immediately offer many children a range of new opportunities, but that a system legally restricted to nonsectarian schools could not, for supply would be quite limited and there would be *nowhere for most kids to go.*" Moe at 394 (emphasis in original). However, over time, the percentage of nonsectarian schools may rise as demand grows and the threat of litigation subsides. In the context of Milwaukee, since the successful outcome in *Jackson v. Benson,* the number of nonsectarian private schools in the parental choice program and the number of students attending nonsectarian schools both have increased substantially. Declaration of Howard Fuller, ¶¶ 18 and 21 (J.A. 234a–236a).

Learning from School Choice at 23 (if gains from the Milwaukee Parental Choice Program were replicated nationally, "they could reduce by somewhere between one-third and more than one-half the current difference between white and minority test score performance").

Parental choice also has evolved from purely a life preserver for kids in failing schools into a crucial facet in the effort to reform and improve public schools through competition. Studies indicate that public schools often perform better when parents have greater educational choices. As Harvard Professor Caroline Hoxby stated in uncontroverted testimony, "a significant effect of school choice is the effect that they have upon conventional public school districts, which have to respond to parents' having alternative school choices." Affidavit of Caroline Hoxby, ¶ 7 (J.A. 62a); see also Nina Shokraii Rees, "Public School Benefits of Private School Vouchers," *Pol'y Rev.* (Jan.–Feb., 1999). The Milwaukee Parental Choice Program apparently has triggered long-overdue reform and improvement in the public schools.[24] The Florida Opportunity Scholarship program, for instance, offers scholarships to children in public schools that have received a failing grade from the State in two academic years. After the program's first year, every public school on the State's failing list lifted itself off (see Greene, *An Evaluation of the Florida A-Plus Accountability and School Choice Program* (Harvard, 2001) at 7–9), and academic gains were most pronounced among the poorest-performing youngsters. *Id.* at 10–11.[25]

Again, none of this background is provided to convince the Court that parental choice is proper public policy, but rather to demonstrate the context in which contemporary parental choice programs arise. A program calculated to expand educational opportunities will look different than one designed to bail out religious schools. That is precisely the case with contemporary parental choice programs,

---

[24] After years of editorializing against the Milwaukee Parental Choice Program, the *Milwaukee Journal Sentinel* changed its position when it became clear that the program was exerting a positive influence on the city's public schools. Remarking on the public school system's recent reforms and improvements, the newspaper acknowledged that "[m]uch of what the system is doing to improve gained impetus because of the expansion of choice in Milwaukee." "MPS and the Virtures of Choice," *Milwaukee Journal Sentinel* (Jan. 31, 2001); see also "Choice: It's Not Only Money," *Milwaukee Journal Sentinel* (June 29, 2001).

[25] This study is available at www.ksg.harvard.edu/pepg.

which comprise one facet of a broader effort to reform public schools and to expand educational opportunities for economically disadvantaged schoolchildren. And it is specifically true with respect to the Cleveland Pilot Project Scholarship Program.

4. The Ohio legislature enacted the Cleveland Pilot Project Scholarship Program "to address an educational crisis in Cleveland's public schools in the wake of a U.S. District Court-ordered takeover of the administration of the Cleveland City School District" by the State of Ohio.[26] *Simmons-Harris v. Zelman*, 72 F. Supp.2d at 836. The educational crisis is severe and continuing. In 1999, the State of Ohio reported that CCSD failed to meet a single one of the 18 performance criteria set by the State. State of Ohio, *1999 School District Report Card* at 150 (6th Cir. J.A. 00475–00481). Among students taking ninth grade proficiency tests, only 11.6 percent of CCSD students passed, compared to 55.6 percent statewide and 22.4 percent of students in districts of similar size, poverty, geography, and tax wealth.[27] *Id.* at 151. The following year, in which expanded performance criteria were used, CCSD met zero out of 27 standards. Janet Tebben and Mark Vosburgh, "Cleveland Schools Score Lowest in State," *Cleveland Plain Dealer* (Dec. 23, 1999) at 1A. The graduation rate for CCSD

---

[26]Newspaper headlines from the mid-1990s, when the program at issue in this lawsuit was created, paint a picture of a school system beset by virtually every conceivable problem, from poor academics to administrative problems to chronic violence. See, e.g., Patrice M. Jones, "9th-Graders Falter on Proficiency Tests," *Cleveland Plain Dealer* (Mar. 20, 1994) at 1B (reporting that only 11 percent of CCSD ninth graders passed the State's proficiency examinations); Scott Stephens, "Officials Continue Test-Cheating Probe," *Cleveland Plain Dealer* (Aug. 3, 1994) at 2B; Scott Stephens, "Transportation Traumas: Cleveland Parents Protest Busing Cuts," *Cleveland Plain Dealer* (Sept. 7, 1994) at 1B; Patrice M. Jones, "Schools Slide Into Disrepair," *Cleveland Plain Dealer* (Sept. 11, 1994) at 1B; Scott Stephens, "School Board Unveils Steps to Curb Violence," *Cleveland Plain Dealer* (Oct. 29, 1994) at 1B; Patrice M. Jones, "[Mayor] White Says It's Time for a Change in Schools," *Cleveland Plain Dealer* (Nov. 13, 1994) at 1A; Mark Skertic, "Cleveland Public Schools: Ohio's Largest District in Chaos," *Cincinnati Enquirer* (Mar. 19, 1995) at A1; Evelyn Theiss, "School Board Repeats Failed Reform Pattern," *Cleveland Plain Dealer* (Aug. 27, 1995) at 6B; "Sweeps Week Continues With 91 More Truants," *Cleveland Plain Dealer* (Sept. 27, 1995) at 4B; Maggi Martin, "East High Student Shot by Man in Ski Mask," *Cleveland Plain Dealer* (Dec. 12, 1995) at 2B; Patrice M. Jones, "Summit on School Woes Draws 2,000: City Parents, Students, Others Look at Ways to Fix System," *Cleveland Plain Dealer* (Jan. 28, 1996) at 2B.

[27]Cleveland Catholic schools boast much higher academic performance. See Buckeye Institute, *Public Choices, Private Costs: An Analysis of Spending and Achievement in Ohio Public Schools* (1998) at 207 (6th Cir. J.A. 00536).

students in 1996 was an appalling 39.3 percent; by 1998 it had fallen to 32.6 percent. Affidavit of Francis H. Rogers III, ¶ 2 (6th Cir. J.A. 01620–01621).

The conditions in CCSD motivated Cleveland Councilwoman Fannie Lewis, who represents the economically impoverished Hough neighborhood, to charter buses to transport parents to the State Capitol to lobby for parental choice. Declaration of Fannie Lewis, ¶ 9 (Dist. Ct. Record No. 37). As Councilwoman Lewis testified, *id.*, ¶ 4, "[T]he scholarship program is essential to improving the educational opportunities for the children of the Hough community.... [F]amilies of limited economic means desperately need educational alternatives beyond those currently available in the Cleveland public schools...."

The children in the program—including those who already were attending private schools—are overwhelmingly poor and minority. Scholarship students have lower family incomes than CCSD students ($15,769 vs. $19,948); they are more likely to be raised in single-parent homes (68.2 percent vs. 40 percent); and they are mostly black (68.7 percent vs. 45.9 percent). Greene (J.A. 215a–216a).

As the official State evaluation of the program found, "The most important factors for applying to the scholarship program were educational quality and school safety," which were identified by 96.4 percent and 95 percent, respectively, of parents in the program. Indiana University, *Evaluation of the Cleveland Scholarship and Tutoring Grant Program (1996–99)* (6th Cir. J.A. 00448). Of the five main factors for choosing a school, religion was identified as least important. *Id.* After the first two years, the State study found limited but positive effects on student achievement. *Id.* at 00453.

The hopes and opportunities for the program resound in the voices of the parents. Senel Taylor, a scholarship father, describes his daughter's experience:

> Our daughter, Saletta, is ten years old and is in the fourth grade at New Hope Christian Academy, a private school.
> When I heard about the Cleveland Scholarship and Tutoring Program, I jumped at the chance to apply for a scholarship for Saletta. She has been in the program for two years. The scholarship has allowed Saletta to receive an excellent education.
> Saletta attended public school for a couple of years. She failed first grade and had to repeat it. Fortunately, it was

245

right at that time that I learned of the [program]. We applied and thankfully Saletta was accepted.

Saletta's progress at New Hope Christian Academy has been excellent. Her grades have improved dramatically. She likes Second New Hope much better than her public school, and as a result is excellent at school. . . .

If the [program] is not allowed to continue, Saletta will have to go back to public school. My wife and I cannot afford to send her to Second New Hope without a scholarship. This would be devastating to Saletta.

Taylor Aff., ¶¶ 2-5 and 8 (J.A. 173a–174a); see also Affidavits of Johnietta McGrady (J.A. 176a–178a), Amy Hudock (J.A. 179a–181a), Christine Suma (J.A. 220a–222a). See also McGroarty, *Trinietta Gets a Chance* (2001).

In the real-world context of education reform, it is plain that the program's primary effect is not to subsidize religion, but to broaden educational options for disadvantaged families. As former Milwaukee Public Schools Superintendent Dr. Howard Fuller testifies,

> The critical issue is not whether children go to private or public schools, to religious or nonsectarian schools, but whether they go to good schools or bad schools. More options for parents means that more families have more opportunities to choose schools best for their children. Cleveland's scholarship program increases educational opportunity. . . . The primary effect of programs like . . . Cleveland's is to expand educational choices for low-income families, which is good for the children and their families, and also good for the educational system by formenting institutional reform and improvement within the public schools.

Fuller Decl., ¶ 19 (J.A. 235a).

For all those reasons, the Ohio Supreme Court categorically concluded, "The primary beneficiaries of the School Voucher Program are children, not sectarian schools." *Simmons-Harris v. Goff*, 711 N.E.2d at 211. It is that court's ruling, and not the erroneous conclusion reached by the federal courts below, that this Court should follow.

III. THE SCHOLARSHIP PROGRAM IS NEUTRAL ON ITS FACE AND FUNDS ARE DIRECTED TO RELIGIOUS SCHOOLS ONLY THROUGH THE TRUE PRIVATE CHOICES OF INDIVIDUAL PARENTS, THEREFORE SATISFYING ESTABLISHMENT CLAUSE REQUIREMENTS.

Throughout this litigation, the respondents have divided the world of establishment clause jurisprudence into two polar opposites—*Nyquist* versus all the cases subsequent to it—and have attempted to shoehorn the scholarship program into the first category with the consequence of pre-ordained unconstitutionality. In reality, there are not two worlds of establishments clause jurisprudence, but one; and the principles articulated have been consistently applied throughout. Viewed against the backdrop of this jurisprudential continuum, the Cleveland Pilot Project Scholarship Program plainly meets this Court's standards.

The Sixth Circuit held that the outcome of this case was dictated by *Nyquist*, even though the question presented here was expressly left open in that case; specifically "whether the significantly religious character of the statute's beneficiaries might differentiate the present cases from a case involving some form of public assistance (*e.g.*, scholarships) made available generally without regard to the sectarian-nonsectarian, or public-nonpublic nature of the institution benefited." *Nyquist* at 782 n.38.

Since *Nyqist*, the Court has answered that question repeatedly.[28] As Justice Powell subsequently observed in *Witters*, 474 U.S. at 490–91 (Powell, J., concurring), "state programs that are wholly neutral in offering educational assistance to a class defined without reference to religion do not violate" the primary effect test.[29] That is true even if government funds an individual's choice to attend religious

[28]But by pigeon-holing this case within a rigid *Nyquist* framework, the panel majority below "refus[ed] to conduct any meaningful analysis of the Supreme Court's several Establishment Clause decisions" in the years since *Nyquist* was decided. *Simmons-Harris v. Zelman*, 234F.3d at 963 (Ryan, J.).

[29]Rather than marking some about-face on the part of Justice Powell, the author of *Nyquist*, it is fairly clear that this is precisely the rule of neutrality intended in *Nyquist*. On the same day the Court decided *Nyquist*, it is also dismissed an appeal in which a state court upheld a student loan program in which students could apply funds to the college of their choice, public or private, religious or secular. *Durham v. McLeod*, 192 S.E.2d 202 (S.C. 1972), *appeal dismissed for want of substantial federal question*, 413 U.S. 902 (1973).

schools, so long as "[a]ny aid . . . that ultimately flows to religious institutions does so only as a result of the genuinely independent and private choices of aid recipients"[30] *Witters*, 474 U.S. at 487. Accord, *Mitchell*, 530 U.S. at 838–41 (O'Connor, J., concurring in the judgment); *Agostini, supra; Zobrest, supra; Witters, supra; Mueller, supra.*

Rather than presenting divergent rules, then, *Nyquist* and the cases decided in the intervening 28 years establish a single set of principles: where tuition aid is directed to a class defined without reference to religion, religious schools may be included so long as the choice of where to spend the funds is made by parents or students.

Applying those principles, the Wisconsin Supreme Court upheld the Milwaukee Parental Choice Program in *Jackson*, 578 N.W.2d at 614 n.9, observing that "[i]n *Nyquist*, each of the facets of the challenged program directed aid exclusively to private schools and their students. The MPCP, by contrast, provides a neutral benefit to qualifying parents of school-age children in Milwaukee Public Schools." The Ohio Supreme Court applied those same principles in sustaining the Cleveland scholarship program, *Simmons-Harris v. Goff*, 711 N.E.2d at 208–11; as did the Arizona Supreme Court in the context of scholarship tax credits, *Kotterman*, 972 P.2d at 615–17; and the Vermont Supreme Court in the context of its tuitioning program. *Campbell*, 641 A.2d at 360–61. See also *Simmons-Harris v. Zelman*, 234 F.3d at 963–74 (Ryan, J.).

It is from these principles that the Sixth Circuit departs. Despite the fact that the scholarship program confers benefits on a class defined without reference to religion, that public funds are transmitted only as the result of independent choices of parents, and that

---

[30] It is that characteristic—"true private-choice"—that distinguishes indirect aid programs such as those at issue in *Mueller, Witters*, and *Zobrest*, from direct aid programs such as the ones sustained in *Agostini* and *Mitchell*. The Court has recognized "special Establishment Clause dangers where the government makes direct money payments to sectarian institutions." *Rosenberger*, 515 U.S. at 842. Hence, in direct aid cases, it is relevant whether public funds "ever reach the coffers of religious schools." *Agostini*, 521 U.S. at 228. Even there, however, the Court has "departed from the rule . . . that all government aid that directly aids the educational function of religious schools is invalid." *Id.* at 225. By contrast, as even the dissenters to the more recent cases have acknowledged, "When government dispenses public funds to individuals who employ them to finance private choices, it is difficult to argue that government is actually endorsing religion." *Zobrest*, 509 U.S. at 22–23 (Blackmun, J., dissenting); see also *Mitchell*, 530 U.S. at 889 (Souter, J., dissenting).

the program creates no incentive to choose religious schools, the court found it had the primary effect of establishing religion. Its decision is untenable. Simply put, *Nyquist* does not control this case, for the program was carefully designed as precisely the type of neutral, indirect student aid program on which the Court expressly reserved judgment in that case, and which the Court repeatedly has sustained without exception ever since.

A. Neutrality. "In distinguishing between [religious] indoctrination that is attributable to the State and indoctrination that is not, we have consistently turned to the principle of neutrality, upholding aid that is offered to a broad range of groups or persons without regard to their religion." *Mitchell*, 530 U.S. at 809 (plurality); accord, *id.* at 838 (O'Connor, J.) ("Our cases have described neutrality in precisely this manner, and we have emphasized a program's neutrality repeatedly in our decisions approving various forms of school aid"). As this Court emphasized in *Zobrest*, 509 U.S. at 8, "Given that a contrary rule would lead to . . . absurd results, we have consistently held that government programs that neutrally provide benefits to a broad class of citizens defined without reference to religion are not readily subject to an Establishment Clause challenge just because sectarian institutions may also receive an attenuated financial benefit."

There can be no doubt that the Cleveland Pilot Scholarship Program confers educational assistance to a class defined without reference to religion. "On its face, the statutory scheme does not define its recipients by reference to religion." *Simmons-Harris v. Goff*, 711 N.E.2d at 209. In contrast to *Nyquist*, in which aid was directed expressly and exclusively to private schools and their patrons, the scholarship program here is available to all Cleveland schoolchildren, with a preference for children attending Cleveland public schools and for children below 200 percent of the poverty level.[31]

---

[31] Respondents repeatedly have noted that despite a cap on the percentage of children in the program who were already enrolled in private schools, a substantial percentage of scholarship recipients in fact never attended CCSD. The assertion is misleading. The phenomenon is attributable to the fact that in its early years, the program expanded one grade each year, meaning that children in the program would progress along and that most new entrants to the program would be in kindergarten—hence, never previously having attended public (or private) schools. Regardless of when their children joined the program, the low average income of scholarship families ($15,769) (see Greene (J.A. 215a)), suggests that most would not be able to afford private school tuition otherwise or could do so only at great sacrifice.

Ohio Rev. Code § 3313.978(A). See *Simmons-Harris v. Zelman*, 234 F.3d at 969 (Ryan, J.). The statute does not disburse aid directly to private schools at all, and eligible schools again are defined "without regard to the sectarian-nonsectarian, or public-nonpublic nature of the institution benefited." *Nyquist*, 413 U.S. at 782 n.38. Accordingly, "[i]t is obvious that the Ohio statute does not have the remotest effect of providing governmental indoctrination in any religion, to say nothing of having such a primary effect." *Simmons-Harris v. Zelman*, 234 F.3d at 968 (Ryan, J.).

1. The program's facial neutrality should end the inquiry; but curiously, the court below embarked upon a far-flung inquiry to identify supposed indicia of partiality. Instead of applying this Court's test of facial neutrality, the panel majority substituted a mathematical analysis, to wit that because at the time of the lawsuit 82 percent of the participating schools were sectarian, and 96 percent of the children were attending religious schools, the program is unconstitutional. *Simmons-Harris*, 234 F.3d at 959.

This Court on at least two occasions has explicitly rejected the Sixth Circuit's proposed standard. In *Mueller*, 463 U.S. at 400–01, the plaintiffs made precisely the same arguments as do the respondents here, presenting almost identical statistics in an effort to invalidate Minnesota's tuition tax deduction:

> Petitioners argue that, notwithstanding the facial neutrality [of the challenged program], in application the statute primarily benefits religious institutions. Petitioners rely . . . on a statistical analysis of the type of persons claiming the tax deduction. They contend that most parents of public school children incur no tuition expenses . . .; moreover, they claim that 96% of the children in private schools . . . attended religiously affiliated institutions. Because of all this, they reason, the bulk of deductions . . . will be claimed by parents of children in sectarian schools.

To this assertion, the Court's response was unambiguous: "We need not consider these contentions in detail. We would be loath to adopt a rule grounding the constitutionality of a facially neutral law on annual reports reciting the extent to which various classes of private citizens claimed benefits under the law." *Id.* at 401. Quoting that language, the Court reiterated in *Agostini*, 521 U.S. at 229, "Nor are we willing to conclude that the constitutionality of an aid program depends upon the number of sectarian school students who happen to receive the otherwise neutral aid."[32]

Substitution of this Court's rule with the statistical formula applied by the Sixth Circuit would result in precisely the "absurd results" against which this Court warned in *Zobrest*, 509 U.S. at 8. First, "[s]uch an approach would scarcely provide the certainty that this field stands in need of, nor can we perceive principled standards by which such statistical evidence might be evaluated." *Mueller*, 463 U.S. at 401. The court below did not suggest any line of statistical demarcation. How many religious schools or students choosing them is too much? Ninety percent? Fifty percent plus one? What if the program is on one side of the tipping point one year, and on the other side the next? In essence, the proposed rule creates a third-party veto over the constitutionality of a facially neutral program— if certain individuals or entities choose not to participate in ways that satisfy some unknown statistical standard, the program is rendered invalid. Surely constitutionality cannot depend on the independent decisions of third parties.

Moreover, the present statistics present only a snapshot in the evolving life of the program, and they are subject to substantial change. As the court below acknowledged, *Simmons-Harris v. Zelman*, 234 F.3d at 949, as many as 22 percent of scholarship students attended nonsectarian schools at one point in the program, compared to four percent when the program was challenged in federal court.[33] Those numbers could change fairly dramatically again, for instance, if suburban public schools decided to participate in the program, or if new nonsectarian schools open. Indeed, the older Milwaukee Parental Choice Program has experienced substantial demographic changes, particularly since litigation ended in 1998. In Milwaukee, the number of nonsectarian private schools participating in the program increased from seven to 30 between 1990 and 2000, and now

[32]Displaying a talent for creating distinctions without a difference, respondents have argued that these admonitions do not apply where the percentage of *schools*, rather than *students*, is disproportionately religious. The reasons for a standard of facial neutrality apply with equal force in both instances, and we reiterate that the program is facially neutral with regard to participation by both schools and students.

[33]The reason for the change is that the two largest nonsectarian private schools participating in the scholarship program converted to community school status, which provides substantially increased remuneration from the State. Affidavit of Caroline Hoxby, ¶¶ 4c and 5c (J.A. 56a, 60a).

comprise 30 percent of the schools in the program; the enrollment of students in nonsectarian schools increased nearly ten-fold during that same period from 337 to 3,025, or 37.5 percent of the 8,066 students in the program. Fuller Decl., ¶¶ 18 and 21 (J.A. 234a–236a). It is not surprising that in the early days of an inner-city parental choice program most of the schools are religiously affiliated, because religious schools often are the only ones that can help subsidize the tuition of economically disadvantaged children. But as the record from Milwaukee shows, that can change as new schools open to serve increased demand.[34]

Further, the statistical approach untenably hitches the program's constitutionality to the way that third parties exercise their independent choices. The court below concludes that because suburban public schools made no spaces available in the program, "[t]herefore, the program clearly has the impermissible effect of promoting sectarian schools." *Simmons-Harris v. Zelman*, 234 F.3d at 959. One can only speculate why suburban public schools declined to open their doors to inner-city Cleveland schoolchildren.[35] But more than 50 private schools decided to participate, agreeing to accept low-income children on a random selection basis for tuition not to exceed $2,500.[36] The import of the ruling below is perverse: because only *some* schools

[34]Litigation, too, can impact the mix. The threat of having the program discontinued obviously impedes the investment necessary to start new schools. In this case, the injunction imposed by the district court drove two nonsectarian schools out of the program. See Declarations of David P. Zanotti, ¶ 9 (J.A. 226a); Dr. Barbara Kurtz, ¶ 4 (6th Cir. J.A. 00573) (injunction "had a devastating effect on our school"); Cassandra Brown-Collier (6th Cir. J.A. 00576–00578). By contrast, as Dr. Fuller testifies in the context of the Milwaukee Parental Choice Program, "Since the litigation cloud was lifted, the growth of the program has been dynamic, in terms of both religious and nonreligious school participation." Fuller Decl., ¶ 18 (J.A. 235a).

[35]Respondents have argued that the State could have ensured public school choices by *requiring* suburban districts to participate. But the program in this regard treats public and private schools exactly alike: both are allowed to opt in or out, as they choose.

[36]As Judge Ryan observed, *Simmons-Harris v. Zelman*, 234 F.3d at 971 (Ryan, J.),
It is probably true that no private school, religious or nonreligious, can educate a child for the voucher value of $2,500. But, in all probability, the participating private schools are willing to accept the voucher as meeting a portion of the actual educational costs for these children and are willing to absorb the differential cost as part of their *pro bono* service in Cleveland to help save as many of these children as possible from the disastrous consequences of continuing in the city's failed public schools.

were willing to provide an educational life preserver, then *none* will be permitted to do so.

All of this underscores why this Court's bright-line rule of facial neutrality—rather than the hopelessly arbitrary and subjective statistical standard proposed by the Court below—is the proper measure of constitutionality.

2. The court below went on to suggest that "[p]ractically speaking, the tuition restrictions mandated by the statute limit the ability of nonsectarian schools to participate in the program, as religious schools often have lower overhead costs, supplemental income from private donations, and consequently lower tuition needs."[37] *Simmons-Harris v. Zelman*, 234 F.3d at 959. Specifically, "[a]t a maximum of $2,250, there is a financial disincentive for public schools outside the district to take on students via the school voucher program."[38] *Id.* at 959.

The premise is factually inaccurate. Under State law, participating suburban schools would receive the scholarship amount *plus* the "average daily membership" expenditure under State law (approximately $4,294 per student), for a total of about $6,544. Ohio Rev. Code §§ 3317.03(I)(1), 3327.06, 3317.08(A)(1). Given the advantageous treatment conferred to public schools, no financial disincentive exists for public schools to participate. The explanation for nonparticipation must lie elsewhere. Whether their motivations are malign or beneficient, however, should be irrelevant to a facially neutral program's constitutionality.[39]

Given the premium that participating suburban public schools would receive, the base amount of the scholarship understandably was set at about the median cost of private school tuition.[40] But the

[37] For this proposition, central to its holding, the court cites to nothing in the record, but only to a law review article.

[38] Again, premising a decision on the notion that the amount of the scholarship is *too low* a hopelessly subjective standard.

[39] As this Court remarked in *Mueller*, 463 U.S. at 401, "[T]he fact that private persons fail in a particular year to claim the tax relief to which they are entitled—under a facially neutral statute—should be of little importance in determining the constitutionality of the statute permitting such relief."

[40] Average private elementary school tuition is $2,138 per year. Average Catholic school tuition is $1,628 annually. See Center for Education Reform, *Elementary and Secondary Education Statistics at a Glance* (2001) (http://www.edreform.com/pubs/edstats.htm).

Table 1
Schools of Choice Available to Cleveland School Children

Type	Public or Private	No. of Students	Per-Pupil Funding	% of Tuition Paid
Magnet	Public	16,184	$7,097	100%
Community	Public	2,087	$4,518 minimum	100%
Scholarship	Private*	3,765	$2,250	90%

*Open to Suburban Public

program plainly creates no financial windfall for private schools, and indeed may not even constitute a break-even proposition. Unlike the Milwaukee Parental Choice Program, which reimburses schools for tuition or actual costs, whichever is greater, see Wis. Stats. § 119.23(4), the Ohio statute caps the amount of the scholarship at 90 percent of the amount of tuition up to $2,250. Ohio Rev. Code §§ 3313.976(A)(8) and 3313.978(C)(1). If the Sixth Circuit's premise is accurate that religious schools subsidize their students, what that means is that everytime a religious school admits a scholarship student, it must raise funds to subsidize that child—hardly a formula for enriching private schools.

3. As the foregoing discussion suggests, the scholarship program is not merely neutral in practical effect, but what might be character-ized as "neutral-plus": *all* of the incentives created by this program and related State programs operate to encourage public schools, or to a lesser extent private nonsectarian schools, rather than religious schools. As this Court observed in *Zobrest*, 509 U.S. at 10, where a program "creates no financial incentive for parents to choose a sec-tarian school," the fact that aid ends up there "cannot be attributed to state decisionmaking."

As Professor Hoxby attested in uncontroverted testimony, "Cleve-land parents have an incentive to choose a public school (community, conventional, or magnet) over a private school." Hoxby Aff., ¶ 4f–g (J.A. 58a). A Cleveland public school student is backed by over $7,000 in public funding. Community schools receive $4,518 per pupil, and are eligible for disadvantaged student assistance and special education funding. *Id.*, ¶¶ 4a, 4c, and 4d (J.A. 56a) (see Table 1 at 41, *infra*). By contrast, scholarship students receive a maximum of $2,250 from the State; and unlike public or community school

Table 2

Distribution of Students in Public, Nonsectarian Private, and Religious Schools of Choice 1999–2000 School Year

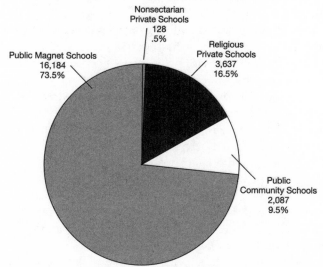

students, they must make up ten percent of the costs of tuition. Moreover, only public school students are eligible for the tutorial assistance grants that the same program created.

In terms of attractiveness to schools, the scholarship program is the poor relative among Cleveland parental choice programs. Nonsectarian private schools may become community schools and receive nearly twice as much in tuition.[41] *Id.,* ¶ 5b–c (J.A. 59a–60a). Religious schools are the only schools whose participation in choice programs is limited to the scholarship program. And to do so, they not only must accept $2,500 as full payment of tuition, but they must also agree to accept students on a random selection basis with a preference for economically disadvantaged youngsters. *Simmons-Harris v. Zelman,* 234 F.3d at 948. If this is a means to funnel subsidies to religious schools, surely it is a strange way to do it.

All of this underscores the wisdom underlying this Court's rule of facial neutrality. Once the State has fashioned a neutral program,

---

[41] And that is exactly what the two largest nonsectarian private schools in the scholarship program did. Hoxby Aff., ¶¶ 4c and 5c (J.A. 56a, 60a).

there is no way to predict with certainty how individuals will exercise their choices. The link between State action and religious school choices is severed. As the Ohio Supreme Court observed, "It is difficult to see how the School Voucher Program could result in governmental indoctrination. No governmental actor is involved in religious activity, no governmental actor works in a religious setting, and no government-provided incentive encourages children to attend sectarian schools." *Simmons-Harris v. Goff*, 711 N.E.2d at 209.

Plainly, under this program, "the aid is allocated on the basis of neutral, secular criteria that neither favor nor disfavor religion, and is made available to both religious and secular beneficiaries on a nondiscriminatory basis." *Agostini*, 521 U.S. at 231. The Cleveland Pilot Project Scholarship steers precisely the course of neutrality that the First Amendment requires.

B. True Private-Choice. As in *Mueller*, 463 U.S. at 399, here "public funds become available only as a result of numerous private choices of individual parents of school-age children." It is not a per-capita aid program, but a scholarship program.

The fact that the aid here is indirect, like under the G.I. Bill, Pell Grants, daycare vouchers, and other forms of general assistance programs, is important for three reasons, as identified by Justices O'Connor and Breyer in *Mitchell*. First, "[t]he fact that aid flows to the religious school and is used for the advancement of religion is . . . *wholly* dependent on the student's private decision." *Id.* at 842 (O'Connor, J.) (emphasis in original). That is true here, too—no one is compelled either to participate in the scholarship program at all, or to choose a religious school.

Second, the distinction "is significant for purposes of endorsement." *Id.* Unlike a direct per-capita subsidy,

> when government aid supports a school's religious mission only because of independent decisions made by numerous individuals to guide their secular aid to that school, "no reasonable observer is likely to draw from the facts . . . an inference that the State itself is endorsing a religious practice or belief." [Citation omitted.] Rather, endorsement of the religious message is reasonably attributed to the individuals who select the path of the aid.

Id. at 843. Here, any link of State sponsorship of religious schools is attenuated by the act of individual choice. Symbolically, as well, the link is further severed by the act of making checks "payable to the parents of the student entitled to the scholarship," and "mailed to the school selected by the parents." *Simmons-Harris v. Zelman,* 234 F.3d at 948. As the Ohio Supreme Court found, "Whatever link between government and religion is created by the School Voucher Program is indirect, depending only on the 'genuinely independent and private choices' of individual parents, who act for themselves and their children, not for the government." *Simmons-Harris v. Goff,* 711 N.E.2d at 209 (citation omitted).

Finally, the distinction "is important when considering aid that consists of direct monetary subsidies," which present special dangers. *Mitchell,* 500 U.S. at 843 (O'Connor, J.). Unlike a per-capita aid program, the scholarship program here is not self-executing. It is an enablement of students, not an entitlement to schools. Not a single dollar crosses the threshold of a religious school unless a parent foregoes public school options, enrolls in the program, and chooses a religious school. The Cleveland Pilot Project Scholarship was designed to—and does in fact—satisfy the concerns addressed by the insistence that public funds must be dispensed through true private-choice.

1. The court below found the promise of choice "illustory."[42] *Simmons-Harris v. Zelman,* 234 F.3d at 959. There can be no question that the program expands the options available to economically disadvantaged Cleveland families. As Judge Ryan observed, even viewing the scholarship program in isolation, Cleveland schoolchildren have the option of remaining in public schools, obtaining a scholarship and choosing a religious school, obtaining a scholarship and choosing a nonsectarian private school, remaining in the public schools and obtaining a tutorial assistance grant, or obtaining a scholarship and attending a suburban public school. *Simmons-Harris v. Zelman,* 234 F.3d at 968 (Ryan, J.). None of the latter four choices existed before the scholarship program. The fifth choice presently is foreclosed as a practical matter not because of the program, but because of independent decision made by suburban public school

---

[42] As one commentator aptly has observed, "To hold that no genuine option exists regarding whether to attend a religious school or nonreligious school is simply to ignore reality that prior to the Voucher Program, low-income students effectively had no choice as to what school to attend." Matthew D. Fridy, "What Wall? Government Neutrality and the Cleveland Voucher Program," 31 *Cumb. L. Rev.* 709, 762 (2000).

districts. No one is compelled or pressured in any way to participate in the program. It merely adds new options to a pre-existing array of parental choices. To exercise that choice, parents must be willing to forego completely free public school tuition and the prospect of a tutorial assistance grant—sacrifices several thousand parents in Cleveland have opted to make to secure what they perceive is a better education for their children.

2. The court of appeals steadfastly refused to examine "other options available to Cleveland parents such as the Community Schools," dismissing them as "at best irrelevant." *Simmons-Harris v. Zelman*, 234 F.3d at 958. In so doing, the court ignored this Court's frequent admonitions to examine a challenged program in its broader context. See, e.g., *Zobrest*, 509 U.S. at 10 ("part of a general government program"); *Mueller*, 463 U.S. at 396 ("only one among many deductions" provided by Minnesota law). As this Court observed in sustaining public funding for a religious publication in *Rosenberger*, 515 U.S. at 850,

> Wide Awake does not exist in a vacuum. It competes with 15 other magazines and newspapers for advertising and readership. The widely divergent viewpoints of these many purveyors of opinion, all supported on an equal basis by the University, significantly diminishes the danger that the message of any one publication is perceived as endorsed by the University.

Unlike the Sixth Circuit's eagerness to go beyond facial neutrality and examine the choices actually made by participants in the scholarship program—which are wholly determined by the independent choices of third parties—it refused to examine the program in the broader context of a educational options even though those choices exist *as a matter of law*. See *Reed v. Rhodes*, 934 F. Supp. at 1557 (commending the State for making a range of school choices available to meet the educational crisis in the Cleveland City Public Schools); Ohio Rev. Code § 3314.01, *et seq.* (community schools program).

Good reasons exist for this Court's instruction to examine the surrounding context. The State could, of course, have adopted magnet schools, community schools, and scholarships in one omnibus education reform package. Had it done so, the entire basis of the Court of Appeals' decision would collapse. As a matter of logic and constitutional law, why is the legal consequence any different if the programs are adopted separately? It is a bedrock principle of constitutional law that States are free to respond to a problem one step at a time. See, e.g., *Williamson v. Lee Optical of Okla.*, 348 U.S. 483 (1955). Here, public school choices (magnet and community schools) were created, then private school (combined with suburban public school and tutorial assistance grant) options were subsequently added. The rule of law advanced below would, strangely, obligate the State to include private school options in the first instance or forever have that option foreclosed.[43]

What the State of Ohio has done, in essence, is to make student funding[44] transportable, and to add one option at a time.[45] The overall system operates like many state systems of post-secondary education: the State maintains its own system of schools, whose tuition is free or subsidized, and also makes scholarships available for use at other institutions, including eligible private and public schools. Like the religious publication in *Rosenberger*, the schools in the scholarship program must compete with many other educational options. *Rosenberger*, 515 U.S. at 850. Unlike *Rosenberger, id.*, however, the schools are not "all supported on an equal basis" by the State— scholarship school pupils receive substantially less funding from the State, as Table 2 on page 41 illustrates.[46]

[43]For a State that already had completely open enrollment in public schools, for instance, such a rule seemingly would make it impossible to add private school options, no matter how neutral the program nor how dependent on true private choices, thus eviscerating the standards this Court has carefully constructed.

[44]For public schools, Ohio bases its State funding on the number of pupils, with a "base formula amount," Ohio Rev. Code § 3317.02, multiplied by a "cost of doing business" amount for each locality, Ohio Rev. Code § 3317.02(N), minus a "charge-off amount." Ohio Rev. Code § 3317.022.

[45]This factor was important to the Wisconsin Supreme Court in sustaining the Milwaukee Parental Choice Program, which was expanded in 1995 to include religious schools, in *Jackson v. Benson*, 578 N.W.2d at 614 n.9 and 618 n.16:

The amended MPCP, viewed in its surrounding context, merely adds religious schools to a range of pre-existing educational choices available to MPS children. . . . Qualifying public school students may choose from among the Milwaukee public district schools, magnet schools, charter schools, suburban public schools, trade schools, schools developed for students with exceptional needs, and now sectarian or nonsectarian private school participating in the amended MPCP. In each case, the programs let state funds follow students to the districts and schools their parents have chosen.

[46]The sources for the chart are Hoxby Aff., ¶ 4c–d (J.A. 56a) and Greene (6th Cir. J.A. 00428–00429).

As Professor Greene found in his study of the racial, social, and religious context of parental choice in Cleveland, "When one looks at the broader system of choice in Cleveland, it is clear that a small percentage of publicly-financed choosers attend religious schools." Greene (J.A. 218a). As Table 2 (p. 41) demonstrates, if scholarships are properly viewed in the overall context of publicly financed schools of choice[47] in Cleveland, *the percentage of students attending religious schools of choice is only 16.5 percent.* Even if the Court of Appeals were correct to adopt a statistical test to determine the program's neutrality, applying it in the proper context of the range of educational choices available to Cleveland parents yields a starkly different result, one that demonstrates beyond doubt that the primary effect of the program is to expand educational choices.

The program is neutral on its face and in effect, and its neutrality is buttressed by a system of true parental-choice. The program therefore comports fully with this Court's establishment clause precedents.

----------◆----------

CONCLUSION

Nothing in this brief is intended in the slightest to disparage public schools or the yeoman's work many of them do in educating our nation's children; nor to diminish in any way the magnitude of the task facing the CCSD and other inner-city school systems. But that is exactly the point: as this Court has recognized in the context of aid for disabled children, sometimes we must go outside the public schools to fulfill the goals of public education. It is essential that the Court preserve this option for policymakers who are trying in good faith to dispatch their most important responsibilities.

Many of the themes in this case reflect those raised 47 years ago in *Brown v. Board of Education.* There, children were forced to travel past good neighborhood schools to attend inferior schools because the children happened to be black; today, many poor children are forced to travel past good schools to attend inferior schools because the schools happen to be private. In the quest to fulfill the promise

---

[47] In other words, this figure includes magnet and community schools, but does not include the vast majority of Cleveland pupils who are in regular district schools. If it included all schools, the percentage enrolled in religious schools using scholarships would be even smaller.

of equal educational opportunity, we must enlist every resource at our disposal.

The Cleveland Pilot Project Scholarship Program was not designed to test the boundaries of constitutional law, but to fit safely within them. We respectfully ask this honorable Court to affirm that it does.

Respectfully submitted,

CHARLES FRIED
1545 Massachusetts Avenue
Cambridge, MA 02138
Of Counsel

INSTITUTE FOR JUSTICE
CLINT BOLICK*
WILLIAM H. MELLOR
RICHARD D. KOMER
ROBERT FREEDMAN
1717 Pennsylvania Ave.,
  NW, Suite 200
Washington, DC 20006
(202) 955-1300
Counsel of Record

PORTER, WRIGHT, MORRIS &
  ARTHUR, L.L.P.
DAVID TRYON
1700 Huntington Building
925 Euclid Avenue
Cleveland, OH 44114
(216) 443-2560
Counsel for Petitioners

Index

education of teachers' children at, 28
individual acceptance of vouchers
by, 210
in Milwaukee, affidavits from, 28
remedial instruction in, 113, 149–53
role in education system, 1
subsidies for, 74–75
supply of, 216
Program design, importance of, 216
Pro hac vice, 19*n*
Property rights cases, 117–18
Protestant hegemony, over public
schools, 2–3
Public education
abandonment of, 96–97
goals of, 37, 99
versus public schools, 209, 213–14
Public interest brief, purposes of,
110–11
Public interest law seminar, Institute
for Justice, 110
Public opinion, 58
in Milwaukee case, 28, 38, 40, 216
in Puerto Rico case, 59–60
in Supreme Court case, 111–12,
157–58, 168–69
Public purpose doctrine, 20, 25, 83
Public school. *See also* suburban public
schools; urban public schools;
specific school
behavioral standards, 22, 207–8
decline in, 5
diversion of funds from, 37, 42, 93,
136
history of, 1–2, 2*n*
Protestant hegemony over, 2–3
versus public education, 209, 213–14
Public school reform, 6, 46, 97
in Florida, 132, 148, 203, 213
legislative efforts at, 160, 201
litigation aimed at, 207–8
market-oriented, 205, 213–14
process of, 207–8
in Puerto Rico, 59
school choice as catalyst for, 97, 101,
148–49, 201, 206–8, 211, 217
and teachers unions, 198–99
Public school teachers. *See also* teachers
remedial instruction by, in religious
schools, 113, 149–53
Puerto Rico, 59–61
Puerto Rico Supreme Court, 59–61
Pullout chart, in Supreme Court brief,
172, 180

Racial preferences (affirmative action),
29, 63*n*, 63–64, 188
Rallies
Cleveland program, 94, 128–29,
151–53
Milwaukee program, 120–22
New York, 156–57
Supreme Court case, 169, 176, 178,
182
Rand, Ayn, 7, 9, 48
Randolph Foundation, 53
Random admissions, 135
Reagan, Ronald, 11, 170
Recusal motions, 140–41, 147, 164
Rees, Nina (Shokraii), 65, 75, 80, 116,
161
Rehm, Diane, 198
Rehnquist, William H., 11, 72, 143, 149,
181, 189
opinion, 191–92
Reimbursement caps, 71
Religion. *See also* separation of church
and state
government endorsement of, 180
Religion clauses. *See also* Establishment
Clause (First Amendment)
state, 83–85
Religious activity, opt-out policies for,
70, 133, 135
Religious schools. *See also* Catholic
schools; *specific school*
disabled students at, 47–48
exclusion of
in Maine and Vermont, 77–78, 95,
112, 117, 122–23, 131, 143, 187
in Milwaukee, 16, 37
financial disincentives for, 192
inclusion of, 46–48
in Cleveland program, 92
in Maine and Vermont, 77
in Milwaukee, 51, 61, 64–65, 67–72,
81, 105, 115
in Puerto Rico, 59
indirect aid to, 48
versus direct, 107, 113–14, 149, 191
vouchers as, 113
remedial instruction in, government
provision of, 113, 149–53
and tax abatement laws, 49
Title I education funds, 106
tuitioning to (*See* tuitioning
programs)
tuition subsidies provided by, 71

About the Author

Clint Bolick serves as vice president and national director of state chapters at the Institute for Justice, which he cofounded in 1991. The purpose of the institute is to engage in constitutional litigation to protect individual liberty and challenge the regulatory welfare state.

Bolick is a leading legal pioneer in several areas. For the past 12 years, he has led the nationwide effort to defend school choice programs, with victories in the Wisconsin, Ohio, and Arizona supreme courts, culminating in *Zelman v. Simmons-Harris* in the U.S. Supreme Court. In the 1980s and 90s, he helped lead the effort to increase judicial scrutiny of racial classifications in such areas as public employment and interracial adoptions. He designed a legal strategy to restore judicial protection of economic liberty, which has produced several landmark rulings invalidating regulatory barriers to enterprise.

In 2001, Bolick moved to Arizona to launch the Institute for Justice's first state chapter. From the Phoenix office, he trains and organizes other state chapters around the nation.

Bolick is one of the subjects profiled in *Gang of Five: Leaders at the Center of the Conservative Crusade,* by Nina Easton, who says that Bolick "confounds his liberal critics because he is something that is not supposed to exist on the right: an idealist."

Bolick received his law degree from the University of California at Davis in 1982 and his undergraduate degree from Drew University in 1979.

Cato Institute

Founded in 1977, the Cato Institute is a public policy research foundation dedicated to broadening the parameters of policy debate to allow consideration of more options that are consistent with the traditional American principles of limited government, individual liberty, and peace. To that end, the Institute strives to achieve greater involvement of the intelligent, concerned lay public in questions of policy and the proper role of government.

The Institute is named for *Cato's Letters*, libertarian pamphlets that were widely read in the American Colonies in the early 18th century and played a major role in laying the philosophical foundation for the American Revolution.

Despite the achievement of the nation's Founders, today virtually no aspect of life is free from government encroachment. A pervasive intolerance for individual rights is shown by government's arbitrary intrusions into private economic transactions and its disregard for civil liberties.

To counter that trend, the Cato Institute undertakes an extensive publications program that addresses the complete spectrum of policy issues. Books, monographs, and shorter studies are commissioned to examine the federal budget, Social Security, regulation, military spending, international trade, and myriad other issues. Major policy conferences are held throughout the year, from which papers are published thrice yearly in the *Cato Journal*. The Institute also publishes the quarterly magazine *Regulation*.

In order to maintain its independence, the Cato Institute accepts no government funding. Contributions are received from foundations, corporations, and individuals, and other revenue is generated from the sale of publications. The Institute is a nonprofit, tax-exempt, educational foundation under Section 501(c)3 of the Internal Revenue Code.

CATO INSTITUTE
1000 Massachusetts Ave., N.W.
Washington, D.C. 20001